THE LAWYER MILLIONAIRE

The Complete Guide for Attorneys on Maximizing Wealth, Minimizing Taxes, and Retiring with Confidence

DARREN P. WURZ, MSFP, CFP®

Solo, Small Firm and
General Practice Division

Cover design by Nick Panos/ABA Design

The materials contained herein represent the opinions of the authors and/or the editors and should not be construed to be the views or opinions of the law firms or companies with whom such persons are in partnership with, associated with, or employed by, nor of the American Bar Association or the Solo, Small Firm and General Practice Division, unless adopted pursuant to the bylaws of the Association.

Nothing contained in this book is to be considered as the rendering of legal, tax, investment, or financial advice for specific cases or individual circumstances, and readers are responsible for obtaining such advice from their own legal counsel or professional financial planners. This book is not a substitute for professional financial services and is intended for educational and informational purposes only.

© 2022 American Bar Association. All rights reserved.

No part of this publication may be reproduced, stored in a retrieval system, or transmitted in any form or by any means, electronic, mechanical, photocopying, recording, or otherwise, without the prior written permission of the publisher. For permission, complete the request form at www.americanbar.org/reprint or email ABA Publishing at copyright@americanbar.org.

Printed in the United States of America.

26 25 24 23 22 22   5 4 3 2 1

Library of Congress Cataloging-in-Publication Data

Names: Wurz, Darren P., 1988- author.
Title: The lawyer millionaire: the complete guide for attorneys on maximizing wealth, minimizing taxes, and retiring with confidence / Darren P. Wurz, MSFP, CFP.
Description: Chicago, Illinois: American Bar Association [2022] | Includes bibliographical references and index. | Summary: "The goal of this book was to provide attorneys a complete financial resource to help make sound financial decisions and avoid costly mistakes so they can maximize their wealth and achieve financial independence"-- Provided by publisher.
Identifiers: LCCN 2022009315 (print) | LCCN 2022009316 (ebook) | ISBN 9781639051472 (paperback) | ISBN 9781639051489 (epub)
Subjects: LCSH: Lawyers--United States--Finance, Personal.
Classification: LCC HG179 .W876 2022 (print) | LCC HG179 (ebook) | DDC 332.0240088/34--dc23
LC record available at https://lccn.loc.gov/2022009315
LC ebook record available at https://lccn.loc.gov/2022009316

ISBN 978-1-63905-147-2

Discounts are available for books ordered in bulk. Special consideration is given to state bars, CLE programs, and other bar-related organizations. Inquire at Book Publishing, ABA Publishing, American Bar Association, 321 N. Clark Street, Chicago, Illinois 60654-7598.

www.shopABA.org

Dedicated to my Dad.

Contents

Foreword .... *ix*
Preface .... *xi*
Acknowledgments .... *xv*

Part I   Foundations of Wealth 1

    Introduction: Financial Challenges of The Legal Profession 3

1   Getting Started 7

2   Paying Off Your Student Loans 15

3   Managing Irregular Income 23

4   Buying a House 29

5   The Biggest Money Mistakes Attorneys Make 37

Part II   Growing Rich: Investing for Attorneys 41

6   The Time Value of Money 43

7   Introduction to Investments 47

8   Investment Strategies 57

9   Assessing Your Risk Tolerance 65

10	Guide to Asset Allocation by Age	71
11	Real Estate Investing	83
12	The Biggest Investing Mistakes to Avoid	89

Part III Tax Minimization for Attorneys ... 95

13	Retirement Accounts	97
14	The Roth Backdoor and Mega-Backdoor	103
15	Turbocharged Tax Deferral	107
16	The Stealth IRA	113
17	Contingency-Fee Tax Deferral	117
18	Charitable Tax Strategies	123
19	Life Insurance Tax Strategies	129
20	10 Tax Tips for Attorneys	135

Part IV Protecting Your Wealth ... 143

21	Life Insurance Protection	145
22	Disability Risk	153
23	Liability Risk	159

Part V Running Your Own Practice ... 165

| 24 | Choosing a Business Structure | 167 |
| 25 | Improving Your Bottom Line | 173 |

26 Business Continuity Planning	179
27 Surviving a Recession	185
Part VI Planning for Retirement	**191**
28 How Much Do I Need to Retire?	193
29 Retirement Income Planning	201
30 Getting the Most Out of Social Security	207
Part VII Law Firm Succession	**213**
31 What's a Law Firm Worth?	215
32 How Do You Sell a Law Practice?	221
33 Making the Sale Successful	227
Conclusion	*231*
About the Author	*233*
Index	*235*

Foreword

Finally, a book by a Certified Financial Planner who specializes in advising attorneys! I commend this book to all private practice attorneys, especially solo practitioners like me. I am a 62-years-young personal injury attorney who works on a contingency fee basis. Thus, my income varies from year to year. Therefore, this book's chapters on "Managing Irregular Income" and "Contingency Fee Tax Deferral" were very insightful for me.

I am planning to retire at the age of 65. As for my financial planning, I have "been there and done that" to acquire a nest egg for retirement—much of it by trial and error. Fortunately, I have been lucky. I wish I could have read Darren's book 30 years ago to make my journey easier. His book is full of valuable information and advice for managing finances to ensure a stress-free retirement.

Attorneys like me who choose to own their own law practice gain substantial freedom to set their own schedules and to choose the cases and clients they want to handle. However, we don't get the large retirement pensions that government lawyers and judges and corporate lawyers command. Law is a noble profession, but I never desired to work until I die like Ruth Bader Ginsburg, may she rest in peace. Managing money over a career in law takes time and planning. Often our time as attorneys is consumed on our clients' causes; and we ignore our own finances.

If, like me, you yearn for an early and secure retirement, then this book is for you. We want sufficient finances to enjoy life in retirement and to have enough to be able to help our relatives who need funds for emergencies or to start their own business ventures. Darren's book is a great first step toward understanding how to achieve financial freedom. I recommend that you then ask Darren about the next steps forward.

Russell S. Kohn, Esq.
Kohn Law Office
Personal Injury Law
Oceanside, California

Preface

If you are an attorney and reading this book, I have great respect for you. I respect the hard work and dedication that it took to get where you are. This respect comes from my own experience building a business, working with clients, and getting to know many attorneys like you. You invested countless hours and lots of money to get through college and law school, pass the bar, and become an attorney. Then you invested even more time and even more capital building your practice and your client base. You have endured many late nights and tough cases. You have fought tenaciously for your clients. You have had to muster your courage, overcome fear, and speak truth to power. Your work is not easy. And I respect that.

WHY I WORK WITH ATTORNEYS

Why did you become an attorney? Did you always know you would be an attorney? Or was this a surprise? I did not always know that I would become a financial advisor. And I definitely did not envision myself working with attorneys as clients. But I suppose my destiny was partly laid out for me in advance.

I grew up in the financial world. My grandpa, John Wurz, was a financial advisor. He brought my dad into the business. And, in turn, my dad wanted me to follow in his footsteps and join the financial advisory business. But as a fiercely independent-minded firstborn son, I was determined to chart my own path. Therefore, I pursued a career as a high school science teacher. I thought teaching was my life's calling! However, after five years of teaching, I was burned out, exhausted, going through a mid-20s crisis, and looking for something different. After much soul searching, I decided to see what this financial advisor business was all about.

I went back to school while I was teaching to pursue a master of science degree in financial planning from Golden Gate University. As I neared the end of that program, I made a huge life-changing decision. I decided to quit my full-time, salaried teaching job with benefits and launch my own financial advisory practice from my dining room. I was in for a surprise. It was a big shock to go from a steady biweekly paycheck to a "feast-or-famine" business.

Here I was—a teacher by trade with all the academic training in financial planning I could obtain but with absolutely no clue about how to market or run a business. So I just started networking like crazy. I joined every organization I could find and went to every networking luncheon and happy hour I could attend. It was grueling work, but slowly and surely, I made connections, connections turned into clients, and I built up my business.

Coincidentally, many of my early clients were attorneys. One day, as I was reviewing my client list, I noticed this and thought to myself, how can I do a better job serving my attorney clients? Could I build a business focused on serving attorneys? What would that look like? What special needs do attorneys have? Is anyone else doing that? I started doing my research. I found out that attorneys actually have some pretty unique financial challenges. Also, many attorneys are business owners themselves and share some of the challenges that business owners have.

You may have seen financial advisors who specialize in serving business owners, retirees, or even doctors. However, as I surveyed the landscape, I saw very few advisors who specialized in the unique needs of attorneys. I decided to completely change my business model and devote my career to helping attorneys like you reap the rewards of your hard work and make the most of your future.

Today, I love what I do and the attorneys I work with. I know—you get a bad rap sometimes. You are the butt of plenty of "lawyer jokes." But the attorneys I know are upstanding members of their communities, good, hard-working people, and incredibly smart and knowledgeable. They are often business owners and entrepreneurs and have a strong sense of right and wrong, committed to justice and a vital part of our democracy. So, for those reasons, I am proud to serve attorneys.

WHY I WROTE THIS BOOK

So why did I write this book? Many attorneys I know are DIY-ers when it comes to their finances. And that is fine! My goal in writing this book was to provide attorneys like you with a complete financial resource to help you make sound financial decisions and avoid costly mistakes so that you can maximize your wealth and achieve financial independence.

If you are just starting your law career, this book will teach you how to start with a solid financial foundation. If you are at your peak earning years, this book will show you how to minimize your taxes so that you can maximize how much you are socking away and growing your portfolio. And if you are near retirement, this book will show you how to make sure you are on track to retire and perhaps fund your retirement with the sale of your law practice.

I wrote this book because I saw a major gap in the literature on financial planning for attorneys. The literature I did find was unsatisfactory. So I decided to use my expertise as a Certified Financial Planner™ (CFP®) with a master of science in financial planning, as well as my real-world experience, to expand the literature.

This book, appropriately titled *The Lawyer Millionaire*, is about helping you maximize your wealth. The important focus of my narrative is not on the number, however, for a million dollars today is not quite what it used to be. Rather, the critical lesson I want you to absorb is the importance of reaching financial independence. This book is meant to help you make all the right maneuvers and take advantage of every opportunity available to you to maximize the growth of your wealth and accelerate your pathway to financial independence.

I know you are busy, but I urge you to read this book right away. Time waits for no one. The earlier you start accumulating and investing, the more money you will have. The earlier you implement the right financial strategies, the greater reward you will reap. So, do not delay. Read this book now. And then put it by your desk as a constant reminder to keep pushing yourself to achieve your goals and go to the next level.

Acknowledgments

This book would not have been possible without some very important people in my life who have supported me, encouraged me, and helped to bring this project to fruition. I would like to acknowledge and thank the American Bar Association. It has been a privilege and joy to partner with such a great organization. In the ABA, I found a great network of warm, kind, and supportive people. I have been impressed by the enthusiasm and encouragement from members and other authors. I would especially like to thank Lorraine Murray, my editor at ABA Publishing. Thank you for believing in me and this project enough to take a chance on it. You have made the process very easy and enjoyable. I look forward to working together on future projects!

A big thanks to Russell Kohn, attorney and owner of Kohn Law Office, for having enough faith in me and this project to be willing to put his good name and reputation behind this book and to author the foreword for the book. Thank you for spending valuable time out of your busy schedule to read the manuscript and write such a thoughtful introduction. I owe you a debt of gratitude.

I also need to thank Christine Luken, my longtime friend and financial coach and the author of *Money is Emotional: Prevent Your Heart from Hijacking Your Wallet*. You were one of my first inspirations to write a book like this. I appreciate your valuable insights and advice from your own publishing journey.

I am thankful to all of my clients. I have learned more in working with you than books and school could ever have taught. Thank you so much for your trust and confidence. It is a joy and privilege to serve the clients that I do. Thank you for choosing to partner with me in your journey to financial independence.

Finally, I need to thank my family. My dad, Richard Wurz, was the one who finally convinced me to join him in the family business. He laid the foundation for my brother, Travis Wurz, and myself. Your daily encouragement and belief in me has been the wind beneath my wings to propel me to succeed and excel. Thank you dad. My mom, Lydia, also played an instrumental role in bringing this book to completion. You were the one who taught me how to write and made me a lover of writing and reading. You have always believed I could do great things and you made me believe it too. Lastly, thank you so much to my loving and patient husband, Chris Minnis. Thank you for putting up with me during the stressful early days of starting my business and the long hours I had to put into building the business and writing this book. You never doubted me, and you've stood steadfastly by my side. Thank you.

PART I

Foundations of Wealth

A good foundation is of utmost importance. Whether you are just starting your career or are late in your career but ready to get serious about your finances, there are some basics that you must get right before anything. In this section, I will cover some of the challenges you will face early in your career, such as paying down debt and buying a house. I will also explore some of the basic money principles that will give you the proper foundation you need to build your wealth, including budgeting and managing cash flow.

Introduction
Financial Challenges of The Legal Profession

One of my favorite TV shows of all time is *Damages*, starring Glenn Close. She plays Patty Hewes, a controversial high-stakes attorney engaged in life-and-death legal battles with powerful and dangerous individuals. Yet, she proves herself to be a formidable and successful adversary.

From Perry Mason to Patty Hewes, Hollywood has romanticized the legal profession. And there is much to admire. However, while the law can be an extremely rewarding career, it is not without its challenges. Here are some of the biggest financial and retirement planning challenges that you will face in achieving your financial goals:

A LATE START

It takes a while to earn a bachelor's degree, four years for most. Then you spend years in law school. Sometimes it even takes a while to get into law school. As a result, attorneys are usually a little behind others their age when it comes to starting their careers.

Not only does that mean attorneys are late bloomers when it comes to earning an income, but they also get a late start saving for retirement, which can be even more challenging. Why does a late start create a challenge? Because when it comes to saving and investing for the future, time is your most valuable asset. The earlier you can start saving and investing, the more you can harness the exponential wealth-building power of compound interest.

When you enter the workforce late and start saving late because of all your years of schooling and student loans, you are missing out not only on years' worth of income but also on years' worth of compounding growth. The situation is even tougher for those who choose to start their own law firms. Although the future payout may be higher, the years spent investing in your own practice and building your client base mean years of missed saving and investing.

STUDENT DEBT

Most attorneys are not just starting their careers late, but they are starting them deep in debt. Law school didn't always cost so much, but today's graduates are accumulating mountains of debt. According to the latest data from the National Center for Education Statistics, in 2015–2016, the average law school graduate finished law school with $145,500 of student loan debt.[1] And for most attorneys, this is much more than their starting salary.

It can take years to dig yourself out from a hundred thousand dollars' worth of student loan debt or more. Every one of those years is a lost year of compounding interest for your retirement savings, and every payment is a lost contribution to your retirement accounts. Student loan debt can be even more detrimental to an attorney's finances than getting a late start in your career.

HIGH TAXES

Although it can take a while to become an attorney, your prospects for making a good living are quite favorable. In 2019, the median attorney salary was over $122,000,[2] and the prospects for going above that are quite good as well. The best-paid 25 percent made over $186,000 in 2019. Partners and law firm owners make significantly more. And of course, if you're a contingency-fee attorney, the sky is the limit.

Unfortunately, a high income usually equates to high taxes. This is especially a problem for contingency-fee and personal injury attorneys. Winning

---

[1] "Trends in student loan debt for graduate school completers," National Center for Education Statistics, 2018, https://nces.ed.gov/programs/coe/pdf/coe_tub.pdf.

[2] "How much does a lawyer make?" *U.S. News & World Report*, accessed October 16, 2021, https://money.usnews.com/careers/best-jobs/lawyer/salary.

a big case means receiving a large settlement fee and being bumped up into a high-tax bracket. In fact, among the attorneys I speak with, reducing taxes is one of their foremost concerns.

UNPREDICTABLE INCOME

Another financial challenge for attorneys is that many have an unpredictable income. This may not be true for salaried associates, but it is an issue for law firm partners who are responsible for their own estimated quarterly tax payments, for solo practitioners whose business fluctuates, and for contingency-fee attorneys who may not know when their next pay day is.

This unpredictability makes it hard to budget and plan for your finances. More importantly, it makes it difficult to put money away into retirement accounts. Tying up money in a retirement account becomes problematic when you are unsure of what the future holds and when your income fluctuates dramatically.

LACK OF TIME

As an attorney, you lead an incredibly busy professional life—and time equates to money in the form of billable hours! This is the way you have been trained to think. Also, you spend a great deal of time worrying about the problems of others and helping others make good decisions. As a result, you will likely spend little time on your own planning.

This can have terrible consequences. First, you are missing opportunities to save money. Lack of planning leads to inefficiency in the use of dollars, missed tax planning opportunities, and ultimately a waste of both time and money.

Second, this leads to a general lack of preparedness for retirement and succession. Unless you are just awesome at saving and have been maxing out your 401(k) forever, you need to start planning for retirement well in advance to make sure you are on track and are saving enough money. Even then, retirement is not something you just one day decide to do. You are going to be facing a lot of decisions, such as when to take social security, how much you can spend, and how you should invest. Planning for retirement and succession needs to start at least five years before you plan to actually retire. However, if you really want to get the most out of life, you need to start much earlier.

My mission is to help attorneys like you overcome these challenges so that you can maximize your wealth and achieve the life you envision for yourself and your family. In the chapters that follow, I will show you how.

CHAPTER 1

Getting Started

As I am writing this book, I am reminded of one of my clients who recently called to tell me that he was literally $1,000 away from his lifetime goal of having $1.5 million in assets. What is your ultimate goal? Is it to get to the $1 million mark? The $10 million mark?

As an attorney, you will likely not find it that difficult to reach the $1 million mark. However, as the worth of our currency has devalued over time, the significance of reaching this goal has diminished considerably. I imagine that within my lifetime, we may have our first trillionaire! We already have some centi-billionaires (that is, over $100 billion). But make no mistake: a million dollars is still a great milestone. The principles of this book will take you there and beyond.

SET YOUR GOALS

A financial plan starts with goals. Be aware that money itself is not the ultimate goal of this plan. If you think it is, you haven't gone deep enough. Rather, it is what that money can do for you that is the goal. Suppose you had $1 million or however much money you are aiming to achieve. What does it feel like? What emotions do you feel? How is your life now different? What does it do for you?

For most of my clients, their real goal is ultimately financial independence. Attorneys often do not have a clearly defined age in mind at which they want to retire. Legal work is not physically demanding, and so they can potentially continue working longer than people in other types of professions. Also, attorneys tend to find a deep sense of purpose and identity in their work, which makes it hard for them to walk away from it. So, rather than shooting for retirement by age 65, your goal might be to reach financial independence by a certain age, perhaps earlier than 65. Financial independence is essentially the ability to stop working if you want to do so. Ultimately, financial independence means having flexibility. It is having enough money that if you wanted to just walk away from your job, you could do so right now. It is the ability to pursue whatever motivates you and whatever interests you and makes you happy. In other words, financial independence is not necessarily about retirement. It is not about not having to depend on anyone or anything for your financial needs. We call this a work-optional lifestyle. For an attorney, a work-optional lifestyle means being able to select the clients and cases you want rather than needing to fulfill a certain quota of billable hours.

So how much money would it take for you to achieve a work-optional lifestyle? Everyone's number is different and it depends on a slew of variables. That number will probably change over time. We will deal more specifically with how to calculate that number later in this book. For now, note that the 4 percent rule is an easy way to estimate how much money you will need. This rule is a general guideline for determining the amount of money you would need to provide a specified income for roughly 30 years of retirement. If you are aiming to be work-optional by age 60, the 4 percent rule should work as a starting point. If you are aiming to be work-optional by 50, perhaps you should use 3 percent.

How does the 4 percent rule work? It is simple. Take your current salary, or the income you would like your portfolio to be able to provide, and divide it by 4 percent. On a calculator, divide your income by 0.04. If you are aiming for a $100,000 income, you would divide $100,000 by 0.04 and come up with $2.5 million. You'll need about that much money to provide an income of roughly $100,000 for 30 years with a sufficiently low probability of running out. This is a high-end estimate and will probably be reduced by supplemental income from Social Security or pension benefits.

For now, let's say you need about $2.5 million. How much would you have to save and invest to get there? This amount will depend on how much time you have and how much you can earn on your investments. For this illustration, let's assume you will earn an average annual rate of return of 9 percent on your investments over time. From 1950 to 2009, the broad US stock market returned 10.9 percent annually.[1] Let's use 9 percent to be conservative.

---

[1] Richard Ferri, *All about asset allocation* (New York: McGraw-Hill, 2010).

Getting Started

Let's also assume you are starting your law career at age 25 and you have 40 years to invest. I've done the math for you. To reach your goal of $2.5 million, you will need to save about $7,399 a year, or about $617 a month. If your current income is about $100,000, this would be about 7 percent of your income.

This amount may seem like a lot, but it is achievable, especially when you factor in potential employer 401(k) matches, profit sharing, bonuses, or settlement fees. As your income grows, your capacity to save will grow as well, and you will be able to put away more money. The key, however, is to start early.

But there's one caveat here: inflation. Thanks to inflation, $2.5 million may not be what it used to be in 40 years. So, you may need to save more. If you continue to increase your savings as your income grows, this will help you combat the corrosive effects of inflation. We will revisit inflation later.

Table 1.1 shows various time frames and the annual savings required at a 10 percent rate of return to reach various goal amounts. As you can see, time makes a big difference.

SPEND LESS THAN YOU MAKE

Reaching the million-dollar plus level over the span of a career is not difficult if you start saving early and stick to your plan. It does, however, require discipline and spending less than you make. This is probably the single most important financial lesson of all: spend less than you make. You could skip the rest of this book if you simply lived by this adage, and you would accumulate plenty of money over your lifetime.

Table 1.1

Time Frame	Goal Amount	Annual Savings Required
30 years	$1 million	$7,336
30 years	$2 million	$14,673
30 years	$3 million	$22,009
40 years	$1 million	$2,960
40 years	$2 million	$5,919
40 years	$3 million	$8,879

In my years of working with attorneys, I have noticed that this wisdom generally leads to great outcomes. Those who have generally spent most of their lives living below their means and saving a good chunk of their income have managed to accumulate large amounts of wealth. Some of my wealthiest clients are not the ones who drive the nicest cars or live in the biggest houses. There are people who drive nicer cars and have bigger houses—but they have less money. Unfortunately, it can be easy to live beyond your means. You may feel pressure to keep up with your colleagues or to display a certain level of affluence for clients. Sudden windfalls from settlements or the nature of fluctuating income may tempt you to go on a shopping spree. You should try to avoid those temptations.

Spending less than you make is a foundational principle of good personal finance. And it's the most important thing that you control. On the surface, it seems easy, but it runs counter to human nature and the society in which we live. We humans are curious creatures who often give in to greed, envy, and materialism. Corporate America capitalizes on these human traits to pump up profits by pushing us to keep buying bigger and better things. Even the government endorses this idea. After all, it is consumer spending that makes the economy go 'round.

The other consideration that makes this principle so hard to follow is that when we get a raise or our incomes increase, we tend to aspire to a higher lifestyle. We tend to spend more because we think we can afford more. There is nothing wrong with living a little. However, as your income expands, it is important that you also expand your savings.

The lesson is this: in your financial decisions, leave some room. Don't buy the biggest house you can afford or the nicest car you can afford. Instead, live a little below your means. This might not be popular advice, but in the long run, you will be happy you followed it.

TRACK YOUR SPENDING

Speaking of spending, one of the best things you can do to improve your financial well-being is to track your spending. When I do retirement planning with folks, one of the first questions I ask them is how much money they spend each month on average. Guess what? Few people know or even have a remote idea about how much, and those who do often vastly underestimate their spending.

Getting Started

Thanks to modern technology, lots of free tools are available for you track your spending. Tools like Intuit's Mint.com (www.mint.com) will aggregate all your transactions from your various credit cards and bank accounts so that you can organize and categorize them. This tool is helpful because you can see exactly how much money you are spending and what you are spending it on. You will be shocked by how much money you spend when you first do this—I guarantee it.

Simply having an awareness of your spending will help you dramatically, but the next step is to be purposeful about where your money is going. Examine where your money goes and discover where you are wasting money or opportunities to save money. Then repurpose this money to be used elsewhere.

Years ago, I worked with a young couple who were trying to save for retirement and their kids' education. They asked to meet with me because they were struggling with credit card debt and needed someone to help them get on the right track. We started with the budget. After close examination, we discovered that they were wasting a lot of money on a cash-value life insurance policy that was losing money and they also had a high interest rate on their mortgage. We replaced the policy with term insurance (which is much cheaper), adding some cushion to the budget. We used the cash value in the policy to fund some retirement accounts and 529 accounts (i.e., college savings plans) for them. Then, they refinanced their mortgage, obtaining a lower interest rate and lower payment, which allowed them to pay off their credit card debt. Now that they had gained extra room in their budget, we set up automatic monthly drafts into their investment accounts.

If you carefully analyze your spending, you will discover extra money that can be used better elsewhere. Also, you can set limits or targets for spending in different categories to keep yourself on track. Sometimes this process is called budgeting—that often-dreaded term. Most people dislike the idea of budgeting, but if you are serious about achieving your goals, you really ought to have a budget. Instead of thinking about this as budgeting, think about it as being purposeful with your money.

The last important aspect of tracking your spending is to keep this system up to date. Spend a few minutes each week (personally, I like to do this on Saturday mornings) reviewing your spending, categorizing transactions, and evaluating any changes that need to be made. For example, if you notice that your food and dining budget for the month, you can put ⌞rant until the next month begins.

⌞VING A BILL

Lastly, ⌞⌞ ⌞re going to achieve your goals, you have got to be serious about savings and treat your savings like a bill. Too many people make the mistake of saving what is left over. Attorneys who have uneven cash flow (as opposed to a steady paycheck) are especially prone to this mistake. If your cash flow is irregular, you will be uncertain as to when and how much money is coming in. Therefore, you will tend to pay the necessary things first, keep a lot in cash, and think about saving last. The problem with this approach is that usually there is not much left over.

Instead, treat saving like a bill and pay it first. Pretend that it is as crucial to give your retirement account its fair share as it is to pay the bank that financed your car. Treating savings like a bill makes a lot of sense because by putting money in your retirement accounts, you actually are paying bills—future bills. You are providing income for your future self, and you are empowering your future self to live a more comfortable life. Be nice to your future self.

The more I have worked with clients over the years, the more I have come to realize that the ones who build wealth are the ones who are serious about saving. They make saving a non-negotiable bill that must be paid first. One easy way to do this is to set up your savings on autopay as you do with your other bills. Have your savings drafted from your bank account on a regular schedule automatically into your investment account. You already use this procedure with your 401(k) if you have one, but you can also do so with your other investment accounts.

SHOULD I HIRE A FINANCIAL ADVISOR?

As a financial advisor myself, my inherent bias leads me to recommend working with a qualified financial advisor. However, most attorneys I know are financial DIY-ers. And truth be told, if you read this book and others and have a good sense of financial discipline, you can accomplish a lot on your own. At the same time, working with a qualified financial advisor can be a worthwhile investment.

First, having a financial advisor can provide additional insight and knowledge that you might not have. Your financial advisor can point out blind spots that you are not aware of and opportunities you may be missing. An advisor also provides another set of eyes to help you avoid costly mistakes.

Second, a financial advisor can be an additional accountability partner to keep you on track to your goals. As I have just explained, it is easy to neglect saving and investing. A financial advisor will help you by pushing you to keep putting money into your investments, encouraging you to periodically review your financial plan, and keeping you focused on your goals.

Finally, a financial advisor can be a big time saver. You are busy running your practice and maximizing your billable hours. Your financial advisor can act as your personal CFO, overseeing your finances and investments for you so that you can focus on other things.

What should you look for in a financial advisor? Not all advisors are created equal. Your financial advisor should first and foremost be a fiduciary—legally bound to always act in your best interests. They should be free from conflicts of interest which would interfere with their ability to provide advice. The best way to ensure their neutrality is to make sure you are working with an advisor who is paid solely for advice or to manage investments, not to sell products. If the first thing your potential new advisor tries to do is to sell you a life insurance policy or annuity—run! Your advisor should derive no compensation whatsoever from the sale of annuities or mutual funds. Their only compensation should come from an asset-based fee deducted separately and directly from your investment accounts or an hourly or flat fee that you pay separately.

Also make sure your advisor has experience and credentials. The unfortunate truth is that the barrier to entry in this industry is quite low. Work with an advisor who has an advanced degree in financial planning or who is a Certified Financial Planner™ (CFP®). There are many designations out there that financial advisors like to earn and put behind their names, but unfortunately many of them are not difficult to achieve and convey little value. The CFP® designation is the gold standard: it requires having three years of experience as well as in-depth educational training and passing a rigorous examination. You can find a CFP® professional near you at https://www.letsmakeaplan.org.

Finally, I would recommend working with a small, independent firm as opposed to one of the big corporate financial firms. You may be easily lost in the shuffle at the big firms. Turnover tends to be less at smaller, independent firms, which means there's less of a chance that your advisor will change careers or switch employers. You will likely receive closer, more personal attention instead of being treated like a small fish in a big pond. In addition, the larger firms have inherent conflicts of interest that you can avoid by choosing an independent advisor. I have been an independent advisor my entire career, and I feel that this has allowed me to focus on serving my clients' needs and putting their interests first, rather than an organization's needs and interests.

In the next chapter, as we continue the theme of "getting started," we will examine strategies for paying off student loans.

CHAPTER 2

Paying Off Your Student Loans

As I mentioned in chapter 1, the average attorney graduates law school these days with around $145,000 in student debt, which is far more than the average college graduate accrues and more than most starting salaries for attorneys. It can cost a lot of money to become an attorney. First, there is your undergraduate degree. And then there is law school, which is often even pricier.

According to *U.S. News & World Report*, the average annual tuition and fees at private law schools in the 2019–2020 academic year was $49,548.[1] The average annual tuition at in-state public law schools was $28,264—considerably less but still expensive. Unfortunately, in the practice of law, prestige matters, and many law students swallow the pill of the higher cost of private schools to attain greater status and a possibly higher salary.

To make matters worse, the rate of inflation affecting college and law school tuition has been outpacing the general rate of inflation for years. What does this mean? College and law school degrees are becoming more and more expensive, and graduates are starting their law careers with increasingly large debt loads.

---

[1] Ilana Kowarski, "See the price, payoff of law school before enrolling," *U.S. News & World Report*, March 31, 2020, https://www.usnews.com/education/best-graduate-schools/top-law-schools/articles/law-school-cost-starting-salary.

HOW MILLIONAIRES THINK ABOUT DEBT

Some money gurus out there will tell you that before you start investing, you need to pay down all your debt, including student loans, car loans, and your mortgage. I meet with plenty of people who are aggressively trying to pay down their mortgage because they received this same advice.

This advice is terribly wrong in an environment where interest rates are relatively low. Yes, it is true that excessive debt or high interest rate debt can be financially harmful. However, debt itself is not a bad thing. In fact, the wealthy think of debt differently. They think of debt as a tool and they use it wisely.

Millionaires think about debt as leverage. In the physical world, leverage is a way to gain mechanical advantage by using a lever. Have you ever used a bottle opener to open a bottle of beer? If so, you have used leverage. The force of your hand was not enough to lift the bottle cap, but the bottle opener (a lever) allowed you to multiply the force of your hand to achieve enough force to remove the bottle cap.

Similarly, debt is a form of leverage: financial leverage. It is a way to gain financial advantage. Without debt, it would be extremely hard to accomplish some things in life. Imagine if you had to first save up enough money to go to college and law school before you could go (assuming you didn't have other sources that could pay for it on your behalf). That wouldn't work. You would waste a lot of time and might never get started. Instead, you used debt to create leverage for yourself. This leverage allowed you to accelerate the start of your money-making years, maximize the efficiency of your time, and ultimately enjoy a higher standard of living.

In the same way, if you wait until all your debts are paid off before you start investing, you may never start investing. You will waste time and miss out on market opportunities. And the most important equation in building wealth is savings multiplied by time. Delaying saving and investing until their student loans are paid off is a big mistake I see a lot of young people making.

My general advice on student loans is to stick to your payment plan. They will get paid off over time. Resist the temptation to pay your debts off early if the interest rate is reasonable. Many people are often concerned about getting "free" from debt payments. If you want to build real wealth, you need to be more concerned about how much you are putting into your investments rather than about paying off your student loans.

Also, here's a very big important tip: never, ever, ever dip into your retirement savings to pay down debt. In my years as a financial advisor, I have seen people time and time again dip into their retirement savings to pay off debt. I used to think that in certain circumstances this is okay. Now, I am convinced that this is never okay.

First, once you start doing this, you have opened a doorway that is difficult to shut mentally. Dipping into your retirement funds is like a drug addiction: once you start, you will do it again. I have seen too many real-life examples of people squandering their retirement savings because they keep pulling money out to pay things off. Each time they tell me that this is the last time; inevitably, it usually is not.

Second, if you pull money from your retirement funds, not only do you reduce those funds, but you also dramatically reduce your earnings and growth potential. It takes money to make money. Not only that, by reducing this growth potential, you rob your future self. The financial cost of that lost opportunity is devastatingly tragic. Be kind to your future self and don't take money out of your retirement funds prematurely. Never! In case you are worried about bankruptcy, retirement funds (IRAs, 401(k)s, etc.) generally are protected from creditors.

In any case, if you are working on paying down your student debts, here are some general guidelines:

Get on a Budget

I already said this in chapter 1, but I'll say it again. By "get on a budget" I mean you should start tracking your spending, set targets for your spending, and monitor your spending to make sure you do not exceed your targets. Your debt payments will be a nondiscretionary part of this budget. If you are serious about paying down your debt, a budget is critical.

Enroll in Auto Pay

This statement may seem like common sense, but auto pay helps you for two reasons. First, it ensures that you will never forget your minimum payments or be late in paying them. In addition, if you are paying more than your minimum payment, the auto pay program will ensure that you stick to your plan. Second, most federal loan providers as well as some private loan providers may reduce your interest rate by as much as 0.25 percent if you are on autopay. That may not seem like a lot, but a mere 0.25 percent can add up over time.

Pay More than the Minimum If It Makes Sense

Earlier, I said it is usually wise to stick to the payment plan. Your loans will take care of themselves over time. However, in some instances it might make sense to pay more than the minimum. When is that? When your interest rate is higher than you could reasonably expect to earn on your investments over time.

The stock market has historically provided an average rate of return of 9 to 11 percent, depending on your time frame. Of course, the market's rate of return in any one particular year can vary widely, and there is no guarantee that a 9 to 11 percent rate of return will hold true going forward. However, this is a good historical benchmark.

When it comes to debt, the interest rate is mathematically the most important consideration. If the interest rate on your debt is equal to or higher than 9 percent, it definitely makes sense to pay it off early. However, if the interest rate on your debt is lower, you will likely have more money down the road by making the scheduled payment according to your payment plan and investing any extra funds that you have.

Let's illustrate. Suppose you have $150,000 in student loans with an interest rate of 6 percent. We will assume interest is capitalized or added to the principal. Your minimum payment according to your payment plan is $1,000 a month, but you could pay $1,500 a month. If you put all of the $1,500 toward your student loans, you'll have them paid off by the end of year 12 (see Table 2.1).

If, instead, you were to pay the minimum of $1,000 a month and invest the extra $500 a month (assuming a 9 percent average annual interest rate), you could accumulate $129,822.20 in your investments by the end of year 12, which will be more than enough to pay off the balance of your loans at that point and have $33,410.50 left over!

This does entail market risk, however, and in spite of the attractiveness of this approach some circumstances might warrant paying more than the payment plan. If you do overpay, make sure you do it the right way. The most effective way to make an extra payment is to apply that payment to your principal if you can. You'll need to tell your lender to do this. Paying down your principal reduces your interest charge because interest is calculated based on your principal balance. The lender will not do this automatically. Usually, they will apply any extra payment to fees and interest first. Some lenders, however, will capitalize your unpaid interest, making this strategy moot.

Table 2.1

	Pay $1,500 per month	Pay $1,000, Invest $500 per month	
	Loan Balance	Loan Balance	Investment
Year 1	$150,000.00	$150,000.00	$0
Year 2	$140,655.80	$146,854.40	$6,300.70
Year 3	$130,735.30	$143,514.90	$13,192.40
Year 4	$120,202.90	$139,969.30	$20,730.70
Year 5	$109,020.90	$136,205.10	$28,976.10
Year 6	$97,149.20	$132,208.60	$37,994.90
Year 7	$84,545.30	$127,965.70	$47,859.80
Year 8	$71,164.00	$123,461.10	$58,650.10
Year 9	$56,957.40	$118,678.70	$70,452.50
Year 10	$41,874.50	$113,601.30	$83,362.20
Year 11	$25,861.40	$108,210.80	$97,482.80
Year 12	$8,860.60	$102,487.70	$112,928.10
Year 13	$0	$96,411.70	$129,822.20

Capitalizing means they add your unpaid interest to your principal. Then, your interest is calculated based on this new, higher principal amount. Make sure to check with your lender on the terms and conditions of your loan.

Pay the Highest Interest Rate Loans First

To attack your debts in the most mathematically efficient way possible, you need to maximize the amount you are putting toward the loans or debts with the highest interest rates first. Prioritize getting rid of these. Pay the minimum on all your debts except the one with the highest interest rate. Put all your extra cash flow towards that one until it is gone. Once that debt is eliminated, target the next highest rate and on down the list.

You may have heard some money gurus talk about targeting the debts with the smallest principal balance first. This alternative may be good for your psyche and make you feel better in the short term, but it takes longer.

Let's say you have two loans. Loan A is for $15,000 and has an interest rate of 4 percent with a minimum payment of $150. Loan B is for $30,000 and has an interest rate of 10 percent with a minimum payment of $300. Let's also assume that you can put a total of $1,000 toward your loans each month.

Paying the minimum on the $30,000 loan and maximizing your payment on the smaller balance loan would pay off the smaller loan in 23 months. Then, if you put the full $1,000 toward the larger loan, you would purge that one in another 23 months for a total of 56 months.

However, if you paid only the minimum on the smaller loan and instead maximized your payment on the higher interest rate loan, you could get rid of the higher interest rate loan in 42 months. Then, putting all your resources toward the other loan, you would pay off the lower interest rate loan in approximately an additional 11 months, for a grand total of 53 months. In this scenario, paying the higher interest rate first pays off your loans 3 months earlier and saves you approximately $2,635.22! See Table 2.2 below.

Refinance If It Makes Sense

In some cases, it may make sense to refinance your student loans, and it can save you a lot of money. When is it a good idea to do this? Generally, you are well advised to refinance if you are moving from a higher interest rate

Table 2.2

Method 1: Pay smallest balance first				
Loan	Interest	Min. Payment	Starting Payment	Time Period to Payoff
$15,000	4%	$150	$700	23 months
$30,000	10%	$300	$300	56 months
Method 2: Pay highest interest rate first				
Loan	Interest	Min. Payment	Starting Payment	Time Period to Payoff
$15,000	4%	$150	$150	53 months
$30,000	10%	$300	$850	42 months

to a lower interest rate. This will save you money in the long run. However, be careful: you may have to pay extra fees to refinance, which can add to your principal balance. Also, I would be cautious about refinancing simply to lower your payment. Doing so may not help you much in the long run.

Finally, be careful about refinancing federal loans. Refinancing this type of loan may cause you to lose some of the benefits and options that federal loans provide, such as forgiveness, deferment, or income-based repayment plans. If your financial situation is not solid, I would not refinance federal loans because they provide you with the greatest flexibility.

Should I Consolidate?

I am not a big fan of consolidating, unless it clearly saves you money in the long run. Consolidating can be tempting because it offers simplicity. You can take several different loans and combine them so that you are just making one monthly payment. However, you will lose the ability to strategically target the high interest rate loans first and accelerate the payoff of your debt this way. I would consider consolidating your student loans if and only if it will lower your overall average interest rate and lead to paying off your loans earlier with an equal or lesser monthly payment, thus saving you money in the long run.

STUDENT LOAN FORGIVENESS

Before I became a financial advisor, I worked as a public high school science teacher in a high-needs district for five years. Because I did that, I was able to have my graduate school loans forgiven. Federal student loans are eligible for a few different types of forgiveness. One type is teacher loan forgiveness. If you teach full time for five years in a low-income school district, you may be eligible for forgiveness of up to $17,500 on federal loans. However, few attorneys probably are willing to put their career on hold for five years. The other major type of forgiveness is public service loan forgiveness. If you are employed by a government or not-for-profit organization, you may be eligible for loan forgiveness after making 120 qualifying monthly payments under an income-driven repayment plan. That means that after 10 years, the full balance of your federal loans could be forgiven. Qualifying employers include government organizations at any level (federal, state, local, tribal, or military), and any 501(c)(3) organization. Labor unions, partisan political organizations, and for-profit organizations are excluded. Those who serve as public defenders or prosecutors for at least 10 years would qualify.

You may want to explore other sources of loan forgiveness available specifically to attorneys. The Department of Justice offers loan assistance of up to $6,000 per year, with a maximum of $60,000 for employees through their Attorney Student Loan Repayment Program. You need to complete at least three years of service for this program. Public defenders can receive repayment of up to $10,000 a year, with a maximum of $60,000, through the John R. Justice Student Loan Repayment Program. You have to complete three years of service. This award is given by individual states, and requirements vary by state. Finally, if you are employed by a legal service corporate grantee such as Legal Aid, you may be eligible for student loan forgiveness through the Herbert S. Garten Loan Repayment Assistance Program offered by the Legal Services Corporation. This program is a lottery system that awards about 70 attorneys a year, with up to $5,600 a year for three years. Funds must be applied to law school loans.

OTHER SOURCES OF FINANCING

One way to cut down your interest rate may be to shift the balance of your student loans elsewhere. For example, if you own a house with significant equity, you may be able to get a home equity line for a much lower interest rate that you can then use to pay off your student loans. This effectively converts student loan interest to mortgage loan interest which you may be able to deduct more on your taxes. Another possibility might be to obtain a loan against your investment portfolio or a 401(k) loan, which can usually be obtained for an interest rate that is similar to the prime rate. However, this approach carries some risk, such as the possibility of margin calls that you should be mindful of.

One factor that makes paying down debt and budgeting particularly different for some attorneys, particularly those who own their own practice or are contingency-fee based, is uneven cash flow. In the next chapter, we will examine some helpful strategies for dealing with uneven cash flow.

CHAPTER 3

Managing Irregular Income

One of the unique challenges that attorneys face, particularly contingency-fee attorneys and law firm owners, is irregular income. If your income is irregular, life can feel like a constant cycle of "feast or famine." You may go weeks or months without seeing much money come in. When you do win a big case, you experience a sudden cash windfall.

This cycle is difficult to manage psychologically and can lead to poor money habits and behaviors that are detrimental to achieving your long-term goals. The natural human tendency is to splurge when we get a sudden cash infusion because we "feel" wealthier. As a result, we end up actually having less money to meet our real needs and to put toward our goals.

Here are some ideas that can help you avoid poor money choices and master your irregular cash flow situation:

ANALYZE CASH FLOW

Start by analyzing your cash flow over a full-year cycle. Whereas most people might budget month-to-month and are accustomed to monthly bills and a monthly or semimonthly paycheck, if your income is irregular you need to look at the full year. This approach will help you understand the things that happen monthly, quarterly, and somewhere in between.

As you analyze your cash flow, create a detailed list of discretionary (nonessential) annual expenses and nondiscretionary (essential) expenses. Be careful because some things can be both. For example, a certain amount of spending on food is nondiscretionary, but spending on dining out is probably discretionary. For some categories, you will need to determine how much is absolutely necessary. After you have looked at the full year, you can divide these expenses by 12 to determine your average monthly discretionary and nondiscretionary expenses.

BUILD YOUR EMERGENCY FUND

Once you have determined your discretionary versus nondiscretionary expenses, you are ready to determine how big your emergency fund needs to be. The emergency fund can be used for times when your income slows down or for when you experience a lull in business activity or the loss of your job. It can also be used for sudden unanticipated expenses like a large medical bill.

For most people, we financial planners generally recommend keeping at least three months' worth of nondiscretionary expenses in a liquid (or easily accessible) cash savings account. If your income is irregular, you probably need a larger emergency fund than most. I would aim for six months' worth of nondiscretionary expenses. If you don't have this fund, start building it today.

CREATE A CASH FLOW ACCOUNT

To help you even out the ups and downs in your income, you will next want to create a cash flow account. Some call this a spending account, but it should be separate from your regular checking account. The best way to deal with irregular income is to turn it into regular income. You can do this by creating a separate cash flow account.

When you get a large influx of cash from a settlement fee or an abundance of legal work, you will put this money into your cash flow account. Using this account, you are going to "pay" yourself a regular monthly or semimonthly income. The idea is that although the amount of money in the cash flow account may fluctuate, up one day and down another, your stream of income will be constant (at least in your mind). This account can also be used to pay your quarterly estimated tax payments.

This account will help you avoid splurging when you get a sudden influx of cash. and it will also help you stick to your budget and your goals. If your cash flow account gets too low, you can supplement it from your emergency fund, but your goal is to avoid dipping into your emergency fund on a regular basis and instead save this fund for real emergencies.

WHAT ABOUT CREDIT CARDS?

Some people use credit cards to manage their cash flow. They put expenses on the card, and then when they finally get a large payment, they pay off the cards or try to. This approach can be very tricky. The problem here is that while your cash flow is irregular, credit cards have interest charges and minimum payments that are very much regular. Typically, a credit card gives you a month of grace before you are charged interest. So, if you pay off your credit card each month, you will not incur interest charges.

If you have used these steps and you are planning to pay off your credit cards each month, this would be a good approach. And using credit cards can provide additional benefits, including cash back rewards and building your credit score. If your income is irregular, however, you may not be able to pay off your credit card every month. Becoming reliant on credit cards to manage your irregular cash flow itself can lead to carrying a balance on your cards and growing interest charges. This becomes a very expensive way to manage your cash flow and can lead to a dangerous buildup of credit card debt.

SHOULD YOU INVEST YOUR EMERGENCY FUNDS?

Clients often ask me if it is wise to invest their emergency funds, especially in today's low interest rate environment. I agree: it is difficult to earn very much on cash deposits at the bank, but you need to keep a certain amount in a low-risk account for emergencies and unexpected expenses. Some banks and credit card companies offer high-yield savings accounts. These banks often do not have branches and are able to keep their expenses exceptionally low. As a result, they can offer above-average interest rates. High-yield savings accounts do not require you to lock up your money like a CD—which would not be wise with your emergency funds—and they usually do not have any expenses. However, it seems that even these "high-yield" accounts are not yielding much these days.

So, how about investing? Here's my take: yes, you can invest your emergency funds, but you'll want to make sure that the way you invest these funds is very conservative.

There are two reasons for this cautionary advice. First, and most obviously, you cannot afford to take a lot of risk with these funds. You need these funds to be there when you need them. If the stock market takes a dip precisely when you need money, you'll be in trouble. Second, difficult economic times tend to be the very times when we need to invade our emergency funds. And these times often correlate with market dips. Therefore, there is a high probability that the time you need these funds is the same time the market will be languishing.

So how should you invest these funds? You could have some stock market exposure, but you'll want to keep this exposure limited. Understand that stocks can decline in value precipitously over the short term, and that's not a risk you can take in full. During the 2008–2009 financial crisis, the S&P 500 declined by over 50 percent. That's not something you can let your emergency fund do. Keep stock exposure limited based on how much of a dip you are willing to experience. Understand that volatility will happen, but how you invest can determine how much volatility you experience. As a general guideline, determine how much of a dip you can handle and then multiply that by two. For example, if the most you are capable of experiencing is a 10 percent dip, keep your stock exposure to less than 20 percent. The bulk of any kind of investment of your emergency funds should be in short-term treasuries, which present the least risk.

Rather than figuring it out yourself, there are conservative asset allocation mutual funds that might be good investment options for short-term reserves. These funds will offer you a diversified mix of stocks and bonds and will manage risk for you in a one-stop shop. Or a qualified financial advisor can help you design your own investment strategy for your short-term reserves with limited risk. We do this for clients at our firm.

ESTIMATED TAX PAYMENTS?

Many attorneys, especially if they are law firm owners or partners, are required to make their own quarterly estimated tax payments. These attorneys do not have the benefit of a payroll department that withholds these funds from their paychecks. Because these estimated tax payments are due quarterly, it can be difficult to plan for them. That's where the cash flow account comes in handy. If you are one of these attorneys, you can simply use your cash flow account to make these payments. That would be the simplest approach. If you need help mentally accounting for these funds, you might consider opening a separate account to deposit money on a regular basis, accumulating enough to pay your estimated payments when they are due.

Having irregular cash flow makes financial decisions more challenging. Managing this cash flow effectively can make decisions easier, especially when you are making one of the biggest decisions of all: buying a house. In the next chapter, I will provide some guidance on buying a house, especially your first house.

CHAPTER 4

Buying a House

Okay—you've graduated law school, you're working on paying down your student loans, you're starting to earn some real income, you've got your cash flow down to a science, and now you're looking to buy a home. Purchasing a house is perhaps the largest transaction you will make during your lifetime, besides perhaps the sale of your practice. Not surprisingly, this large transaction will have a huge impact on your financial future.

The experience can be a challenging and daunting one, especially if it is your first time. If you've been through the home-buying experience, I bet there are some things you wish you had done differently. Because this is such a critical part of your life that will have big consequences, it is important to get it right. So, here are some thoughts to guide you through the process.

BUYING VS. RENTING

First, let's deal with the buying versus renting debate. I'm sure someone has told you that buying a house is key to building wealth. My parents told me that. The government even tells us this! In general, over a long enough period of time, I think buying is preferable to renting.

After the real estate and financial crisis of 2008–2009, however, many people started to question the wisdom of buying a house. During that crisis, home values fell, and many homeowners fell "under water." That is, they owed more money on their house than it was worth. Today, younger people are showing a preference for living in urban areas, and so more people are renting these days.

In deciding what is right for you, here are some things to consider. First, how long are you planning to stay in your residence? The longer you are planning to stay, the more likely buying will be a better bet in the long term. That is because buying a house involves additional costs such as closing costs and broker commissions. The longer you live there, the longer your home's value can appreciate so that you can recoup your costs.

Second, you need to consider how owning a home will affect your taxes. Your mortgage interest and property taxes are deductible expenses. If your itemized deductions are greater than the standard deduction, you can reap some significant tax savings. However, thanks to the tax law enacted in 2017, the cap on mortgage interest deductibility was lowered, and in addition, a cap was put on the amount of property tax that can be deducted. Also, the standard deduction has been raised significantly. If your combined itemized deductions are less than the standard deduction, you won't get any extra tax benefit from your mortgage interest and property taxes. Raising the standard deduction greatly reduced these benefits.

Finally, you need to consider the true cost of renting versus buying. One of the nice things about renting is that certain costs are paid for, such as certain maintenance items. Add up all the extra monthly expenses incurred by owning a home (not just principal and interest) and compare that to the cost of renting a similar-size place. And don't forget things like property insurance, taxes, extra utilities, maintenance costs, repairs, and the potential replacement of big-ticket items like a roof.

If adding up all the costs of owning is still less than renting, then you have your answer. However, if the true cost of owning a home is more than renting, what could that extra money do for you if you invested it over the lifetime of owning a home? If you invested the difference, how much money could you accumulate? And how would that compare to how much you could make selling your house after you pay off the mortgage? Thankfully, there are renting versus buying calculators online that can help you answer this question.

HOW MUCH HOUSE SHOULD YOU BUY?

Let's say you've done the calculation and determined that buying a house will be best for you in the long run. How much house should you buy? Remember when I said back in chapter 2 that you should spend less than you make? This is a great time to follow that principle.

Buying a House

Ultimately, how much you should buy depends on what your monthly payment will be. This in turn depends on how much you borrow, the term of the loan, and the interest rate you qualify for. And don't forget to factor in taxes, insurance, and perhaps Homeowner Association (HOA) fees.

How much banks will lend you will depend on your lender's underwriting standards and your financial details, such as debt-to-income ratio and credit history. However, generally banks will lend you as much as you want up to a monthly housing cost of 28 percent of your pretax income. That means that on a $100,000 salary, they figure you can afford up to a $2,333 mortgage payment. But the ability to borrow that much does not necessarily mean you should borrow that much.

A $2,333 mortgage payment would be a strain on a $100,000 pretax budget. See Table 4.1 for an example. In this example, I have made some assumptions, but it shows how little could be left over on a $100,000 pretax salary if you are spending $28,000 a year on housing, especially if you are trying to save enough to meet your future financial goals. That monthly leftover amount needs to be enough to pay for everything else: gas, cars, groceries, dining, utilities, repairs, insurance, entertainment, and so on. I think the 28 percent rule is too high—especially if you are serious about building wealth. Hopefully, you agree.

Instead, look at your current budget. Before you consider buying a house, ask yourself some questions. Are you saving enough to achieve your long-term financial goals? Make sure your house payment doesn't prevent you from saving what you need to reach your goals. Make saving a priority. Is there enough wiggle room in the budget to accommodate for unplanned expenses?

Table 4.1

Starting salary		$ 100,000.00
Minus payroll tax	7.65%	$ 92,350.00
Minus 401(k) contribution	10%	$ 82,350.00
Minus health insurance	$ 2,000.00	$ 80,350.00
Minus federal, state, local taxes	25%	$ 60,262.50
Minus mortgage	$ 28,000.00	$ 32,262.50
Monthly leftover		$ 2,688.04

How will owning a house increase your expenses (other than your mortgage payment)? Adjust your current budget for the extra expenses a house would add. Then, determine how much you can spend a month on your mortgage payment. Use that number to inform how much of a house you can afford.

WHAT TYPE OF LOAN SHOULD YOU HAVE?

You can take out various types of loans. One consideration in taking out a loan is its term. The most widely used terms are 15-year or 30-year loans. By far, most home buyers opt for the 30-year mortgage. This is probably because a 30-year mortgage allows you to buy more house with a lower payment.

Fifteen-year loans do have some advantages. Normally, the interest rate on a 15-year loan is lower. That, coupled with the fact that the term is half the time, means you end up paying less than half as much on interest as you would with a comparable 30-year mortgage.

However, a 15-year mortgage may mean less money in the budget and may therefore result in putting less money toward your investments and retirement. As an investment guy whose goal is to maximize wealth, my primary concern is making my money work as hard as possible for me. With mortgage rates around the 5 percent range and the expectation that I could earn 9 percent on my investments over time, I favor the mortgage with the lowest payment possible, even if it means I'll pay more in interest over time. This is because a lower payment will mean I can maximize how much I am investing and putting toward retirement.

Let's say you are buying a $200,000 house with a 20 percent down payment ($40,000), so that you need to borrow $160,000. You have two options: a 30-year mortgage with a 5.2 percent interest rate and a 15-year mortgage with a 4.4 percent interest rate. Some money gurus will tell you that getting the 15-year mortgage and eliminating your debt early will let you accelerate your savings once it is paid off and build more wealth. However, in this case, the 30-year mortgage is far better over time (see Table 4.2).

In this illustration, we've assumed that if you get the 30-year mortgage, you invest the difference and earn 9 percent a year (compounded monthly). If you get the 15-year mortgage, you start investing the full mortgage payment after the first 15 years. How do they compare? The 30-year mortgage plan leaves you with $159,011.20 more in the end! Why does it make such a huge difference? Because when it comes to investing, your most valuable commodity is not money—it's time. Starting earlier even with a smaller amount can yield much greater results.

Buying a House

Table 4.2

	15 years	30 years
Interest rate	4.4%	5.2%
Principal	$ 160,000.00	$ 160,000.00
Monthly payment	$ 1,211.40	$ 874.80
Investable difference	$ –	$ 336.60
Assumed rate of return	9%	9%
Savings after 15 years	$ –	$ 128,326.70
Savings after 30 years	$ 461,838.80	$ 620,850.00

Another consideration is the fixed rate versus variable rate mortgage. Many borrowers got in trouble in the lead up to the Great Financial Crisis because they bought variable-rate mortgages and then when those interest rates went up, they were faced with higher payments and they were in trouble. Do yourself a favor: instill some constancy in your financial life and go with the fixed rate. If rates go up, you will be protected. If rates go down, you can always refinance.

HOW MUCH SHOULD YOUR DOWN PAYMENT BE?

Traditionally, lenders want you to have a 20 percent down payment on your house. This helps give the lender confidence in you as a borrower because you start off with a significant financial stake in the house you are purchasing. It is often possible to pay less than 20 percent. But if you do, you will likely pay for private mortgage insurance (PMI).

This insurance insures the lender against the risk that you will default on the loan. Generally, PMI costs anywhere from 0.20 percent to 1.00 percent of the loan value per year. This cost is divided by 12 and factored into your monthly payment. After you have built up 20 percent equity in the home, you generally can get rid of this PMI.

Many financial gurus will tell you to pay the 20 percent down payment and avoid PMI because it will save you money. But does it? Let's assume you are purchasing a $200,000 home and are considering either a 20 percent down payment or a 3.5 percent down payment.

If you go with the 20 percent, the monthly payment will be less, and you can plan to invest the difference at a 10 percent assumed annual rate of return (compounded monthly). If you go with the 3.5 percent down payment, you could invest the difference in the down payment immediately. Later, once the PMI goes away, you plan on investing the cost of the PMI. We are assuming you pay 0.7 percent in PMI premiums annually and the PMI goes away after 9 years. We are also assuming a higher interest rate on the lower down payment option. See Table 4.3.

In this example, going with the lower down payment nets you over $30,000 more in the end. This is because, once again, time is your most valuable commodity. Investing a larger amount up front puts more money to work sooner, harnessing more of the power of time. However, several factors may make the larger down payment net more wealth in the end: lower assumed rates of return, higher mortgage interest rates, a greater difference in interest rate based on the down payment size, and higher PMI rates.

Table 4.3

Down payment	20%	3.50%
Term	30 years	30 years
Interest rate	4.5%	4.8%
Principal	$160,000.00	$193,000.00
Monthly payment	$811.00	$1,013.00
PMI	$ –	$117.00
Term of PMI		10 years
Initial investment	$ –	$33,000.00
Monthly investment	$319.00	$ –
Savings after 9 years	$55,523.13	$80,864.77
Monthly investment after 9 years	$319.00	$117.00
Savings after 30 years	$721,095.65	$754,496.96

HOW SHOULD YOU PREPARE FINANCIALLY?

Now, while I have advocated for putting less money down, that does not mean you should go into a home purchase ill prepared. Before you begin the home-buying process, there are some things you need to do to prepare financially.

First, you need to beef up your emergency fund. Buying a home involves additional expenses you may not have thought of, such as the home inspection, appraisal, and closing costs. Closing costs include real estate agent commissions and all the legal fees involved in completing the transaction. Often closing costs can be shared between buyer and seller and can be bundled into the loan itself.

Then, there are moving costs and furniture costs if you plan to purchase any new furniture. Most people spend more money than they anticipate on things for their new home. According to a study from the National Association of Homebuilders, the average buyer of a new home spends over $10,000 in their first year on new furnishings.[1]

On top of that, you never know what surprise expenses may pop up. My first home purchase involved ripping up an entire floor and replacing a subfloor to fix a pinhole leak that had led to severe rot and termite damage—damage that I was completely unaware of at the time of purchase! So, make sure you've put aside some extra money.

Second, take steps to improve your credit. A better credit score can mean a lower interest rate and save you thousands of dollars. Many websites and services can help you track your credit and show you what steps you can take to improve it. Try to lower your debt-to-income ratio and reduce your total credit usage.

Third, get a preapproval letter before you go looking for a house. A preapproval letter tells a seller that you are serious about buying and assures them there will not be any hiccups in obtaining financing if they accept your offer. You can obtain a preapproval letter from the lender you intend to use to finance your home purchase.

---

[1] Natalia Siniavskaia, "Spending patterns of home buyers: Appliances, furnishings and property alternations," National Association of Home Builders, July 5, 2017, https://www.nahbclassic.org/fileUpload_details.aspx?contentTypeID=3&contentID=257993&subContentID=698841&channelID=311.

Fourth, if you are a first-time homebuyer, find out if any first-time homebuyer assistance programs are available to you. Some states and municipalities will offer first-time homebuyers down payment assistance, assistance with closing costs, or even special interest rates.

Also, one source of funding you could use (although I generally recommend that people avoid invading their retirement savings) is your IRA or Roth IRA. If you are a first-time homebuyer or have not owned a principal residence within the last two years, you can withdraw up to $10,000 without penalty to put toward a home purchase. This amount applies individually, so a married couple can potentially draw up to $20,000. Although the penalty is waived, you may still owe taxes. Generally, you will owe taxes on IRA distributions and any Roth IRA distributions over your cost basis.

Lastly, make sure you are ready to use this money because this money must be used within 120 days, or it will count as a premature distribution if you are under $59\frac{1}{2}$ and it may be subject to penalty. If for some reason your purchase is delayed, you can generally put the money back into your IRA to avoid penalties and tax by classifying it as a 60-day rollover, but you can do this only once every 12 months.[2]

In establishing the right foundation for growing wealth, it is important to avoid mistakes when buying a home that could cost you in the long run. In the next chapter, I will show you the major financial mistakes attorneys often make and how to avoid them.

---

[2] "Publication 59-B (2020), distributions from individual retirement arrangements (IRAs)," IRS, accessed October 16, 2021, https://www.irs.gov/publications/p590b#en_US_2019_publink1000230925.

CHAPTER 5

The Biggest Money Mistakes Attorneys Make

In the previous few chapters, I have covered some of the basic principles of starting with a solid financial foundation. I discussed some key considerations related to setting savings goals, budgeting, dealing with student loans, managing your cash flow, and making a home purchase that will set you on the pathway to financial independence. As we wrap up this section, I want to highlight some of the most common financial mistakes that attorneys make. Hopefully, you will avoid these tragic mistakes and by doing so, set yourself up for success.

INSUFFICIENT SAVINGS RATE

Saving can be tough. Thanks to law school, you got a late start in your career, and you have student loans to pay. If you are part of a small firm or are running your own practice, the ups and downs in your income can make saving a challenge. It is even tougher if your employer does not provide a matching contribution or if you do not have an employer plan at all.

For these reasons, many attorneys are not saving enough money for retirement. To reach financial independence, you need to start saving aggressively. The earlier you start saving and the more you save, the more you will accumulate. You cannot change what the stock market will do. What you can change is how much you are saving and when you start. Get realistic with yourself about how much you need to save and get started now.

NEGLECTING SAVINGS TO PAY OFF DEBT

One factor that makes saving so difficult is debt. From student loans to mortgages, young attorneys are often saddled with large amounts of debt. When it comes to debt, it seems like today's mainstream thinking is that you need to pay down all your debt before you do anything else. I see a lot of attorneys and others buying into this concept and aggressively paying down all their debts, including mortgages, before they start investing.

This is a big mistake. When it comes to investing, your most valuable commodity is time. The earlier you start investing, the greater your compound growth will be over time. The opportunity cost of missing out on your early years of investing is enormous and can set you back considerably. While paying down high interest rate debt should be a priority, do not make the mistake of neglecting your savings and investing.

LIVING TOO LARGE

You get a big windfall, you get a bonus, or you get promoted to partner and what happens? You start spending more. This is human nature. Most people who experience an increase in income expand their lifestyle and neglect to expand their savings. If your lifestyle gets upgraded, you will need to upgrade your retirement savings too if you want to eventually maintain that lifestyle in retirement.

The secret to building wealth is to live below your means. One of the biggest mistakes attorneys make is living too large. The long hours and high stress of your job might lead you to splurge on food, alcohol, and entertainment. The desire to keep up with your neighbors and colleagues might lead you to buy a bigger house or nicer office than you can afford. The increase in your income might tempt you to splurge on things you never thought you would have.

A little splurging is okay. After all, we're human. We need to enjoy life from time to time. You can build some splurging into your budget, but stick to your plan. Make sure that you are not jeopardizing your financial future by living too large.

NOT MAXIMIZING TAX ADVANTAGES

One of the biggest problems attorneys face, especially those who own their own practices, is paying high taxes. Because you are extremely busy and your time is valuable, you may not have the time to spend researching and doing tax planning. I have also seen many attorneys simply assume (rightly or wrongly) that their accountant or financial advisor will proactively tell them what they need to do. Often, they do not.

As a result, many attorneys are paying more in taxes than they need to because they are not maximizing their tax deferrals through tax-advantaged investment vehicles. Knowing what is available to you and taking maximum advantage of your options can save you thousands in taxes. We will explore this topic more in-depth later.

TOO MUCH TIED UP IN REAL ESTATE

Among the attorneys I work with, it seems that many have an interest in real estate either for passive income or as investment property. While some real estate can be a nice diversifier to your overall portfolio, be cautious about tying up too much money in it. As an investment, you might be better off buying stocks and bonds.

There are several reasons real estate is not ideal. First, it may be illiquid. Some properties, especially commercial real estate, can be difficult to sell. If you cannot sell it, you cannot use that money for other needs or opportunities. Second, it involves additional costs that will subtract from any revenue, such as maintenance or utilities. A portfolio of stocks and bonds does not incur these costs. Third, physical real estate as an asset class is not guaranteed to grow in value and may actually decline. Of course, this is true of stocks and bonds too. However, many people are attracted to real estate because they are certain it will be worth more down the road. This is not always the case.

NOT HAVING A PLAN

By far, the biggest mistake of all is simply not having a financial plan. A financial plan is a written document that describes your goals in detail (such as retirement) and how you plan to use your resources to work toward those goals most efficiently.

At a minimum, a plan should describe how much money you are aiming to accumulate to be able to retire or be financially independent, how much money you need to save to get there, and checkpoints to measure your progress along the way. A plan can also include where the money is going (what type of accounts), budgets for spending, short-term goals, debt-reduction goals, insurance coverage, your social security strategy, and so on. If you are operating with no plan, it's like trying to navigate in a foreign country with no map. You might get where you're going, but it will probably take you longer and cost you more money. Also, this plan needs to be documented and written down. By writing down your plan, you commit to it and ensure that it will not be forgotten.

TOO MUCH PLANNING, NOT ENOUGH DOING

Finally, the biggest mistake of all is inaction. Most attorneys I know are meticulous researchers, voracious readers, and analytical thinkers. These are great skills, but they can be a detriment if you are "overly" analytical. I suffer from this fault myself as an analytical, mathematical person. I can spend an hour in a store debating with myself between purchasing two similar items and then go home with nothing.

Do not allow yourself to get stuck in the researching and planning phase and never take action. Too many people I know neglect their finances because they are still trying to figure things out or they are overwhelmed. Neglecting our finances makes the process of budgeting and planning even more daunting, and so we get stuck in this cycle of neglect. A decent, simple plan acted on is better than a meticulously perfected plan never implemented. Start with a simple plan and then work the plan.

A qualified financial planner can help you not only with crafting a quality financial plan, but also with implementing a plan. Be careful: some will offer free "plans" that are little more than a quick retirement calculator. These plans are often just a way to get you in the door and sell you a product. As the saying goes, you get what you pay for. You don't want a free plan—you want to pay a qualified planner to help you create and implement a plan and hold you accountable for following it. Also, be sure to seek out a qualified, fee-based financial planner, such as a Certified Financial Planner™, not a commission-based sales representative.

My mission in life is to help attorneys and law firm owners like you avoid these common mistakes and make the right moves to maximize your wealth over time. The mistakes described in this chapter can cost you dearly in the long run. We all have limited time. Make the most of your time by making smart decisions, having a plan and acting on it, and avoiding costly financial mistakes.

PART II

Growing Rich: Investing for Attorneys

If you're going to grow your wealth and reach financial independence, you will need to put your money to work for you by investing, and you are going to need to be smart about your investment decisions from the start. Long-term investing for your future is not the same thing as stock market speculation. In this section, I will cover basic investing concepts that will set you up for success.

CHAPTER 6

The Time Value of Money

According to the legend, what is now known as Manhattan Island, boasting some of the most expensive real estate in the world, was at one time purchased by Dutch settlers from Native Americans in 1626. Purportedly, a man named Peter Minuit, the leader of the Dutch settlers, purchased the land from a local Native American tribe for the equivalent of approximately 24 dollars.

Whether or not this story is true is the subject of debate. Supposing it is true—was it a good deal? Manhattan comprises approximately 14,600 acres. As of 2019, the average cost of an acre of land was $3,160.[1] According to that math, this amount of land on average would today cost about $46 million. But Manhattan is special—it is not just any old land. According to an article in Bloomberg in 2018, the land value of Manhattan was approximately $1.74 trillion.[2] So, in terms of real estate deals, this was a great deal!

But what if instead of buying Manhattan for $24, you had invested that money in the stock market and earned an average 9 percent rate of return for the next 395 years? Assuming you could earn that rate of return over that time frame, today you would have a whopping $14,577,328,081,832,802.00. That's

---

[1] "Land values 2019 summary," US Department of Agriculture, August 2019, https://www.nass.usda.gov/Publications/Todays_Reports/reports/land0819.pdf.

[2] Richard Florida, "What's Manhattan's land worth?" Bloomberg, April 24, 2018, https://www.bloomberg.com/news/articles/2018-04-24/manhattan-s-land-value-is-an-incredible-1-74-trillion#:~:text=Manhattan's%20Land%20Value%20Is%20an%20Incredible%20%241.74%20Trillion%20%2D%20Bloomberg.

$14 quadrillion. Wow! Right now, you're probably scratching your head, asking: is that right? I did the calculation several times just to make sure.

That staggering figure helps illustrate the awesome power of compounding interest over time. It is the singular most powerful force of wealth creation that exists. Because of the power of compounding interest, a sum of money today has more value than the same sum of money in the future. We call this concept the time value of money. As I have mentioned in previous chapters, time is in fact your most valuable commodity and money compounding over time grows exponentially.

COMPOUND INTEREST

Compound interest is the ability to earn interest on interest earned. If you are earning interest on the interest that you earn each year, the total value of your interest earned each year will keep increasing, resulting in exponential growth. This happens when interest (or dividends, capital gains, etc.) is reinvested into the same investment.

Let's consider a simple example. Suppose you put $10,000 in an investment account and earn 9 percent interest this year (compounded annually). You will earn $900 in interest. You leave the $900 in the account, and now you have $10,900 in the account to earn interest on. The following year, you earn 9 percent again. Only this time you are earning 9 percent on a larger amount ($10,900), so your total interest earned is $981 instead of $900. If you leave all the money in the account the following year and earn 9 percent again, you'll earn $1,069.20. See Table 6.1 below.

Table 6.1

Year	Starting Amount	Interest	Ending Amount
1	$10,000.00	$900.00	$10,900.00
2	$10,900.00	$981.00	$11,881.00
3	$11,881.00	$1,069.29	$12,950.29
4	$12,950.29	$1,165.52	$14,115.81
5	$14,115.81	$1,270.42	$15,386.23
6	$15,386.23	$1,384.76	$16,770.99
7	$16,770.99	$1,509.39	$18,280.37

EXPONENTIAL GROWTH

As you can see in Table 6.1, the growth increases exponentially over time as the dollar amount of interest earned increases each year. This is what we call exponential growth, as opposed to linear growth. You can see the effect of exponential growth in Figure 6.1. Note how the line curves upward over time, reflecting the increasing rate of growth in dollar terms.

At a 9 percent rate of growth, a sum of money will double in about 9 years (or achieve 100 percent growth), triple in about 13 years, quadruple in 17 years, and quintuple in 20 years. A higher rate of growth would lead to your investment doubling faster. There is a quick and easy way to estimate how quickly an investment will double at different rates of growth. In the investment world, we call this the rule of 72. To determine how long it will take to double an investment, divide 72 by the rate of return. For example, if you want to know how long it will take an investment to double at a 6 percent rate, divide 72 by 6 to get 12. At a 6 percent rate, your investment should double approximately every 12 years. This method is not completely accurate, however, and gets less accurate at the extremes—but it serves as a good estimation.

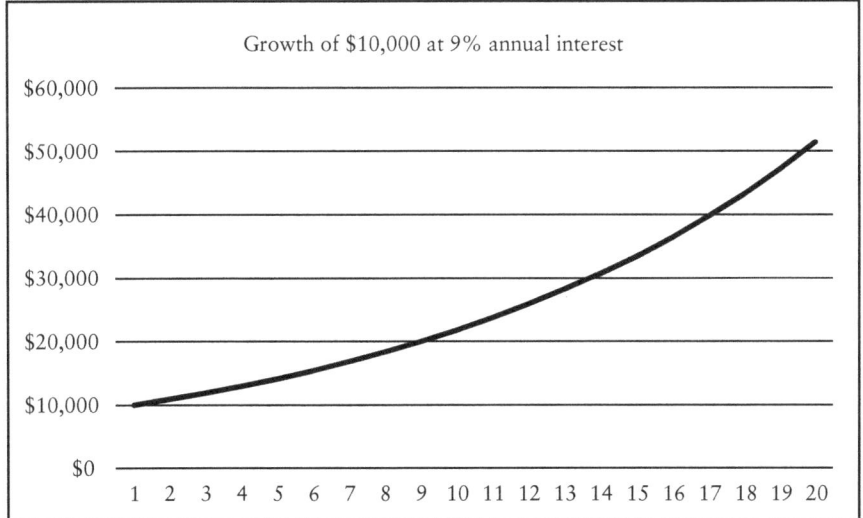

Figure 6.1

THE SECRET TO GROWING RICH

Hopefully, my example at the opening of this chapter is now looking less absurd. The secret to growing rich is simply time. The odds of getting rich some other way—such as picking the right stock or winning the lottery—are slim. You may earn more than your peers, or you may earn less than your peers. I have seen attorneys who earned relatively little accrue very large retirement balances by starting early and continuing to save regularly. On the other hand, I have witnessed my share of attorneys who make great money and have no accumulated assets to show for it.

True, you can probably do some things that will tilt the scales in your favor. But there is one tried and true method for building wealth. That method is simply to maximize the amount of time your money has to grow, thereby maximizing the potential growth of your money. You can put time on your side by starting early and making saving and investing a priority in the beginning, even if you are still paying down student loans and other debts.

The other really critical thing is not to withdraw money prematurely from your retirement accounts. Sadly, some of my attorney clients keep dipping into their retirement accounts when they are running short on cash. The result? Their accounts have barely grown. Why? Withdrawing money prematurely greatly reduces your earning potential by cutting short the power of compounding.

Now that you have a clear understanding of the power of compounding and the importance of investing, let's dive into the world of investments so that you can put this power to work for you. In the next chapter, we will discuss the different types of asset classes you can invest in.

CHAPTER 7

Introduction to Investments

What do I invest in? In this chapter, I will provide you with an overview of the major investable asset classes: fixed income, equities, commodities, and real estate. Are there more? Certainly. But having a firm understanding of these basic asset classes will give you the foundational understanding you need to get started.

FIXED INCOME

Fixed income refers mostly to bonds. Bonds are lending instruments, unlike stocks which represent ownership in a company. By purchasing a bond, you are lending money to the organization or company that is offering the bond.

There are various types of bonds: government bonds issued by the federal government; municipal bonds issued by state and local municipalities; and corporate bonds issued by companies. Some bonds issued by companies can be converted to stock later; these are referred to as convertible bonds. There are also foreign bonds issued by foreign governments or companies.

Another type of bond, one that gained infamy during the Great Financial Crisis, is the mortgage-backed bond. Since then, this type of bond has been subject to much greater regulatory scrutiny. As the name implies, mortgage-backed bonds are created from mortgages. Financial institutions purchase mortgages, bundle them together, and sell them as bonds. By purchasing a mortgage-backed bond, you are buying small pieces of hundreds or even thousands of mortgages.

This asset class is called fixed income because investors or owners of these securities receive regular interest payments (or dividends). Most often this is a fixed dollar amount. Companies or governments are obligated contractually to pay these dividends because they are debt obligations. Failure to pay results in default, which harms the company's credit rating and can bring legal action against the company. The rate of yield is correlated to the risk of the bond. Government bonds, for example, are considered less risky and usually offer lower interest yields than corporate bonds.

Another important characteristic of bonds is their maturity, or the specified length of time during which interest payments are paid to the investor. At the end of maturity, usually the face value of the bond is repaid to the investor. The maturity of a bond can also affect the interest yield. Bonds are often classified as short term, intermediate, and long term. Longer-term bonds are considered higher risk and therefore usually have higher yields.

Bonds are subject to various types of risk, primarily the ability of the issuer to continue making interest payments to the investor. This is called default risk. Government bonds (or treasuries) have the lowest default risk because the government tends not to default on its debt and can always raise more money through taxation or debt issuance. For corporate bonds, the risk of default hinges on the company's financial strength. Companies with strong balance sheets and cash flow should have lower default risk. Bonds from these companies are considered "investment grade." Bonds issued by companies that are less creditworthy are considered junk or high-yield bonds and normally yield higher interest rates due to the higher risk.

Another key risk of bonds is interest rate risk. Because bonds typically pay out a fixed dollar amount, the value of the bond can rise or fall depending on changes in the broader market's interest rates. Suppose you purchase a 10-year bond for $1,000 yielding 5 percent interest (or $50 annually). If, a year later, bonds from similar companies with 10-year bonds are yielding 6 percent interest, the value of your bond will decline because it is less attractive. If you try to sell the bond, you will get less than the $1,000 you paid for it.

Investors are attracted to bonds for their relatively low risk as compared with equities. If a company were to go bankrupt, the bondholders would receive payment before the stockholders, so bonds are a degree less risky than stocks from similar companies. Because they have less risk, bonds tend to have less volatility, and fluctuations in value are less extreme than stocks.

Investors also use bonds as a diversifier and risk hedge in portfolios, especially government bonds. Government bonds tend to do well during times of economic distress and when stocks are doing poorly. Also, during recessions the government usually tries to lower market interest rates through the powers of the Federal Reserve. Because bonds are sensitive to interest rates, the value of bonds will go up during these times. Therefore, government bonds can serve as a buffer against investment losses during economic and market downturns.

However, bonds tend to offer a lower rate of return over time than stocks, especially government bonds. This is the trade-off for a less risky asset. From 1802 to 2010, bonds produced an average rate of return of 3.6 percent after inflation. On the other hand, stocks earned an average rate of return of 6.7 percent after inflation over that same time frame.[1]

EQUITIES

The term *equities* refers to stocks. Stocks are the preferred asset class for long-term growth and wealth creation. They are considered ownership securities. When you buy a stock, you are buying a piece of that company and becoming a shareholder or owner of that company. As an owner of the company, you may have certain rights, such as the right to elect board members, vote on issues like mergers and acquisitions, or receive dividends. However, to have any real sway over these decisions, you must be a significant shareholder.

Why do companies issue stock? Issuing stock is a primary method of raising money for companies. Most often, investors purchase stock in the secondary market; that is, we buy it from other investors. However, those shares originally were sold from the company directly to investors either in an initial public offering (IPO) when the company first "went public" or in a secondary offering. Companies go through IPOs and secondary offerings to raise capital. They will sometimes buy their own stock back to deploy excess cash and attempt to boost their stock price and reward investors.

You can make money owning stocks in two ways: dividends and capital appreciation. Profitable companies will often pay dividends to their shareholders. These dividends are mostly discretionary, as opposed to fixed income securities, which have fixed dividend payments. Usually, dividends

---

[1] Jeremy Siegel, *Stocks for the long run: The definitive guide to financial markets and long-term investment strategies* (New York: McGraw-Hill, 2014).

are not the primary method of earning money owning stocks, however. The average dividend yield for companies in the S&P 500 between 2009 and 2019 was just 1.97 percent. Dividend yields have been higher historically. Between 1871 and 1960, the average dividend yield in the S&P 500 was never below 3 percent.[2]

Today, however, we face two dynamics that have put pressure on dividends. First, interest rates are historically low. Companies do not feel that they need to have high dividend rates in this low interest rate environment. Second, the biggest components of the S&P 500 are growth-oriented tech companies that favor investing in innovation instead of paying dividends to investors.

Luckily, there is another way to make money owning stocks: capital appreciation. As a company's profitability grows, the company's value and the value of its shares should increase as well, providing reward to the stockholders. Capital appreciation accounts for most of the growth of the stock market over time.

However, just as the value of stocks can go up, the value of stocks can go down. Even on a day-to-day basis, a stock's share price can swing wildly in the positive or negative direction. And an increase in profitability does not always produce a commensurate increase in the share price. Stock prices are subject to the whims of investors and how investors view a particular stock and its prospects.

Generally, stocks are riskier than bonds. Many risks affect stocks, but you should be aware of two main types: market risk and company-specific risk. Market risk refers to the risk of the broad stock market as a whole and the general economic cycle. During positive economic periods, when the stock market is rising, most stocks also tend to increase in value. Conversely, during negative economic periods or when the stock market is in decline, most stocks also tend to decline. During the 2008–2009 Great Financial Crisis, as mentioned earlier, the S&P 500 declined in value by over 50 percent. Most stocks saw similar declines during this period, some more and some less.

Company-specific risk refers to the risks associated with the business activities of a particular company and how financial conditions may affect that company. For instance, a grocery store will have very different company-specific risks than an oil company. The grocery store may be more stable

---

[2] Sean Ross, "A history of the S&P 500 dividend yield," Investopedia, May 5, 2020, https://www.investopedia.com/articles/markets/071616/history-sp-500-dividend-yield.asp.

during recessions, whereas the oil company may struggle during recessions as economic activity slows.

There are various types of stocks and ways to categorize stocks. Stocks are often categorized by size: small, mid, and large. Smaller companies tend to experience larger swings in share price (greater volatility) and therefore may represent more risk. Sometimes they are categorized by the terms *growth* and *value*. Growth stocks are focused on growing sales and earnings and often do not pay dividends, instead reinvesting profits in the company to accelerate growth. Technology companies are often growth stocks. Value stocks are usually companies that are in relatively stable and cash flow-oriented industries like utilities.

Geographically, there are foreign and domestic stocks. Foreign stocks can be further divided into developed countries, such as most of Europe and parts of Asia, and emerging markets, such as China, India, Brazil, and Russia. Stocks can face unique geopolitical opportunities and risks depending on where they do business.

Stocks can also be categorized by sector. Eleven sectors are commonly recognized: technology, health care, communications, consumer discretionary, consumer staples, energy, financials, industrials, materials, utilities, and real estate. Each of these sectors has different characteristics, offers different growth opportunities, and is subject to different underlying risks.

COMMODITIES

Commodities are an often overlooked, yet crucial, ingredient in a portfolio. Whereas fixed income securities are lending securities and equity securities are company-ownership securities, commodities represent real assets. Examples of commodities include precious metals such as gold, silver, and copper; fossil fuels such as oil and natural gas; agricultural products such as wheat and cattle; and others including timber, sugar, and coffee.

What makes commodities valuable in a portfolio is their low correlation to equities and fixed income. Correlation is a measurement that quantifies how similarly two different asset classes behave. Commodities tend to have a low correlation to stocks and bonds, meaning they behave differently. They may perform well during periods when stocks or bonds perform poorly, helping to reduce overall risk and smooth out returns over time.

Equities tend to do well during expansionary periods, where economic growth is strong and interest rates are low. Fixed income tends to do well during contractionary periods, when economic growth is weak, interest rates are falling, and inflation is low. But there is a third type of economic environment, called stagnation—periods characterized by weak economic growth, rising interest rates, and high inflation. Stocks and bonds tend to perform poorly during these periods. Although various types of commodities may behave differently, in general, they tend to do well during these periods.

Commodities can serve as a hedge against inflation because they tend to do well during inflationary periods. Inflation refers to the general increase in prices due to the devaluation of currency. Inflation has been relatively low for many years, but there have been times in our history, such as the 1970s, when inflation was abnormally high. During this time, stock returns were dismal, and bonds suffered losses as the Federal Reserve increased interest rates to combat inflation.

In the old days, commodities were bought and sold directly in markets; today, they are most often traded using futures contracts. Futures contracts are agreements to pay a specified price at a date in the future for a commodity such as wheat. Futures contracts allow producers of commodities to hedge price risk by locking in a future price. The price risk is then taken up by traders who buy and sell the futures contracts.

Fortunately, owning commodities can be much simpler. To do so, you can buy mutual funds and exchange-traded funds (ETFs). You can buy the entire commodities market with a general commodities mutual fund or an ETF, or you can purchase specific commodities like oil and gas with an oil and gas fund, for example.

Commodities have fallen out of fashion as they have been outpaced by stocks and bonds in recent years. From 2009 to 2017, commodities posted an annualized gross return of –4.84 percent (according to the S&P Goldman Sachs Commodity Index). However, over a longer time frame that includes periods of high inflation, they have fared better. From 1970 to 2017, the same index returned an average of 6.99 percent annually.[3]

REAL ESTATE

Although real estate is a sector of the stock market, it should be regarded as its own asset class. As is the case with commodities, this is because

---

[3] Craig L. Israelsen, "A sector to watch as inflation ticks up," Financial Planning, June 21, 2018, https://www.financial-planning.com/news/how-commodities-funds-can -help-your-clients-portfolios.

Introduction to Investments 53

real estate as an asset class shows a low correlation to fixed income and equities. According to the Pension Real Estate Association, from 1984 to 2018, real estate showed a correlation to bonds of −0.15 and a correlation to stocks of 0.07. That is even less correlation to stocks and bonds than commodities.[4]

Better yet, real estate has shown historical returns similar to the high returns enjoyed by the stock market. From 1930 to 2009, real estate total returns averaged 9.1 percent per year compared with 9.2 percent for the total stock market.[5]

You can invest in real estate in your investment portfolio primarily through real estate investment trusts (REITs) and real estate developers. REITs are companies that own and operate portfolios of mostly commercial, income-generating properties. As an investor in the REIT, you make money by receiving pass-through income in the form of dividends and in capital appreciation as the portfolio of real estate increases in value.

Real estate should be treated as a separate piece of your portfolio because it serves a valuable role. As an asset class, real estate historically has shown less volatility and therefore less risk than equities, but higher yields and stronger returns than fixed income. Due to the nature of real estate, it may provide positive returns when equities and fixed income are not faring so well. Specifically, real estate tends to do well during periods of strong economic growth and rising inflation. This is what gives real estate its low correlation with equities and fixed income.

Because of its higher yield and connection to physical property, real estate tends to stand up well in times of inflation. Furthermore, when prices rise, real estate owners tend to increase rents, hopefully increasing dividend payments to investors and thereby keeping pace with inflation. Theoretically, then, real estate, like commodities, can provide an inflation hedge.

However, real estate is not without significant risks of its own, as we saw during the 2008–2009 crisis. In addition, due to its dividend-oriented nature, real estate can be interest-rate-sensitive and lose value when rates rise.

---

[4] Greg MacKinnon, "Yes, stocks, bonds, and real estate are exposed to different risk factors," PREA Quarterly, 2018, https://docs.prea.org/pub/45CA1E42-A07F-E5EA-C448-19C346183AAF.

[5] Richard Ferri, *All about asset allocation* (New York: McGraw-Hill, 2010).

MUTUAL FUNDS AND ETFS

The most prudent way to invest most of your portfolio is by owning a large cross section of stocks, bonds, commodities, and REITs. You can buy individual stocks and the like, but such purchases entail a lot of risk, which I will discuss later. It is okay to speculate with a small portion of your portfolio (I suggest 5 to 10 percent to my clients), but the majority of your portfolio should be broadly diversified. It is difficult to achieve diversification by buying individual stocks. There are 500 different stocks in the S&P 500. You could buy all 500 individually, which would be extremely tedious, or you could simply buy a mutual fund or an ETF that tracks the S&P 500 and buys all those companies for you.

Mutual funds are securities offered by companies that pool investor money to purchase a portfolio of stocks, bonds, or other assets. Like stocks, investors purchase shares of a mutual fund to invest in the fund. By investing in a mutual fund, you are investing in all the holdings of that fund all at once. This is a great way to achieve diversification without much effort.

There is a broad variety of mutual funds and ETFs. Some are multi-asset funds that invest broadly in a mix of different asset classes; these are often called asset allocation funds or balanced funds. Others offer exposure to an entire asset class like stocks or bonds or are focused on particular subcategories like large-cap stocks, intermediate treasuries, or gold.

How are ETFs and mutual funds different? ETFs are like mutual funds; except, like stocks, they trade during the day. Mutual funds, on the other hand, can usually be bought and sold only at the market's closing price for the day. When purchasing a mutual fund, you can put your order in anytime throughout the day, but your order will execute at that day's closing price.

There are some other key differences between ETFs and mutual funds. ETFs are usually passive or algorithm-driven; that is, the securities the ETF owns are predetermined by an index or a formula. Mutual funds can be passive or actively managed. Actively managed funds have a team of investment professionals who make investment decisions and have discretion over the holdings of the fund. These funds rely on the skill of the managers to achieve results.

What about fees? One fee that ETFs and mutual funds have in common is their expense ratio. This fee is expressed as a percentage and describes the percentage of fund assets used to pay expenses. For you as the investor, this fee will reduce your gains by the percentage expressed. For example, if the expense ratio is 1.0 percent, you can expect that your returns will be reduced by 1.0 percent to pay expenses. Because ETFs are most often passively managed and traded like stocks between investors, managers have less work to do and therefore ETFs tend to have lower expense ratios.

Mutual funds often have additional fees. Some mutual funds have front-end loads (commissions paid when you buy the fund) or back-end loads (commissions paid when you sell the fund). Back-end loads often go away after you have owned the shares for a certain period of time. These commissions may be as high as 8.5 percent in some cases. Obviously, then, your potential returns will be greatly reduced.

Although ETFs do not have inherent commissions, sometimes you must pay a commission to your broker to purchase them. These commissions are usually not a percentage, but rather a flat dollar amount per order—often somewhere around $5 to $10. If the commission is five dollars, you pay five dollars to place an order for any number of shares—not per the number of shares you purchase. So, one order for 10 shares would be subject to a commission of $5, not $50. Nowadays, many online trading platforms offer commission-free ETF trading.

Mutual funds have extra fees used to pay marketing costs called 12b-1 fees. These fees may go to the broker through whom you purchase the fund. These fees may range from 0.25 percent to 1.00 percent. An extra 1.00 percent fee on your investment each year will greatly reduce your potential returns over time.

In general, I favor passive ETFs over mutual funds. The first and biggest reason is the lower expenses. One of the world's most popular ETFs (as of this writing) is State Street's SPDR® S&P 500 ETF, which goes by the symbol SPY. As of August 31, 2021, this ETF had a gross expense ratio of 0.0945 percent—an infinitesimal amount.[6] Similar actively managed mutual funds can have expense ratios of more than 1.00 percent, more than 10 times higher! This ETF allows you to instantly invest in the entire S&P 500 with little cost.

Another reason to favor ETFs is their liquidity. Liquidity refers to how readily something can be sold and converted to cash. ETFs do not have any minimum hold times (as mutual funds sometimes do) and can be sold at any point during the day, making them much more liquid.

---

[6] "SPDR S&P 500 ETF Trust," State Street Global Advisors, accessed October 16, 2021, https://www.ssga.com/us/en/individual/etfs/funds/spdr-sp-500-etf-trust-spy.

You can purchase mutual funds and ETFs through a financial advisor or you can go it alone. If you do go it alone, I recommend using a low-cost online brokerage such as Charles Schwab, which has zero commissions on online ETF trades.

Before you buy a mutual fund or ETF, you will want to do your research. Many online brokerage platforms offer research tools that give you information about funds you want to purchase. Plenty of third-party research sites are also available. One of the industry favorites, Morningstar.com, provides an abundance of information about stocks and funds. There is a free version for general information and a paid version that offers deeper insights.

The universe of mutual funds and ETFs is so vast and diverse that it can quickly become confusing and overwhelming. I therefore recommend sticking to the basics. A few good ETFs representing the major asset classes is really all you need. At our firm, we prefer to use the largest, cheapest, and most liquid ETFs available. But what do you do with these funds? Which ones do you buy and how many shares do you purchase? Do you just buy them and hold them? In the next chapter, we will review various investment strategies you might consider employing in your own investment plan.

CHAPTER 8

Investment Strategies

In the old days you might have received a phone call from a broker on Wall Street trying to pitch you the latest and greatest initial public offering (IPO). Those days are mostly gone, but the environment remains the same. We have websites, TV, our email inboxes, and our phones now pitching stocks to us daily. Technology has inundated us with more information than we need or ask for.

Investing can be confusing and daunting, and you cannot afford to be distracted by all the noise. You need a simple, reliable, and efficient investment strategy that is appropriate for your risk level and will help you reach your financial goals. You don't have time to waste messing around. In this chapter, I will break down the most fundamental investment strategies and what I believe is the best approach for the individual attorney.

CONCENTRATION

You have heard the word "diversification" before, but let's start with its polar opposite: "concentration." Concentration refers to when an investor holds a large portion of their portfolio in one particular stock or other security.

Some investors intentionally hold a concentrated position in an individual stock as part of their overall portfolio if they feel that that particular stock will perform well and if they have a lot of faith in that particular company. This strategy holds out the carrot of potentially outsized gains as in the case of early investors in behemoths like Amazon and Google or other stocks that have come to dominate the market over time.

However, I do not think this is a wise approach for most attorney investors. First, managing stock picks requires time, and your time is already at a premium. Do you really have the time to monitor and manage individual stock trading? Second, your odds of picking the next unicorn are slim to none. The risk of potentially picking the wrong stock and missing out on years of stock market growth or, worse yet, losing money while the market climbs higher, could be devastating.

According to Tim Kochis in *Managing Concentrated Stock Wealth*, only 0.14 percent of tech start-ups reach "unicorn" status. It takes an average of seven years for a tech start-up to go public, and even then, only 39 percent reach that point. When they do, most IPO share prices underperform the market after debuting to the public.[1]

Stock market history is a graveyard littered with the tombstones of bankrupt companies. Even "blue chip" names that were once thought invincible, or steady and reliable dividend payers, have gone belly up from time to time. One great example is Sears, once a retail giant, a household name, and, at one point, the builder of the world's tallest skyscraper. The company declared bankruptcy in 2018, and its stock lost nearly 100 percent of its value.

Nevertheless, the temptation to pile into the next hot stock is great. I have had many clients who insist on including concentrated positions in individual stocks in their portfolios. In my experience, in the best scenarios, these stock choices have performed about as well as the market. But more often, my clients invest in a particular name at exactly the wrong time and lose money. They choose to invest in a particular stock because they see it on the web or on TV, note how dramatically it has gone up, and so want to get in on the action. Often that's the worst time to get in.

Individual retail investors are usually last to the party and leave with an empty bag after the pros take their profits and run. I encourage you not to pursue this strategy. If you insist, as some of my clients do, keep any individual concentrated positions limited to no more than 5 percent of your overall portfolio.

DIVERSIFICATION

Instead of trying to pick the next big winner, it's best to be diversified. Instead of buying individual stocks, buy a mutual fund or an ETF that

---

[1] Tim Kochis and Michael J. Lewis, *Managing concentrated stock wealth: An advisor's guide to building customized solutions* (Hoboken, NJ: Wiley, 2016).

represents the whole stock market. Instead of buying bonds from a particular company, buy a mutual fund or an ETF that represents the whole bond market. One and done.

Diversifying your portfolio reduces your overall level of risk and volatility. Individual stocks can be extremely volatile and fluctuate in price greatly. The market tends to fluctuate in price much less than individual stocks.

Finally, and more importantly, diversification reduces the risk of not achieving your financial goals. While the stock market is not predictable and future stock returns are uncertain, they have been relatively consistent on a long-term basis. And the future returns of individual companies are far more uncertain and unpredictable.

Another great reason to diversify is that it takes a huge burden off your shoulders. Diversification requires no thinking—no trying to read the tea leaves, no charting, no research. It is simple. You do not have to invest time and energy (and stress) trying to pick the right stock. And, most importantly, you will avoid making investment mistakes that can derail your financial plan.

SMALL VERSUS LARGE

Within the stock market there is a lot of variety. One of the most basic distinctions is small versus large. Small-cap stocks typically have a total market capitalization (the value of all their stock) of $300 million to $2 billion. The Russell 2000 is a small-cap index and tracks the performance of roughly 2,000 of these companies. Large-cap stocks, on the other hand, are usually considered companies that have a market capitalization of greater than $10 billion. The S&P 500 is a large-cap index that tracks the performance of the 500 largest companies in the United States. What about the stocks in the middle? These are called mid-cap, and there are indices that track mid-caps as well.

Some investors have historically favored small caps because they are thought to offer better opportunities for long-term growth, whereas large-cap companies are thought to be more mature companies with fewer growth opportunities. Therefore, small caps are believed to perform better than large caps over time. This is sometimes called the "small-cap premium."

As John Bogle demonstrates in his book *Common Sense on Mutual Funds*, this is not always the case. Sometimes small caps perform better, but there are long periods of time when large caps can perform significantly better as well. From 1925 to 1997, the compound annual rate of growth for small caps was 12.7 percent, whereas large caps achieved 11.0 percent. However, most of the outperformance for small caps occurred during a single decade—1973–1983. Excluding that period, large caps returned 11.0 percent and small caps 10.4 percent. Bogle suggests that periods of outperformance and underperformance of small caps and large caps can largely be explained by the phenomenon of "reversion to the mean."[2]

Also, small caps tend to have higher volatility and can represent higher risk. Smaller companies can be more affected by changes in economic conditions. Based on Bogle's work and the higher risk of small companies, I do not think it is wise to favor small caps over large caps. Rather, both should be represented appropriately in your portfolio.

VALUE VERSUS GROWTH

Another distinction that investors often make is between value and growth. Value stocks are companies perceived to be undervalued by the market. They often are well established companies with strong cash flow that offer dividends. These are often companies whose stock is trading at a discount relative to book value or sales and profits. Growth stocks, on the other hand, are valued for their potential to grow and expand their business faster than other companies. These companies often do not have strong cash flow but are expected to achieve it in the future. Rather than pay dividends, these companies usually reinvest earnings in the business to accelerate growth. These companies usually are priced at a premium relative to sales or profits.

Value stocks are favored by those investors who feel that these stocks will do better over the long term because they are currently undervalued. Warren Buffett is perhaps the most famous value investor. Value stocks did very well in the 1980s and 1990s, leading investors to believe this would always be the case. This was termed the "value premium."

However, as with small- and large-cap stocks, value stocks do not always outperform. Bogle contrasted value and growth stock performance from 1937 to 1997 and found that over the cumulative time frame they performed very similarly, with growth stocks averaging 11.7 percent and value stocks averaging 11.5 percent in total return. However, growth stocks outperformed significantly for over half of that time frame—from 1937 to 1968. Value stocks

---

[2] John C. Bogle, *Common sense on mutual funds: New imperatives for the intelligent investor* (New York: Wiley, 1999).

enjoyed a huge comeback through 1976, and growth stocks then took the lead through 1980. Finally, value stocks outperformed until 1997.

In recent years, we have seen this rotation as well. From January 1, 2000, to January 1, 2007, the Vanguard Value Index Fund Admiral Shares (VVIAX) returned a cumulative 19.19 percent, whereas the Vanguard Growth Index Fund Admiral Shares (VIGAX) returned a cumulative -7.06 percent, a time frame clearly favoring value. However, from January 1, 2007 to September 1, 2020, VVIAX returned a cumulative 58.05 percent, while VIGAX returned a whopping 319.99 percent.[3]

While some argue that there is a "value premium" and that you should therefore tilt your portfolio toward value, I fail to see evidence that this idea is a wise one in the long run. Myriad factors are at play that can contribute to performance of value or growth. Rather, your portfolio should be equally weighted between value and growth or, better yet, just buy the entire stock market with a fund that represents the entire market.

STRATEGIC ASSET ALLOCATION

Strategic asset allocation is by far the most common approach by investors and investment professionals alike. It involves using long-term characteristics of various asset classes to plan what investments will be in your portfolio and what percentage you will allocate to each (your target allocation), largely leaving that unchanged.

This strategy, which often goes by nicknames such as "buy and hold" or "passive investing," is the easiest and simplest investment strategy you can employ. That is because it requires little thought or maintenance other than the initial setup and periodic rebalancing.

Strategic asset allocation is grounded in two ideas: modern portfolio theory and efficient market hypothesis. Modern portfolio theory postulates that by combining different asset classes, you can reduce overall risk, and holds that there is an optimal way to combine asset classes to achieve the highest possible return for a given level of risk.

In practice, strategic asset allocation uses historical risk and return data to determine this optimal blend of asset classes at a given level of risk. For example, if your maximum acceptable drawdown is 20 percent, what mix of asset classes would give you the highest historical rate of return without exceeding

---

[3] Data sourced from: YahooFinance.com.

a 20 percent drawdown? Determining a precise answer to that question usually requires complex calculations or the help of computer software.

The second supporting doctrine of strategic asset allocation, efficient market hypothesis, states that current stock prices reflect all current publicly available knowledge and information. A corollary of this hypothesis is that you cannot outperform the market by picking which stocks will do better, since everything that can be known is already priced in by other investors. Therefore, according to this doctrine, it is best to simply be diversified and not try to outsmart the market or get ahead of market movements.

In accordance with this idea, a strategic asset allocation is one that does not change. Once you set your target allocation, you make no changes except for perhaps adjusting your allocation to a more conservative mix as you get older and closer to retirement or rebalancing.

Strategic asset allocation usually involves rebalancing periodically. Because the market is volatile and ever changing, your targets will drift. Suppose you put 50 percent of your portfolio in large-cap stocks. If the US market has a bad year, you may discover that your large-cap stock allocation has drifted down to 45 percent. Rebalancing at that point would mean selling assets that have risen in value to buy those that have dropped in value, such as your large-cap stock allocation. This helps your portfolio stay true to its original intent and maintains your desired risk level. It is also a way to automatically buy low and sell high. However, rebalancing does not necessarily improve your returns over time. I usually recommend rebalancing at least once a year.

TACTICAL ASSET ALLOCATION

An alternative to strategic asset allocation is tactical asset allocation. Unlike strategic asset allocation, this approach is an active investment strategy through which you frequently change the weightings of different asset classes in your portfolio to take advantage of market trends or opportunities and attempt to avoid market downturns.

Tactical asset allocation is grounded in behavioral finance theory, which is a budding field of study. Behavioral finance argues that markets are driven by investor psychology more than anything else and are inherently irrational. Investors buy when markets are going up and sell when markets are going down. This is called herd behavior, and it results in the existence and persistence of trends over time, and ultimately market bubbles and market crashes.

A tactical strategy tries to capitalize on these trends. While modern portfolio theory adherents widely critique this approach, some tactical strategies have shown themselves to be effective over time. Many of these strategies are based on the concept of momentum, which is the idea that asset classes that have outperformed in the recent past are likely to continue to outperform in the near term. A momentum-based investment strategy will seek to identify those asset classes that have the strongest momentum, weight those asset classes more heavily, and periodically reevaluate and update its positioning.

This approach is not easy, is often counterintuitive, and requires intense discipline and the willingness to be wrong at times. The best tactical approaches I have studied are based on specific quantitative rules that leave no guesswork and therefore eliminate human, error-prone judgment. We use strategies like this in my practice with client portfolios. However, because of the psychological difficulty in implementing a tactical strategy and the maintenance work required, most attorneys investing on their own would be better suited to avoid this approach and stick to a simple "buy and hold" portfolio.

To begin building your investment strategy, the next thing you need to know is your risk tolerance level. In the next chapter, we will discuss risk, and I will show you how to determine your own personal risk tolerance level.

CHAPTER 9

Assessing Your Risk Tolerance

I sometimes hear people compare investing to gambling because both activities involve probability and the risk of loss. This is an unfair comparison, however. While both activities do involve risk, investing has an advantage that gambling does not: expected return. It is for this reason that investors invest their money; they take a degree of risk in exchange for an expected return. Investors expect to be rewarded for the risk they take.

Stock-picking may be a bit more akin to gambling. Placing all your chips on one individual stock involves a lot more risk than investing in a diversified S&P 500 index fund. Most long-term investors do not do this because the risk is too high. Although they might own individual stocks, they are diversified, and they are in it for the long haul. The key to growing rich isn't necessarily picking the right stocks. True, there are some lucky individuals who have amassed fortunes this way. But there are just as many, if not more, who have lost big time. Your odds of picking the next Amazon and making it rich are quite slim.

WHAT IS RISK?

The two main types of risks are systematic and unsystematic. Systematic risks are risks faced by the broad stock market—economic risk, inflation risk, interest rate risk, and so on. Unsystematic risks are the unique risks faced by individual companies because of their business operations. These risks can be reduced through diversification. In general, taking unnecessary unsystematic risk does not provide commensurate expected return.

We can define risk in many ways. Investment professionals often define it as volatility or in other academic terms. I like to define risk the way my clients see it: drawdown. The term *drawdown* refers to how far an investment or portfolio could decline before recovering to new highs. Drawdown is how much something can drop in value.

I think this is the best way to define risk because it gets at the core of the issue which is how much are you capable of seeing your portfolio decline before you throw in the towel? All of us have a breaking point, so this is an important question and perhaps the most important one.

Drawdown helps illustrate the difference between systematic and unsystematic risk. Companies can and do go bankrupt often. As noted earlier, even large, seemingly safe companies have gone bankrupt. When this happens, a company's stock can drop to essentially $0. That is, it can become entirely worthless. If that happens, investors in the stock can see their investment vanish into thin air. The drawdown risk of investing in an individual stock is 100 percent: you could lose everything.

Contrast that with the stock market. It is highly unlikely (though theoretically possible) for the value of every stock in the stock market to drop to zero simultaneously. Therefore, by investing in the broad market through a diversified stock fund, you already greatly reduce your risk level.

HOW RISKY IS THE MARKET?

The market can be highly risky. Every asset class—stocks, bonds, real estate, and commodities—has a certain level of drawdown risk. During the aftermath of the tech bubble in the early 2000s, the S&P 500 fell 50 percent below its previous highs. During the Great Financial Crisis of 2008, the S&P 500 fell by over 50 percent. During the COVID-19 pandemic of early 2020, the S&P 500 declined by over 30 percent. And of course, nothing compares to the crash of 1929, a bear market that saw the S&P 500 decline by over 80 percent.

Markets can be incredibly risky, and drawdowns can and do occur regularly. In fact, the stock market is almost always in a state of drawdown. Figure 9.1 shows the maximum monthly drawdowns of the S&P 500 from January 2000 to September 2021.

The big drawdowns of the early 2000s and the Great Financial Crisis stand out markedly in Figure 9.1. But smaller drawdowns also occur regularly.

Assessing Your Risk Tolerance

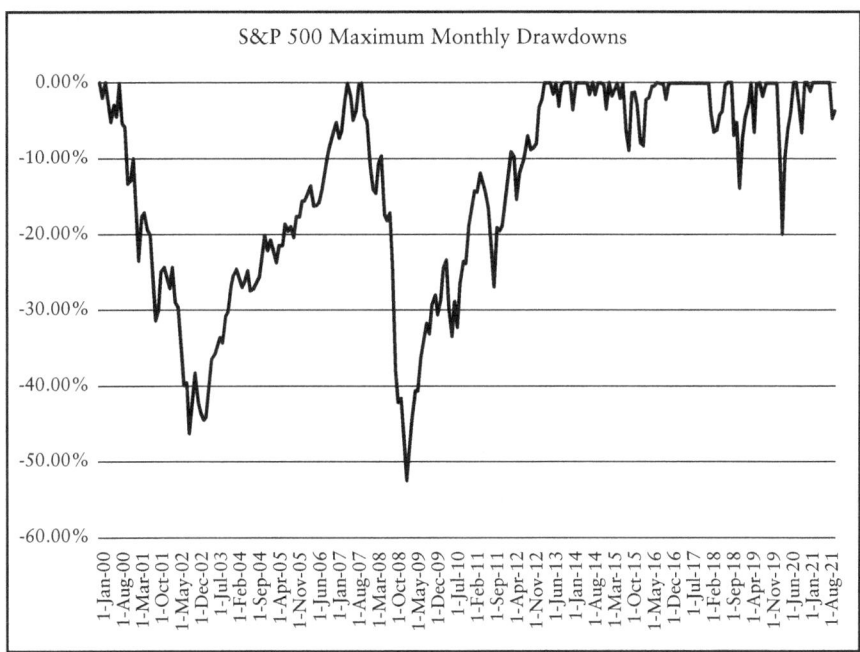

Figure 9.1[1]

Drawdowns of about 5 percent happen almost every year. Drawdowns of 10 percent or more for stocks are often called corrections. These types of drawdowns should be expected every few years. A drawdown of 20 percent or more is considered a "bear market." Drops of this magnitude are much less frequent, seeming to occur about once every 10 years or so. But just because bear markets tend to be rare, do not ignore the fact that they do happen from time to time. They are also incredibly hard to predict.

The stock market tends to be less risky over longer periods of time. Jeremy Siegel demonstrates this concept in his book *Stocks for the Long Run*. Siegel examined the real returns on stocks, bonds, and treasury bills over 1-, 2-, 5-, 10-, 20-, and 30-year periods from 1802 to 2012. Stocks have provided one-year periods as rewarding as +66.6 percent and as poorly as −38.6 percent.[2]

However, looking at the 10-year time frames, we find that stocks have enjoyed 10-year periods with annualized rates of return as high as 16.8 percent

---

[1] Data sourced from Yahoo! Finance.
[2] Jeremy Siegel, *Stocks for the long run: The definitive guide to financial markets and long-term investment strategies* (New York: McGraw-Hill, 2014).

or as low as −4.1 percent. Stretch that out to 20 years and you get a high of +12.6 percent and a low of +1.0 percent. In other words, from 1802 to 2012, while there were some great years and some quite nasty years, there was never a 20-year time frame over which the stock market was negative.

DETERMINE YOUR RISK TOLERANCE

When it comes to investing, risk and return are related. If you are a litigator, you may have been trained to think negatively about risk. But in the markets, some risk is good. You need to take a certain level of risk to achieve sufficient returns to reach financial independence. If you take no risk at all, keeping all your money in cash in a safe or in your mattress—you will never earn anything. You need to take as much risk as your risk tolerance will allow. Determining your tolerance for risk will determine how you should invest. You can reduce risk by altering the mix of assets in your portfolio. Certain asset classes, like bonds, can offset the risk of other assets like stocks. But to understand the correct makeup of your portfolio, you need to understand your risk tolerance.

Risk tolerance has two components. The first is what I call "risk capacity," which is how much risk you are capable of handling financially. Your risk capacity is a function of your age and the steadiness of your income. If you are younger and liquidity is not a concern, you likely have a high degree of risk capacity. Conversely, if you have retired and are depending on your portfolio to support yourself financially, your risk capacity is quite low.

Why is that? It has to do with your time horizon—that is, how long until you need the money. If you are retired and are actively pulling money from your account, you cannot afford to experience major drawdowns. Withdrawing money during a down market "locks in" your losses. This greatly reduces the growth rate of your portfolio, which in turn greatly increases the probability of running out of money in retirement. If you are actively pulling money from your portfolio or may need to do so soon either because you are retiring or because your income is unpredictable, risk management becomes more important.

The second component of risk tolerance is what I call "risk attitude," which describes how comfortable you are taking risk. Even if your risk capacity is high, if you freak out when your portfolio declines, your risk attitude may be quite low. Risk attitude is important to understand because if your portfolio is riskier than you are capable of handling psychologically, a major drop in the markets could cause you to alter your investment strategy at just the wrong time and make a terrible and irreversible investment mistake.

The easiest way to determine your risk tolerance is to ask yourself how much drawdown you are capable of going through (risk capacity) and how much drawdown you are comfortable going through (risk attitude). Are you comfortable and capable of enduring a 50+ percent drawdown like the one we experienced in 2008? Or does the thought of that terrify you? Would that take you too far off course from your financial goals?

Another key consideration is how long you can wait for the market to recover if it does drop. The market usually recovers from small drops quickly. Larger drops of the magnitude of 20 percent or more can mean the passage of several years for recovery to take place. Do you have the patience and ability to wait several years for the market to recover?

If your portfolio is $500,000, a 50 percent drawdown would reduce your portfolio to $250,000. Plug in your own numbers. How would you react? Would you be able to wait several years for your portfolio to recover?

RISK MANAGEMENT

You can manage risk in many ways. The easiest way to DIY your risk management is to first determine how much of a drop you can tolerate and then use that information to determine what percentage of your portfolio should be in stocks versus bonds. If you can tolerate a 50 percent drop in your portfolio, you should have a majority of your holdings in stocks—90 percent or above. If you are young and have a high tolerance for risk, a 90 percent stock portfolio may make sense. Stocks will likely provide the best returns for you over the long term if you are able to endure the ups and downs along the way. If you are closer to retirement, you need to think carefully about how much risk you can afford to take and align your portfolio in accordance.

Whatever drop you can tolerate, divide that amount by 50 percent; that's a quick and easy way to estimate how much you should have in stocks versus bonds. For example, let's say you can only tolerate a 25 percent drop in your portfolio, half of 50 percent. Therefore, using this method, you would want to put 50 percent of your portfolio in stocks and 50 percent in bonds. But understand that by doing so, you may sacrifice about 50 percent of the returns of the stock market. Be careful about being overly conservative. You need to be comfortable with some risk in order to experience sufficient long-term returns.

In my work with clients, I have noticed that when markets are doing well, clients are more risk tolerant and when markets are doing poorly, they are more risk averse. Pay attention to these changes in yourself. Pick a level of risk that you can tolerate in both good and bad markets. Remember that market selloffs do happen. You want to pick a risk level that will not cause you to change your investments when the market sells off. In the next chapter, I will give specific examples of portfolios for different levels of risk.

CHAPTER 10

Guide to Asset Allocation by Age

Truth be told, the biggest contributor to your risk tolerance level is your time horizon. If you are just starting your career and have 30 years or so until you even think about retiring, you can, and should, be more aggressive with your investments. On the other hand, if you are planning to retire in a few years, you ought to be more conservative. In this chapter, I suggest portfolios for different ages based on a moderate risk tolerance. If you wish to be more aggressive, you should allocate more to stocks and real estate and less to bonds. If you wish to be more conservative, you should allocate more to bonds and cash, and less to stocks and real estate.

Because not every investment option may be available to you, at each age I provide both a basic and a full model. The basic model includes just four asset classes: US stock market, international developed markets, total bond market, and US real estate. Most 401(k) providers have at least these four options. If real estate is not an option in your 401(k), this portion could be allocated to US stocks. The full model lists a more comprehensive set of asset classes.

THE YOUNG ATTORNEY

You've just graduated law school and landed your first job at a big law firm. As part of your orientation, you are setting up your 401(k) and learning about the options available to you. Because you are young and early in your career, you have a long time horizon.

Therefore, you have a high capacity for risk. If the market tanks, you need not worry because you have time to wait for it to recover. You still might not like the idea of participating in a market selloff, but you need to be aggressive during these early years if you are going to reach financial independence.

Now, you might think that being aggressive means putting all your money in stocks and nothing else. That is not necessarily the best approach. First, not everyone can stomach being 100 percent in stocks because of the higher degree of volatility and potential for large drawdowns. Second, being 100 percent in stocks does not give you the opportunity to rebalance and buy stocks when they fall in value. If you have some in bonds, or other asset classes, you can take advantage of these opportunities. Finally, in some time periods bonds, real estate, or commodities outperform stocks. These time periods can last many years.

For young attorneys with a moderate risk tolerance, Table 10.1 contains a basic suggestion for allocating your portfolio.

Table 10.2 shows a more comprehensive portfolio for the moderate risk young attorney.

I used PortfolioVisualizer.com (a free tool available on the web) to test these allocations. This test does not include potential fees or transaction costs. I primarily used the example exchange-traded funds (ETFs) in tables 10.1 and 10.2 but made some substitutions to extend the back test as far as possible: Fidelity Emerging Markets (FEMKX) for iShares Emerging Markets ETF (EEM), Vanguard Long-Term Treasury (VUSTX) for iShares 20 Plus Year Treasury Bond ETF (TLT), Vanguard Intermediate-Term Investment Grade Corporate Bond

Table 10.1

Moderate Risk Basic Portfolio for Young Attorneys		
Stocks	**Allocation**	**Example Low-Cost ETF**
US stock market	40%	SPY
International developed markets	24%	EFA
Bonds		
Total bond market	17%	BND
Real estate		
US real estate	19%	VNQ

Table 10.2

Moderate Risk Full Portfolio for Young Attorneys		
Stocks	Allocation	Example Low-Cost ETF
US large cap	23%	SPY
US small cap	15%	IWM
International developed markets	14%	EFA
Emerging markets	13%	EEM
Bonds		
Long-term US treasuries	6%	TLT
US corporate bonds	6%	LQD
Intermediate US treasuries	4%	IEF
International treasuries	2%	BWX
Commodities		
Gold	2%	GLD
Diversified commodities	2%	DBC
Real estate		
US real estate	13%	VNQ

(VFICX) for iShares Investment Grade Corporate Bond ETF (LQD), Vanguard Intermediate-Term Treasury (VFITX), T. Rowe Price International Bond (RPIBX) for SPDR® Bloomberg International Treasury Bond ETF (BWX), US Global Investors Gold and Precious Metals (USERX) for SPDR® Gold Trust (GLD), PIMCO Commodity Real Return Strategy (PCRIX), and Vanguard Real Estate Index (VGSIX) for Vanguard Real Estate Index Fund ETF (VNQ). Assuming annual rebalancing, we see that full portfolio allocation would have produced a compound annualized growth rate of 9.95 percent from January 2003 to August 2021. The maximum drawdown on a month-end basis of this model would have been −46.95 percent (November 2007 to February 2009). The worst one-year period for our portfolio was −41.32 percent.

By comparison, putting 100 percent of your money in State Street's SPDR® S&P 500 ETF (SPY) would have yielded a compound annualized growth rate of 10.51 percent, with a maximum drawdown of –50.80 percent and worst one-year period of –43.44 percent. SPY performed better but with more risk. Our model significantly reduced the risk level and would have recovered faster than SPY during the Great Financial Crisis by more than a year. Our portfolio recovered from the crisis by the end of February 2011, whereas SPY did not recover until the end of March 2012.

Furthermore, our model would have outperformed SPY for the first 15 years of the back test, with SPY pulling ahead only in the final three years of the test period. If we ended the test period at the end of 2017, our model would have produced a growth rate of 10.01 percent with 9.82 percent for SPY by itself. That is primarily due to the significance of the impact of the Great Financial Crisis.

This model was designed with more than just past performance in mind. Our primary concern is how these assets behave together collectively and how they may behave in the future. Past performance is no guarantee of future results and should not be used as the primary basis for designing a portfolio.

THE MIDCAREER ATTORNEY

You have worked hard to build up your practice or you have climbed up the ladder at your firm. Perhaps you've just been named partner. Business is flowing and you have had some nice wins. You may be married, and perhaps the kids are getting ready to go off to college.

At this stage of life, you want to remain fairly aggressive. You are earning more than ever before in your career, and you need your portfolio to stay aggressive to maximize your growth. Even at midcareer, you still have a fairly long time horizon, and therefore you can afford to keep your risk level elevated. You have plenty of time to recover from market downturns. Also, at this point in your career, liquidity should no longer be a concern, and you should have a significant emergency fund well established. However, you may want to make some tweaks to reduce the risk level slightly at this stage of life.

Table 10.3 shows a sample basic portfolio for a midlife attorney with a moderate risk tolerance. Table 10.4 shows the more comprehensive portfolio.

If the same constraints and assumptions as above were used, the midcareer full portfolio would have produced a compound annual growth rate of 9.52 percent with a maximum monthly drawdown of –42.75 percent. As you can see, the historic growth rate is slightly less, but the risk level has been

Table 10.3

Moderate Risk Basic Portfolio for Midcareer Attorneys		
Stocks	Allocation	Example Low-Cost ETF
US stock market	37%	SPY
International developed markets	22%	EFA
Bonds		
Total bond market	26%	BND
Real estate		
US real estate	15%	VNQ

Table 10.4

Moderate Risk Full Portfolio for Midcareer Attorneys		
Stocks	Allocation	Example Low-Cost ETF
US large cap	20%	SPY
US small cap	14%	IWM
International developed markets	13%	EFA
Emerging markets	11%	EEM
Bonds		
Intermediate US treasuries	7%	IEF
US corporate bonds	7%	LQD
Long-term US treasuries	8%	TLT
International treasuries	3%	BWX
Commodities		
Gold	2%	GLD
Diversified commodities	3%	DBC
Real estate		
US real estate	12%	VNQ

reduced. The worst 12-month period for this portfolio was −37.91 percent. In addition, this portfolio would have experienced a faster recovery from its maximum drawdown during the Great Financial Crisis, recovering fully by December 31, 2010.

PRERETIREMENT

You are about 5 to 10 years away from retirement and contemplating your next moves, including your exit strategy or how you might sell your firm. You are starting to think seriously about what life might look like after the law. When you hit preretirement, it is time to start making some bigger changes. This is perhaps the most critical period of your investing life. You want to ensure that you can retire when you want to and that a major shift in the market will not throw those plans off track. The biggest risk to any retirement plan is a major drop in the markets in the few years leading up to retirement or just after retirement. Major market drops during these years can dramatically alter the trajectory of your retirement plans.

At this point in life, it is time to start reducing your risk level considerably. You still want to achieve a healthy level of growth to ensure you can meet your financial goals, however, so this is a delicate balance of risk and reward.

Table 10.5 shows a sample basic portfolio for an attorney with moderate risk tolerance who is close to retirement. Table 10.6 shows a more comprehensive portfolio.

Table 10.5

Moderate Risk Basic Portfolio for Preretirement Attorneys		
Stocks	**Allocation**	**Example Low-Cost ETF**
US stock market	29%	SPY
International developed markets	19%	EFA
Bonds		
Total bond market	39%	BND
Real estate		
US real estate	11%	VNQ
Cash	2%	N/A

Table 10.6

Moderate Risk Full Portfolio for Preretirement Attorneys		
Stocks	Allocation	Example Low-Cost ETF
US large cap	14%	SPY
US small cap	11%	IWM
Emerging markets	10%	EEM
International developed markets	10%	EFA
Bonds		
Intermediate US treasuries	10%	IEF
US corporate bonds	10%	LQD
International treasuries	7%	BWX
Long-term US treasuries	10%	TLT
Commodities		
Gold	4%	GLD
Diversified commodities	3%	DBC
Real estate		
US real estate	9%	VNQ
Cash	2%	N/A

In this portfolio, you will notice that cash is included as part of the allocation. As you near retirement, you may want to set aside a small portion of your portfolio in cash, which you will use to support withdrawal needs. The cash can be replenished regularly or opportunistically—that is, when the market has had a nice runup and it is a good profit-taking opportunity.

Using the same constraints and assumptions as before, we see that this portfolio would have produced a compound annual growth rate of 8.81 percent, less than the previous portfolios. However, the most important thing here is the risk reduction. This portfolio's maximum monthly drawdown would have been −34.64 percent, a significant reduction. Recovery time is faster as well: this portfolio would have recovered from the GFC by the end of September 2010. And the worst one-year period for this portfolio would have been −31.57 percent.

POSTRETIREMENT

At this stage, you are settled comfortably into retirement. You've perhaps sold your practice, bought yourself a second home on an island somewhere, and you're enjoying spending time sailing and visiting family and friends. Maybe your picture of retirement is different, but you get the idea. At this point, you cannot afford to take a great deal of risk. Your earning years are behind you, and you cannot afford to run out of money. You are perhaps actively taking withdrawals from your investments, and you cannot be exposed to a lot of volatility.

At this point, you need to minimize drawdown risk and achieve as consistent and stable a rate of return as possible to sustain your lifestyle in retirement. You may have to shift even more from high-risk assets like stocks to lower risk assets like bonds. When do you make this shift to a lower risk portfolio? I would suggest 5 to 10 years after retirement.

Table 10.7 shows a sample basic portfolio for a postretirement attorney with a moderate risk tolerance. Table 10.8 shows a more comprehensive portfolio.

You will notice that there is significantly more cash to support your withdrawal needs and temper volatility. This portfolio is designed to minimize drawdowns as much as possible without sacrificing long-term growth.

Using our testing constraints and assumptions, we find that this portfolio would have produced a compound annual growth rate of 7.97 percent with

Table 10.7

Moderate Risk Basic Portfolio for Postretirement Attorneys		
Stocks	**Allocation**	**Example Low-Cost ETF**
US stock market	21%	SPY
International developed markets	13%	EFA
Bonds		
Total bond market	48%	BND
Real estate		
US real estate	11%	VNQ
Cash	7%	N/A

Table 10.8

Moderate Risk Full Portfolio for Postretirement Attorneys		
Stocks	Allocation	Example Low-Cost ETF
US large cap	13%	SPY
US Small Cap	8%	IWM
Emerging markets	6%	EEM
International developed markets	8%	EFA
Bonds		
Intermediate US treasuries	24%	IEF
Long Term US treasuries	10%	TLT
US corporate bonds	9%	LQD
International treasuries	5%	BWX
Commodities		
Gold	3%	GLD
Diversified commodities	1%	DBC
Real estate		
US real estate	9%	VNQ
Cash	4%	N/A

a maximum monthly drawdown of -25.92 percent, a very significant reduction in risk. This portfolio would have recovered from the Great Financial Crisis much faster, by the end of March 2010; the worst 1-year period was -23.83 percent.

Obviously, a drawdown of 24 percent is still very significant, and you may want to be even more conservative if you are uncomfortable with that level of risk. However, it is important to achieve a healthy enough long-term rate of growth to support withdrawals and combat the risk of inflation.

Are these the most perfect portfolios you could design based on back-testing? No, and they are not meant to be. We start with theory and build a portfolio. Then, we test it to make sure it works. You should never design a strategy based purely on back-testing. This is called data-snooping or over-fitting. The problem with data-snooping is that history will never repeat itself in exactly the same fashion and data-snooping can lead to portfolios that simply will not work in the future.

For example, from January 2000 to December 2020, long-term treasuries outperformed the S&P 500 significantly with considerably less risk. A portfolio allocated 100 percent to VUSTX would have yielded an annualized return of 7.60 percent with a drawdown of only −16.68 percent. Meanwhile, VFINX, which tracks the S&P 500, yielded only 6.50 percent, with a maximum drawdown of −50.97 percent. Based on that information, should you allocate all your money to long-term treasuries? That would assuredly be a mistake.[1]

TARGET DATE FUNDS: A SIMPLE SOLUTION

One very simple and elegant solution is a one-stop shop known as a target-date fund. Target-date funds are asset allocation funds, meaning they give you exposure to a broad, diverse range of asset classes—everything from stocks to bonds to commodities. Instead of buying multiple funds to represent different asset classes, you can buy just one target-date fund.

As the name implies, target-date funds are based on a particular target retirement year. As that year approaches, the managers of the fund will automatically adjust the portfolio to match the shortening time horizon. Instead of you having to make changes to your investments as you approach retirement, they do it for you. For example, a target-date 2040 fund is designed for people who are planning to retire around the year 2040. As that year draws near, the portfolio will automatically shift in a more conservative direction. If you are intimidated by the idea of managing your investments on your own or simply do not have time, target-date funds may be a good solution.

There are some things to be aware of, however. Not all target-date funds are created equally. They all have their own approach, and some are more aggressive than others. For example, not all 2040 funds have the same mix

---

[1] Data obtained from www.portfoliovisualizer.com and other third-party sources assumed to be accurate and reliable. Past performance is no guarantee of future results. Not investment advice. Not a recommendation to buy or sell securities. For educational and illustrative purposes only.

of asset classes. You will want to closely examine how they are allocated and determine what is best for you. Also, you lose flexibility and the opportunities that may arise from rebalancing since the allocation is done for you. Finally, target-date funds may be more expensive than simply doing it yourself.

On the other hand, if you want a more individualized and sophisticated approach, you may want to work with a personal financial advisor. An advisor can work with you to develop a customized strategy that fits your own personal risk tolerance and needs. Be sure to choose an advisor who is a fiduciary and is paid on a fee-basis, rather than a commission. A fee-based advisor is paid based on a percentage of your portfolio—usually around 1 percent per year. This ensures that the advisor is incentivized only to grow your account and not to make a sale.

What is best for you will depend on your own unique circumstances and risk tolerance. The models I have provided could serve as a good starting point. But there are other places besides the stock market to invest. One example is real estate—as in direct real estate ownership, not investing through real estate investment trusts as we have discussed. I will deal with direct real estate investing in the next chapter.

CHAPTER 11

Real Estate Investing

While we have discussed different types of accounts for stock market investing, there is another very popular way to invest money: direct real estate ownership. The growing popularity of channels like HGTV demonstrates how popular direct real estate investment has become in recent years. Many are drawn to real estate for its promise of low-risk, passive income. I have found the idea to be particularly popular among attorneys and law firm owners looking for ways to build alternative streams of income. But is direct real estate investing all it is cracked up to be?

ADVANTAGES OF DIRECT REAL ESTATE INVESTMENT

Investing directly in real estate has its advantages. You can invest in real estate in two ways: flipping or renting. First, flipping can offer extremely attractive returns. According to data from ATTOM Data Solutions, homes flipped in the first quarter of 2021 generated an average gross profit of $63,500 or an impressive 37.8 percent return on investment.[1]

The other way to invest in real estate is to buy rental properties with the objective of building up a passive income stream and holding on to the properties for long-term capital appreciation. The idea of passive income can be very attractive to attorneys who experience irregular income. Home prices

---

[1] "Home flipping rate and gross profits decline across U.S. in first quarter of 2021," ATTOM Data, June 17, 2021, https://www.attomdata.com/news/most-recent/q1-2021-u-s-home-flipping-report.

can appreciate over time and tend to do a decent job of keeping pace with inflation. Moreover, you can increase the rent you charge over time to allow your income to rise with inflation.

Investing directly in real estate offers unique tax benefits. Some areas that are seeking improvement, often urban areas undergoing revitalization, may offer tax abatements and other incentives. As an owner of the property, you can deduct ordinary and necessary expenses related to maintaining the property. You can depreciate the acquisition cost of your property over time. In addition, your rental income is not subject to payroll taxes. Finally, by taking advantage of 1031 like-kind exchanges, you can potentially defer taxes on the sale of a property by purchasing a new property.

Direct real estate investing may also offer you the ability to exercise leverage through financing. If you finance the acquisition of a property and you put 20 percent down, you have obtained 100 percent of the value of a property for only 20 percent of the initial cost. This is leverage—doing more with less. While you still owe money on the house, you have been able to put a lot more money to work than you otherwise would be able to do.

An added benefit is that investment can be insured. Having property insurance insulates you from certain risks associated with owning a property, such as catastrophic loss. This advantage is one you cannot get from stock ownership. At the same time, insurance does not protect you against every risk, including the loss of market value.

Finally, direct investment offers greater control. For some this aspect is the most appealing one. Real estate is a tangible asset, which many feel better about than they do about owning nontangible assets like shares of a company. Having complete ownership of this tangible asset, you are free to do with it as you please. Your effort and investment will be directly tied to your profitability.

DISADVANTAGES OF DIRECT REAL ESTATE INVESTMENT

Before you become too enamored with direct real estate investment, it is important to understand that it does come with risks and costs. First, let's examine flipping. Flipping is a high-risk investment in which you can easily lose money inasmuch as it is associated with a lot of costs and uncertainty. For example, it entails remodeling, transaction, and holding costs. Each month that you hold a property without selling it, you are losing money. As flipping has become more competitive and home prices have surged in recent years, it is getting more difficult to make money, even though the average profit margins are wide. The common wisdom is that most flippers need to make at least 30 percent above their purchase price to be profitable.

Real estate investing, whether flipping or renting, requires a large investment of time and energy. If you are flipping, remodeling work will need to be done. Rental properties may involve possible tenant issues and maintenance emergencies. As an attorney, you already have a premium on your time. Unless you have a lot of time you can devote to this endeavor and some expertise in the real estate market, it may be best to steer clear. Yes, you could hire professionals to do most of the work for you, but that will eat into your profits.

In addition to time and energy, direct real estate investing may require more capital. Owning stocks does not require you to add money. Companies are not going to come crawling to you for more money to keep your investment afloat. But if you own a property, you may find yourself having to inject more capital. Some items must be paid, especially property taxes, insurance premiums, and possible assessments. If you are renting and you have vacancies, you can run into a cash flow problem.

Another consideration is that physical real estate is a relatively illiquid investment. Even though houses seem to be sold at an increasingly fast pace these days, it still takes time to complete a real estate transaction. By contrast, you can sell a stock in seconds. If you need to unload real estate quickly because you are facing a cash crunch, you may be in trouble and lose money.

Lastly, and most importantly, direct real estate investing is a nondiversified investment and therefore poses a significant amount of unsystematic risk. If you recall, unsystematic risk is risk associated with a singular company or other investment. With real estate, one of the biggest unsystematic risks is location. If you get the location right, you will be handsomely rewarded. But if the neighborhood changes for the worse, you may lose money. You have little control over future changes to the location of your property.

WHY REITS MAY BE BETTER

A real estate investment trust (REIT), or better yet a real estate mutual fund that buys a diversified portfolio of REITs, may be a better option. First, this approach offers broad diversification among properties and property types. REITs allow you to invest in numerous properties at once without having to own or manage physical properties. If you are following one of our models of asset allocation, you already have some REITs in your investment portfolio.

REITs and real estate mutual funds or exchange-traded funds (ETFs) are also very liquid. They are bought and sold throughout the day on major stock exchanges. Many can be bought or sold instantaneously through an online broker. And they have a much lower barrier to entry than direct real estate. You do not need to obtain financing and you do not need as much money. You can buy as few or as many shares as you like.

The icing on the cake is that returns on REITs may be as good as or better than direct real estate investing. REITs pay a high dividend yield: they must pay at least 90 percent of their income to shareholders to avoid corporate taxes. They can also appreciate as the underlying properties appreciate. According to an article in *Forbes*, REITs may outperform direct investment. From 1977 to 2010, they delivered an average return of more than 12 percent annually, while private real estate funds achieved only 6 to 8 percent.[2]

REITs do have some downsides, however. First, REIT dividends are not qualified dividends, so they are taxed at your ordinary income tax rate. Moreover, because REITs are very dividend focused, they can be sensitive to interest rates and other market fluctuations, making them potentially more volatile than direct investment.

WHY STOCKS MAY BE BETTER

Stocks may be a better long-term bet than real estate. Certainly, this opinion reflects my bias toward the stock market, but there are some sound reasons for this viewpoint. First, the stock market shares many of the same advantages of REITs and real estate funds, including diversification, low point of entry, liquidity, and no maintenance required. But more importantly, stocks tend to provide a better hedge against inflation and better long-term returns. Just think back to the story about the property value of Manhattan in chapter 6.

Over long periods of time, the S&P 500 has delivered total returns in the range of 9 to 10 percent. According to CNBC, from 1940 to 2000 the annualized rate of increase in the median home value in the United States has

---

[2] Marc Prosser, "Data proves REITs are better than buying real estate," *Forbes*, July 19, 2017, https://www.forbes.com/sites/marcprosser/2017/07/19/data-proves-reits-are-better-than-buying-real-estate/#21f618c6d6b7.

been about 5.5 percent.[3] But much of that increase may be due to an overall increase in the size of the average home as well. If you factor that in, long-term returns in real estate do not look as attractive as returns for stocks.

But here, I am not trying to burst your real estate bubble. Real estate ownership can be an attractive alternative stream of income and help to even out the ups and downs in income associated with owning a law practice or contingency work. Just be sure that real estate investing does not detract from funding your retirement accounts and saving enough to reach your long-term goals. That would be a big mistake. In the next chapter, I will close out this section with some of the biggest investment mistakes to avoid.

---

[3] Emmie Martin, "Here's how much housing prices have skyrocketed over the last 50 years," CNBC, June 23, 2017, https://www.cnbc.com/2017/06/23/how-much-housing-prices-have-risen-since-1940.html.

CHAPTER 12

The Biggest Investing Mistakes to Avoid

During my career, I have witnessed some terrible investment mistakes. In this chapter, I will show you 10 of the most egregious investment mistakes that I have encountered or that I was taught to avoid by my own father. Admittedly, even I have had to learn from some of these mistakes the hard way, mistakes made during my early days of investing my own money. The most detrimental consequence of investment mistakes is that they rob you of one of your most precious commodities: time. By avoiding mistakes and saving the time you would waste making those mistakes, you can maximize your wealth and your life.

1. HAVING NO PLAN

The first and most obvious mistake is having no plan at all. This is probably the most common mistake people make. When folks come to my office to have me review their investment accounts, they often have no idea what they are invested in, what the plan is, and why that plan makes sense for them. I will sometimes see a long list of mutual funds and stocks that overlap each other redundantly or a hodgepodge of different stock funds that are missing key ingredients. You need to have a plan. Know what you own and why you own it. Having an investment plan that is aligned to your overall financial plan will give you confidence in your investment strategy and lead to success.

2. NOT STARTING EARLY ENOUGH

Another glaring error is the failure to start investing early enough. Why do people not start early enough? Because they are waiting for the chance to pay down debt, for their income to grow, or for the kids to graduate. Others may delay investing simply because they do not know where to start and they are afraid of losing money. I have seen this with some young investors that I have worked with. If you have never experienced market volatility, the idea of the value of your investments fluctuating can be hard to stomach at first. Do not let fear or other excuses stand in your way. You need to start investing early and stay committed to your plan if you are going to grow wealth. The longer your money can stay invested, the more you can harness the power of exponential growth.

3. TOO MUCH OR TOO LITTLE RISK

You need to make sure that the level of risk in your portfolio is appropriate for your overall financial plan. If you are young, you need to be willing to be aggressive and comfortable with a high level of risk if you are going to maximize your wealth over time. This means having a portfolio with a high allocation given to stocks. It does not necessarily mean pursuing excessively risky ideas like individual stock speculation or options trading.

If you are closer to retirement, you need to have a healthy amount of risk for your portfolio to achieve enough growth to last through retirement, but it should be less risk than when you were younger. You cannot afford to be 100 percent allocated to stocks and see 50 percent of your portfolio vanish during a major downturn like 2008. Lots of people have made this mistake and have had to put their plans for retirement on hold.

4. LACK OF PATIENCE

Once you have chosen an appropriate investment strategy, you need to be patient. One of the biggest mistakes I witness is a lack of patience. Your investment strategy is not going to be profitable from day one. Markets do not move higher in a linear fashion. They ebb and flow. In fact, markets are almost always in a period of drawdown, with little spurts to take us to new highs along the way. When you start an investment strategy, it is quite common to see it lose value initially. You need to be patient.

A lack of patience leads people to constantly change their investment strategy, and this approach leads to poor performance over time. Every strategy has good periods and bad periods, but you will never experience the good periods unless you have the patience to wait out the bad ones. For example, people often seek out the mutual funds that have the best recent performance or have achieved a five-star rating by Morningstar. However, evidence suggests that these high ratings are fleeting. Mean reversion takes over, and most of these high-rated funds tend to underperform in subsequent years.[1]

5. MAKING EMOTIONAL DECISIONS

Lack of patience is closely related to another big mistake: making emotional decisions. Without a doubt, money is emotional: it is easy to feel emotional about our investments. Emotions lead us to make poor investment decisions. When our investments are up, we are elated, we are overconfident, and we want to take more risk. When our investments are down, we are panicky, and we want to take less risk.

I have often witnessed these emotions in the clients I serve. When markets are at all-time highs, I get calls from clients wanting to up their risk exposure or invest in the hot stocks they have seen on TV. This is often the wrong time to make such changes. Markets will pull back, and these same investors will panic. When markets are dropping, the opposite scenario emerges. Clients call wanting to "go to cash" or to take all their money out of their investments and put it in cash. Again, this is almost always a big mistake. It is at about the time I start getting these calls that the market starts to rebound. Those who get out miss the upswing and have a difficult time overcoming the psychological barrier to getting "back in." What is more, they miss out in a big way. A good investment strategy is designed with market drops in mind, and so it is important to be patient and stick with your strategy even through trying times.

6. STOCK PICKING

Stock picking is a mistake. I sometimes have clients who want to engage in stock picking. They call me with great excitement about a particular stock

---

[1] Kirsten Grind, Tom McGinty, and Sarah Krouse, "The Morningstar mirage," *The Wall Street Journal*, October 25, 2017, https://www.wsj.com/articles/the-morningstar-mirage-1508946687.

and ask me to add it to their portfolio. Generally, I will entertain the idea if it is limited to no more than 5 percent of their overall portfolio and if they commit to holding it for a long period of time. Some of these calls make money and some lose money. Stock picking is a very difficult game even for the so-called professionals. In previous chapters, I have explained how this risk is qualitatively different from and greater than overall stock market risk.

7. LISTENING TO THE EXPERTS

I strongly encourage my clients not to watch CNBC or to listen to other market commentary. Most of the people you see on TV are there to entertain you and not necessarily to help you make better investment decisions. If a particular stock they recommend is so good, why are they telling you all about it? Are they just that generous? I think you know the answer.

How about off-camera experts? You shouldn't listen to them either for the most part. First, the stock market experts almost always forecast the market to go higher. This is because they usually work for big banks or brokerage firms, and they have a vested interested in keeping investors invested. As we all know, the market is not positive every year.

Second, the same thing happens with the "buy" and "sell" recommendations that analysts give to individual stocks. Even in times of downturns, there are almost always far more buy than sell recommendations. In fact, sell recommendations are fairly rare.[2]

Finally, expert market forecasts are often wrong and sometimes disastrously so. All you need to do is look at 2008. Many firms, analysts, and experts forecasted a nicely positive year for 2008. And they were terribly wrong: the S&P 500 was down −37 percent for the year.

8. INSUFFICIENT LIQUIDITY

Whatever investment strategy you have chosen, it is essential to maintain an appropriate level of liquidity. What does this mean? You need to have enough money in your emergency fund to prevent yourself from invading your investments. This is especially true if you have irregular income. If you

---

[2] Mark Fahey, "Why Wall Street analysts almost never put 'sell' ratings on stocks they cover," CNBC, January 26, 2017, https://www.cnbc.com/2017/01/26/sell-ratings-by-wall-street-analysts-almost-never-happen.html.

do not keep enough in liquid savings and an emergency arises, you may be forced to dip into your investments. Taking money from your savings will severely hamper your long-term growth, especially if you do so repetitively or if you withdraw funds at a point when the market is down.

9. OBSESSING OVER TAXES OR EXPENSES

Another big mistake occurs when people obsess too much over taxes or expenses, thereby influencing their investment decisions. Concern about taxes mostly affects taxable brokerage accounts where you may be taxed on capital gains. As the saying goes, two things in life are certain: death and taxes. Taxes are a fact of life.

Holding on to a particular stock only because you are afraid of paying the taxes on the realized gain is a mistake. Some of my clients who have a large position in a particular stock are often hesitant to sell it and diversify because of the tax implications. But be aware that in order to use that money, you will eventually have to pay those taxes. Even if you are going to hold the stock until you die to get the step up in basis for your heirs, it usually makes sense to sell it and pay the taxes. Reducing the single stock exposure risk is often well worth any taxes you might pay to do so.

Similarly, do not get too hung up on expenses. In today's world, investors and investment companies seem to be laser focused on reducing expenses. I love it that investing costs have come down over the years. However, when it comes to your portfolio, you should not invest in a particular fund, choose a particular strategy, or select a specific advisor solely for the opportunity to reduce your expenses. That should be a secondary consideration. You should always make that decision only because the investment opportunity or the advisor is qualitatively better. Expenses should be a factor only when two very similar funds, strategies, or advisors are being compared.

10. USING LIFE INSURANCE OR ANNUITIES AS INVESTMENTS

My biggest pet peeve of all and the most glaring mistake I see is using life insurance or annuities as investment vehicles. Life insurance and annuities are not investments; rather, they are insurance products meant to insure against a specific risk. Life insurance insures against the risk of premature death. Annuities insure against the risk of running out of money in retirement. These are not investments.

There are slick, smooth-talking salespeople who will try to convince you otherwise. And there are insurance products that will tell you your investment is tied to the S&P 500 or some other index. Don't be fooled. Your money is never truly invested. These are just different formulas that the insurance company will use to determine how much interest to credit to your account. And if you read the fine print, you will usually find a clause in the disclosures that states these products are not investments and should not be viewed that way.

Life insurance and annuities are not inherently bad. They serve a specific purpose, but that purpose is not investing and growing wealth. Insurance products have excessively high expenses that will eat into any returns you anticipate. They often involve locking away your money for many years, and they are frequently subject to complex formulas like caps and participation rates that may limit your growth. In addition, they usually offer a very limited assortment of "investment" options.

Do yourself a favor: use insurance and annuities only for their intended purposes and not to accumulate wealth. Steer clear of these products for wealth-building. Instead, use a low-cost brokerage firm like Charles Schwab or Fidelity for investments.

Investment mistakes don't just lead to subpar performance; they also rob you of precious time. My sincerest hope for you is that you will avoid the above mistakes and thereby avoid wasting time and losing money. Make a plan and stick to it. Have a well-thought-out investment strategy. Do not let your emotions take over, and also exercise discipline and patience even in tough times. If you can do all these things, I am confident you will be successful.

PART III

Tax Minimization for Attorneys

If you are a successful attorney, you will likely face some large tax bills. Minimizing taxes is one of the chief concerns of most of the attorneys I meet. However, while reducing your current tax rate is important, it is even more important to think about the big picture. Planning ahead can ensure that you minimize taxes over your lifetime and thereby maximize your wealth. In the following chapters, I will present some ideas to help you minimize your taxes now and in the future.

CHAPTER 13

Retirement Accounts

One of the chief ways to reduce taxes is through a retirement account. The terms IRA, Roth IRA, 401(k), and the like refer to the type of account that you set up—not the investment strategy. The only major difference between different account types is the tax treatment of the investments inside the account. The most basic account that you can set up is a taxable account, sometimes called a brokerage account or a standard account. With this type of account, your investments will be subject to taxation each year. If you receive dividends or other distributions from your holdings, these are taxable. If you sell a holding for a profit, the profit (or capital gain) is taxable. You will receive a 1099 to report these taxable events on your taxes.

IRAs and other types of tax-advantaged accounts were set up to provide a way to defer these annual taxes and encourage Americans to invest and save for retirement. There are two main types of IRAs and other retirement accounts: traditional and Roth.

THE TRADITIONAL TAX-DEFERRED ACCOUNT

Traditional tax-deferred retirement accounts provide big tax advantages. These types of accounts include the traditional IRA, 401(k), and 403(b). Contributions to these accounts can be tax deductible. This can be a great way to reduce your taxable income in a particular year and, therefore, also reduce your tax liability for that year. The basic concept behind these accounts is that you are deferring income until later in retirement. Rather than being taxed on money you put into the account today, you will pay taxes later when you take the money out to use it in retirement.

Each type of account has its own set of limitations and requirements. As an employee, you can contribute up to $20,500 to a 401(k) or 403(b) plan per year, and you can contribute up to $6,000 to an IRA or Roth IRA per year (as of 2022). Those who are over the age of 50 can contribute more thanks to the provisions for "catch up" contributions. Individuals over 50 can contribute an extra $6,500 to their 401(k) or 403(b) and an extra $1,000 to their IRA. Deductibility for an IRA contribution is subject to certain income limitations if you have a retirement plan through your employer. Roth IRA eligibility is also subject to certain income limitations.[1]

The traditional IRA or 401(k) has another tax advantage in that any gains or dividends inside the account are tax-deferred. This means that as long as the money stays inside the account, you do not owe any taxes, but if you take a withdrawal, you will owe. Pre-tax amounts withdrawn from a traditional retirement account will be included on your taxable income and taxed at your ordinary income tax rates. To encourage saving for retirement, if you withdraw money prematurely (prior to $59\frac{1}{2}$ for IRAs and 55 for 401(k)s and 403(b)s), you will also face a 10 percent tax penalty on your withdrawal.

THE ROTH ACCOUNT

The Roth account is named after Senator William Roth of Delaware, who originated the Roth IRA as part of the Tax Relief Act of 1997. This account shares some similarities with the traditional tax-deferred retirement account. Also, 401(k)s and 403(b)s often have a Roth option for employee contributions. Like a traditional IRA, your investments inside a Roth account are tax-deferred, so that you do not owe taxes on gains or dividends as long as they stay inside the account. The Roth account also has an early withdrawal penalty of 10 percent if you take money out prematurely.

However, there are some key differences between the Roth account and traditional retirement accounts. First, unlike the traditional retirement account, you do not receive a tax deduction for making a contribution. Money that you contribute is income that you have already paid taxes on. Second, the really big difference (and advantage) of the Roth account is that

---

[1] "Retirement topics—IRA contribution limits," IRS, August 18, 2021, https://www.irs.gov/retirement-plans/plan-participant-employee/retirement-topics-ira-contribution-limits.

once you reach retirement age (59½), assuming you have had the account for at least five years, you can take money out tax-free. That's right: you will not pay taxes on any of your earnings over the years. This is a big deal. Whereas the traditional IRA gives you a tax break today, the Roth IRA essentially gives you a tax break in the future.

Another key feature of Roth IRAs is the ability it gives you to access your contributions at any time. The early distribution penalty of a Roth IRA does not apply to your direct contributions. And because these contributions are not tax-deductible, there is no tax to take them out either. In other words, you may withdraw your contributions at any time without tax or penalty. This provides an additional source of potential liquidity, which could be helpful to younger attorneys or attorneys with irregular cash flow.

WHICH IS BETTER?

Traditional and Roth accounts both have their own tax advantages. To determine which is better, let's run some numbers. Let's say you have an extra $6,000 you can either put in your traditional 401(k) account or a Roth 401(k) account. Putting $6,000 in a traditional 401(k) will reduce your taxable income by $6,000 and reduce the amount you pay in taxes at your marginal income tax rate. For our illustration, let's assume you're in the highest tax bracket (37 percent), and so you will receive the greatest benefit. For a $6,000 traditional 401(k) contribution, you will save yourself $2,220 in taxes.

Let's assume that you earn a 9 percent annual return on your investment over 30 years. Let's also assume that you put your tax savings amount of $2,220 in a taxable brokerage account, invest it similarly and can earn 9 percent per year on this money as well.

After 30 years, you will have accumulated $817,845 in your traditional account. If this was a Roth account, assuming you are 59½ or older, that money is now tax free. You have contributed a total of $180,000 and have accumulated earnings of $637,845. With a Roth account, all these earnings become tax-free once you reach retirement age.

Because this is a traditional account, however, anything that you withdraw is now subject to ordinary income tax. At the highest tax bracket of 37 percent, your after-tax value of your account is actually only $515,243. However, it is very possible that you will be in a lower tax bracket in retirement.

But let's not forget your after-tax account where you have been stashing your tax savings. Because this is a taxable account, you will likely be subject to capital gains and dividend taxes each year. At the highest tax bracket, your long-term capital gains tax rate is 20 percent; we are being generous here and are assuming only long-term gains. So, we will assume a tax drag of 20 percent on your returns, resulting in an after-tax return of 7.2 percent instead of 9 percent. After 30 years, your after-tax account will have grown to $233,055.

So, which is better in this scenario? The traditional retirement account strategy I have outlined above would net you $748,298 in after-tax dollars. Meanwhile, the Roth account strategy would net you the full $817,845 in after-tax dollars. Here, the Roth is the clear winner by a margin of nearly $70,000. You may be asking yourself: What about other tax brackets? See Table 13.1 for how our test looks with different tax brackets.

Based on our test, the Roth account is preferable in most cases. However, the traditional retirement account may be better over the long term at the lower end of the tax spectrum. Also, if you are in a significantly lower tax bracket in retirement than you are during your working years, the traditional retirement account may provide a higher benefit.

There are some very important things to consider here. First, the only way that the traditional retirement account leads to more wealth over time than the Roth over time is if a person actually invests their tax savings from the deduction. Many people do not have the discipline to invest their tax savings. Failure to invest those dollars makes the Roth account far more valuable regardless of your tax bracket now and in the future because both strategies would result in the same amount of money, but the Roth bucket would be tax-free.

Table 13.1

Tax Bracket	Capital Gains/ Dividend Tax Drag	After-Tax Value of Traditional Account	After-Tax Value of Taxable Account	Roth Account Difference
10%	0%	$736,061	$ 89,145	($ 7,361)
12%	0%	$719,704	$106,974	($8,833)
22%	15%	$637,919	$150,995	$28,931
24%	15%	$621,562	$164,721	$31,562
32%	15%	$556,135	$219,628	$42,082
35%	15%	$531,599	$240,219	$46,027
37%	20%	$515,243	$233,055	$69,547

Second, having tax-free income from your Roth account in retirement has other benefits. This income will lower your taxes on other sources of income such as social security and potentially reduce the cost of your health insurance. Also, if you are married, when one of you passes away, the surviving spouse will be forced into a higher tax bracket as a result of having to file as single instead of married. The surviving spouse will pay more in taxes on distributions from traditional retirement accounts. Having Roth accounts is one way to mitigate this risk.

Third, the Roth IRA has a major advantage with respect to estate planning. When you pass a traditional IRA to a spouse, the spouse can treat it as their own. Other heirs must distribute the funds within 10 years—and pay the taxes. The SECURE Act of 2019 did away with the old stretch IRA rules which used to allow heirs to stretch distributions out over their lifetime. Roth IRAs, by contrast, are inherited tax free if they were held for at least five years.

Finally, the Roth account provides what some like to call "tax insurance." If taxes are higher in the future, having chosen a Roth account will have looked like a genius move. Putting money in the Roth locks in today's tax rate in exchange for future tax-free money. We do not know how tax laws will change in the future. Taxes could be higher or they could be lower. So, it is not possible to know for sure if this is the right move, but it is one way to provide some protection against the possibility of higher taxes down the road.

In terms of building wealth, the Roth strategy is a powerful tool that should not be neglected. Unless your income is exceedingly high, in most cases the Roth account is preferable over the long term. It is especially valuable for younger attorneys because the Roth has its greatest potential over a long period of time. You should take advantage of it especially in years where your income is lower than normal and you are in a lower tax bracket.

Now, before you get too excited about Roth IRAs, there is an income limit that determines if you are eligible to contribute to a Roth IRA (this does not apply to Roth 401(k) or Roth 403(b) accounts). Unfortunately, our high-income earners in our test would be ineligible to make a Roth IRA contribution because of their high income. In 2022, this limit was $144,00 modified adjusted gross income for single filers and $214,000 for those married filing jointly.[2] Thankfully, there are some loopholes that will allow you to get around these limitations. We will explore these loopholes in the next chapter.

---

[2] "Amount of Roth IRA contributions that you can make for 2021," IRS, June 26, 2021, https://www.irs.gov/retirement-plans/amount-of-roth-ira-contributions-that-you-can-make-for-2021.

CHAPTER 14

The Roth Backdoor and Mega-Backdoor

In the previous chapter, I made the case for the value of the Roth IRA. However, it presents one big problem: there is an income limit that determines your eligibility to make Roth IRA contributions. Thankfully, high-income earners can get around this limitation in two ways: the backdoor Roth and the mega-backdoor Roth.

THE ROTH BACKDOOR

If you can't get in the front door, go around to the back! While Roth IRA contribution eligibility is subject to income limitations, your eligibility to make a traditional IRA contribution is not. You can always contribute to a traditional IRA, regardless of your income. If you are already covered by an employer retirement plan, your ability to receive a deduction for your contribution is subject to income limitations. Anyone, regardless of income, is able to make an "after-tax" contribution to their traditional IRA. You will not receive a deduction for this contribution, but you will receive the benefit of tax deferral on your earnings.

Another key feature that makes the Roth Backdoor strategy possible is your ability to convert traditional IRA funds to a Roth IRA. When you elect to make this conversion, you must pay ordinary income taxes on any pretax contributions (contributions for which you received a tax deduction) and earnings. However, you do not have to pay taxes on any after-tax contributions.

So, here's how the Roth Backdoor strategy works. First, you make an after-tax contribution to a traditional IRA. (You do not take a tax deduction.) Then, you immediately convert these funds to your Roth IRA. And voila—you have made your Roth IRA contribution. Simple, right?

There's one caveat here. If you already have a traditional IRA with pretax money in it, you will encounter some difficulties. This is because when you do a conversion, a portion of your conversion will be taxable. Whatever percentage of the account is pretax, the IRS will deem that same percentage of the conversion amount to be pretax and therefore taxable.

For example, let's suppose you have $6,000 in pretax funds in a traditional IRA. You want to do a backdoor Roth contribution, so you make an after-tax contribution of an additional $6,000 to your traditional IRA. Now you have $12,000 in your traditional IRA: $6,000 pretax and $6,000 after tax. Because 50 percent is pretax, any amount that you convert to your Roth IRA will be deemed to be 50 percent pretax, and therefore 50 percent of it will be taxed. This applies across the board to any IRAs you own, so you cannot set up a separate IRA to get around this complication.

Therefore, this works best if you start with no traditional IRA money at all. Then, set up your accounts, make the after-tax contribution, and convert it. If you already have IRA money, you can transfer these funds to your 401(k) or convert those funds over to your Roth to eliminate any pretax traditional IRA money in advance.

THE MEGA-BACKDOOR ROTH

The Roth backdoor strategy allows you to put the maximum allowable IRA contribution into a Roth IRA, regardless of your income. But what if you want to do more?

Let me introduce the "mega-backdoor." This strategy involves using your 401(k) to do a backdoor Roth contribution. Because a 401(k) allows much higher contributions, this strategy lets you to put as much as $61,000 (or $67,500 if you are over 50) in a Roth account for 2022! That's huge.

How does this strategy work? First, you need to understand a couple of things about 401(k)s. The maximum combined employer and employee contribution to a 401(k) for 2022 is $61,000 (or $67,500 if you are age 50 or over). Of that amount, up to $20,500 (or $27,000 if you are over 50) can be contributed from the employee as pretax or Roth money. The rest (up to $40,500) can come from the employer *or the employee as an after-tax contribution*. You are going to use that after-tax opportunity to funnel extra money into a Roth. To figure out how much you can contribute to your 401(k) on an after-tax basis, subtract any employer contributions or matches from $40,500.[1]

Just like the Roth backdoor strategy, after you have made your after-tax contribution, you are then going to convert these after-tax funds to a Roth account. You can accomplish this conversion in two ways. If your 401(k) allows in-plan conversions, you can simply convert these funds to the Roth account in your 401(k) plan. If your plan does not allow these conversions or does not have a Roth feature, you will need to do an in-service withdrawal or rollover to move these funds to an outside Roth IRA.

Your 401(k) must have two features for this strategy to work: the ability to make after-tax contributions and in-plan Roth conversions or to take in-service distributions. If you can only make after-tax contributions, but not in-plan conversions or take an in-service withdrawal, you can still make your after-tax contributions and wait until you leave your current firm or retire to complete the Roth conversion. Doing that will trigger taxes on any earnings. To get around this regulation, you can split up the money and roll the contributions to your Roth IRA and the earnings to your traditional IRA. However, this reduces the benefit of the Roth in the first place—tax-free earnings.

This strategy works very well if you are a solo practitioner and you have your own 401(k), or if you are part of a small firm. You can then control and change the terms and conditions of the 401(k) to add the features you need if you do not already have them.

The Roth backdoor and mega-backdoor strategies allow high-income earners to funnel more money into a Roth IRA. But suppose you are looking for just some good old-fashioned tax deductions. Since we are on the topic of 401(k)s, let us now take a look at how you can use an employer retirement plan to maximize your tax deferral.

---

[1] "Retirement topics—401(k) and profit-sharing plan contribution limits," IRS, June 26, 2021, https://www.irs.gov/retirement-plans/plan-participant-employee/retirement-topics-401k-and-profit-sharing-plan-contribution-limits.

CHAPTER 15

Turbocharged Tax Deferral

If you are a solo attorney or the owner of a small firm, some extra tax advantages can apply to you specifically. Owning your own firm affords you the opportunity to set up your own retirement plan and take tax deferral to a whole new level.

THE SIMPLE IRA AND SEP IRA

If you have not yet set up a retirement plan for your firm, you may want to start by exploring a SIMPLE IRA or SEP IRA. Both plans are simple to set up and often free, which makes them ideal for smaller firms or attorneys that are just starting out and trying to keep overhead low. The SIMPLE IRA allows each participant to contribute up to $14,000 from their salary on a pretax basis (in 2022). Then, the firm can provide either a 3 percent matching contribution or a nondiscretionary 2 percent contribution regardless of each participant's contribution. These funds are pretax as well, allowing you to put away more pre-tax dollars than is possible with a traditional IRA.[1]

The SEP IRA allows you to contribute up to the lesser of 25 percent of your salary or $61,000 for 2022, which is a lot more than the SIMPLE IRA. However, there is a catch: only an "employer" contribution is allowed. Employees cannot make their own contributions. In addition, the percentage of salary contributed to each participant's account—those of both owners and

---

[1] "SIMPLE IRA Plan," IRS, July 6, 2021, https://www.irs.gov/retirement-plans/plan-sponsor/simple-ira-plan.

employees—must be the same. So, if you have employees, this option may not be ideal.[2] One of my clients is a small criminal defense firm. When they started working with me, they had a SEP IRA into which they were putting a lot of money each year. This arrangement was fine because the firm only consisted of the two founding partners at the time. However, when a couple of new attorneys joined their firm, they realized they needed a new plan because they did not necessarily want the new, younger attorneys to be given the same contribution percentage.

THE 401(K) FOR SOLO/SMALL FIRMS

The 401(k) provides considerable flexibility in plan design. You can customize your 401(k)'s options such as vesting, eligibility, and employer contributions as long as the plan meets the IRS's nondiscrimination requirements. The 401(k) can also permit Roth and after-tax contributions as we discussed earlier.

If you are a solo practitioner or you are part of a small partnership made up solely of owners/partners and no W-2 employees, the 401(k) is by far the most advantageous plan because it permits you to set up what is called a "solo" 401(k). The solo 401(k), or owners-only 401(k), offers you the opportunity to maximize your retirement contributions with the lowest cost and greatest flexibility. Solo 401(k)s can be set up for sole proprietors and for owner-only businesses with no W-2 employees. You can have 1099 employees but not W-2 employees.

First, the 401(k) allows you to contribute more than is possible with most other retirement plans. Using a solo 401(k), you can make an "employee" contribution of up to $20,500 in 2022, or $27,500 if you are over 50. This can be either a pretax contribution or a Roth contribution. Then, you can make an additional "employer" contribution of up to 25 percent of your compensation up to the total contributions limit. In 2022, total contributions could not exceed $61,000 or $67,500 for those over 50.[3]

Second, if you are married, you can include your spouse! If your spouse takes income from your business, he or she can make contributions to a solo

---

[2] "Simplified employee pension plan (SEP)," IRS, June 10, 2021, https://www.irs.gov/retirement-plans/plan-sponsor/simplified-employee-pension-plan-sep.

[3] "One-participant 401(k) plans," IRS, September 28, 2010, https://www.irs.gov/retirement-plans/one-participant-401k-plans.

401(k) just like you do. In this way, you may effectively double the amount of money put toward the 401(k) plan. To do so correctly, you will need to pay your spouse as you would a W-2 employee. Even though W-2 employees disqualify a business owner from using the solo 401(k), spouses are an exception to the rule. If your spouse is an attorney, you can make them a part owner of the business, file as a partnership, and pay them as you would yourself.

Finally, unlike a regular 401(k), the solo 401(k) does not have IRS testing requirements. Normally, 401(k)s must perform nondiscrimination testing to make sure the plan is fair to employees. Because you do not have employees, you do not need to hire someone to perform this testing and can save money on skipping this requirement.

If you have employees, the 401(k) is still a great option; there are just some additional requirements. The 401(k) is great because you can customize how much of a match or employer contribution you want to provide to employees, if at all. You can also have additional requirements such as vesting. Vesting is the amount of time an employee must work at your firm before they have the right to employer contributions.

Unlike a SIMPLE IRA or SEP IRA, you do not necessarily have to treat owners and employees the same way. The 401(k) can have a profit-sharing feature that allows certain employees to receive additional contributions. Profit-sharing contributions are discretionary to the employer. To do so, the plan needs to have a formula to determine how contributions are divided among employees. You can separate employees into different categories and provide profit sharing only to select categories, such as attorneys versus support staff.

Running a 401(k) with nonowner, employee participants is a bit more expensive. The plan must make certain IRS filings and undergo annual testing to ensure it meets IRS nondiscrimination requirements. Typically, you need to hire an accounting firm to complete these tasks. The cheapest way to set up a 401(k) plan is to use a "safe harbor" plan. As a template plan, it automatically meets IRS requirements and therefore does not need to undergo annual testing.

THE CASH BALANCE PENSION PLAN

Even though the 401(k) permits you to stash away quite a lot of money for retirement, for some it will not be enough. If you need to put away more, the cash balance plan is another option. This plan is like the 401(k) on steroids, and it allows you to stash a lot of money away on a pretax basis—over $100,000 annually. Also, a cash balance plan can be paired with a 401(k) allowing you to turbocharge your retirement savings. Technically, the cash balance plan is a type of defined benefit pension plan. However, it operates similarly to a 401(k).

Contributions to a cash balance plan are made on a pretax basis, similar to a traditional IRA. This plan does not permit Roth contributions. Because cash balance plans are defined benefit plans, a different set of rules governs how much can be contributed. The maximum annual benefit for a participant in a defined benefit plan must be less than 100 percent of the participant's average compensation for their three highest consecutive years and less than $245,000 for 2022. That is the absolute maximum.[4]

The sum you ultimately contribute will likely be less because your actual contribution limit is an actuarial calculation based on your age. The older you are, the more you can contribute. Without going into the computations, however, you can clearly see that you can contribute a lot on a pretax basis to a cash balance plan. Moreover, if you pair that with a 401(k) plan, you can put away even more.

Cash balance plans can be used by solo attorneys, small partnerships, and even firms with W-2 employees. Of course, if you have employees, you will need to include them in the plan and make contributions to their accounts. When you set up the plan, you will determine how much you will contribute to participants based on age and salary. The formula for cash balance plans favors older participants who receive higher compensation, which means that these participants can receive larger contributions. Often, it is the case that law firms want their senior partners to receive larger retirement contributions. Since senior partners are often older and more highly compensated, they will naturally receive larger contributions under a cash balance plan.

In a cash balance plan, all the assets are pooled and invested in one account. Therefore, the plan sponsor (firm) bears all the investment risk. Employees do not have separate accounts but will receive statements that show a hypothetical account value calculated on the basis of the contributions they have made plus a guaranteed interest rate of 3 to 5 percent. You as the employer are guaranteeing this interest and bear the risk of not meeting it. This may be

---

[4] "Retirement topics—defined benefit plan benefit limits," IRS, November 10, 2020, https://www.irs.gov/retirement-plans/plan-participant-employee/retirement-topics-defined-benefit-plan-benefit-limits.

a disadvantage, but if you are a sole proprietor, you will obviously not need to worry about this risk.

Among other possible downsides, these plans are costly to set up and maintain, and the amount you contribute each year must stay relatively the same. This can be difficult to do if your income experiences dramatic fluctuations.

Cash balance plans are not for everyone, but they are great for highly profitable law firms with stable revenues where the owners (or partners) are generally older and receive a salary significantly higher than the employees. This plan can provide you with significant tax savings if you are already maxing out your other tax-deferral avenues.

At our company, we help law firm owners examine all the facets of different plan options and design an overall retirement plan that fits their needs. The strategy that provides the largest possible tax deferral is to pair a cash balance plan with a 401(k), but you need to make sure this arrangement is right for your firm.

So far, we have covered various ways to defer income taxes through retirement accounts. However, there is one additional type of account that is seldom used but can be an important source of tax savings. We call it the stealth IRA, and we will discuss that next.

CHAPTER 16
The Stealth IRA

If your goal is to maximize how much you are saving for retirement on a tax-advantaged basis and you have already signed on to IRAs and a 401(k), there is another often overlooked way to save money for retirement. It is the Health Savings Account (HSA). Some refer to it as the stealth IRA because while it is meant to take care of health care costs, it can also be used as a "stealthy" way to save for retirement.

HIGH-DEDUCTIBLE HEALTH INSURANCE AND THE HSA

The HSA was authorized by legislation in 2003 to help people with high-deductible health plans pay for medical costs. To qualify for an HSA, you must be enrolled in a high-deductible health insurance plan (HDHP) whose deductibles are at least $1,400 for an individual and $2,800 for a family for 2022. If in the future you leave your HDHP for a different plan, you can keep your HSA, but you cannot make contributions.

You can contribute up to $3,650 a year if you have self-only coverage and $7,300 a year for family coverage (as of 2022). Money contributed to an HSA is tax deductible, can be invested in the stock market, and grows tax-deferred, much like a traditional IRA. Funds withdrawn to pay for qualified medical expenses are not subject to tax, allowing you to use pretax earnings to pay for medical expenses tax free. This is a major tax advantage! However, any funds withdrawn that are not used for qualified medical expenses are subject to a 20 percent penalty plus ordinary income taxes.[1]

USING THE HSA AS AN IRA

The HSA should be used as an additional retirement vehicle. The legislation passed in 2003 allowed people to accumulate money from year to year in an HSA account. Before that time, these accounts were called Flexible Spending Accounts, and funds had to be used up each year or the owner would risk forfeiture. With an HSA, however, any money not used by the end of the year can remain in the account, stay invested, and continue to grow tax deferred. In fact, you can leave the money in the account for as long as you want, even until retirement.

Once you reach age 65, your HSA can be treated like an IRA. You can take withdrawals from the account for any reason—medical or not—without penalty. Like an IRA, however, if these funds are not used for qualified medical expenses, you will owe ordinary income taxes on any withdrawals.

Therefore, your HSA can be treated much like an additional traditional IRA, allowing you to contribute more on a pretax basis toward retirement. The attractive feature of the HSA is that, unlike the traditional IRA, it does not impose income limitations on making contributions or receiving a deduction for those contributions. Thus, the HSA is ideal for lawyers. Furthermore, it can serve as a potent tax-advantaged health care emergency fund if a major health event occurs in the future.

DISADVANTAGES OF AN HSA

Like other types of accounts, an HSA does have its downsides: namely, having an HSA requires you to be enrolled in an HDHP. Thus, you may pay more for health care costs than you would on a different type of plan. However, this may not be an issue if you are in good health and do not pay very much in health care costs anyway. Also, HDHPs have lower premiums, saving you some money, and people enrolled in HDHPs are not prone to abusing the system and requesting more health care services than they truly need. Being on

---

[1] "Publication 969 (2020), health savings accounts and other tax-favored health plans," IRS, February 16, 2021, https://www.irs.gov/publications/p969.

an HDHP may prompt health care services to give you a break on certain costs and lower your cost of care.

Finally, when choosing an HSA provider, you will want to choose a provider that allows you to actually invest the funds. Some HSA providers only offer cash deposits that earn minimal interest. You should employ a long-term investment strategy similar to your retirement accounts.

In the previous few chapters, we have covered various types of investment accounts that attorneys and nonattorneys alike can use to save for retirement and achieve maximum tax efficiency. However, some attorneys can take advantage of one additional method of tax deferral that others cannot. We will explore that in the next chapter.

CHAPTER 17

Contingency-Fee Tax Deferral

One of my clients is a solo attorney who does some personal injury work. Before he and I started working together, he won a rather large case in which he received a $1 million fee. Sounds great, right? Yes—except for the fact that he owed the IRS a whole lot of money that year. Personal injury attorneys and others working on a contingency-fee basis have a unique problem: they may go years without seeing any compensation from a particular case, and then when a case finally settles, they experience a major cash windfall. This is a major headache as far as taxes are concerned, because receiving a large settlement fee in one individual year means being pushed up into a higher tax bracket and paying a lot in taxes. Thankfully, attorneys can structure their legal fees to avoid this sudden tax hit. Structuring your fee means delaying receipt and setting up an agreement to receive your fee over a period of years rather than all at once.

WHO CAN STRUCTURE LEGAL FEES?

Attorneys have been able to structure their fees for years. Any attorney working on a contingency-fee basis, whether a physical injury or a nonphysical injury case (qualified or nonqualified), can structure their fees. Structures can be set up for attorneys working on their own or at large firms. The payee can be either the attorney or the firm. These structured arrangements can be set up on stand-alone basis for just the attorney if needed. The ability of the attorney to structure their fee does not depend on the client's decision about structuring their own settlement and can be done regardless. However, the defendant must agree to this arrangement as part of the settlement agreement. To preserve your right to structure your fee, you will want the fee award to include the possibility of a structure as early as possible.

WHY DEFER CONTINGENCY FEES?

Deferring a contingency fee makes a lot of sense in terms of taxes and financial planning. If you receive a $1 million settlement fee as an immediate cash payment, you will pay taxes on that fee in the tax year you receive it. That includes federal, state, and local income tax, and you will be at the highest tax bracket. Your tax rate on your fee could easily exceed 40 percent. Such a tax will result in a tax bill of $400,000 or more, leaving only $600,000 to invest. You will also be taxed on the growth of that money, amounting to double taxation! You will be taxed on the growth you need to gain back what you paid in taxes in the first place!

By contrast, a structured fee arrangement would allow you to invest your entire $1 million fee up front, minus any costs to set everything up. Because it is tax deferred, you won't be taxed on any of the growth while it is within the structure. Instead, you will receive portions of that fee over time and pay taxes on the amount you receive each year.

To illustrate, let's assume you can achieve a 10 percent rate of growth on your investments. Let's assume that you are in the highest tax bracket (federal, state, and local combined)—40 percent. The amount left over after taxes is $600,000. You invest this money in an after-tax account, which will be subject to capital gains and dividend taxes. Let's assume your tax drag from these taxes is 15 percent, bringing your after-tax rate of return down to 8.5 percent. Under these assumptions, after 10 years you will have $1,356,590.

On the other hand, if you invest your full fee up front and let it grow for 10 years, you will have $2,539,743. If you take it out all at once and pay 40 percent in taxes, you will have $1,523,846. That's almost a $150,000 difference. However, if you take distributions over a period of years, your tax rate might be significantly less, making the structured fee arrangement strategy even more attractive. See Table 17.1.

Not only does fee deferral provide great tax benefits, but it can also be very helpful from a financial planning perspective. The ability to structure your fee so that you receive it over a period of years can help solve some of

Contingency-Fee Tax Deferral

Table 17.1

	Immediate Cash Payment	Structured Fee Arrangement
Initial amount	$1,000,000	$1,000,000
Up-front taxes	$400,000 (40%)	$0
Amount invested	$600,000	$1,000,000
After 10 years	$1,356,590	$2,539,743
After tax value	$1,356,590	$1,523,846

the problems of irregular cash flow and smooth out the financial turbulence that contingency-fee attorneys often experience. You can set up a structured arrangement to provide enough income to cover your operating expenses over a period of years to give you peace of mind.

Additionally, a structured fee arrangement provides protection from creditors and judgments. Because you do not have constructive receipt of the funds until they are actually paid out to you from the structured arrangement, you do not own the funds and they are not subject to the demands of creditors.

Finally, a structured fee arrangement can be used to enhance your retirement planning and create a stream of income for yourself in retirement. This is perhaps its most attractive feature. You can defer receipt of your fee all the way until retirement age and then set it up to pay you over a period of years in retirement. This could allow you to avoid invading other investments sooner than necessary.

THE LEGAL BASIS FOR FEE DEFERRAL

As an attorney, you may be wondering what the legal basis is that allows these arrangements to be set up. The primary doctrine that allows this strategy is the doctrine of constructive receipt. The IRS will only tax you on income that you have constructive receipt of. Constructive receipt exists when you have the unrestricted right to receive income. Even if you have not physically received money, having the unrestricted right to receive a sum of money as income makes you liable to be taxed on it. If your right to receive income is restricted and you do not control it, the IRS does not deem you to have received this income.

The structured fee arrangement avoids constructive receipt because of two important characteristics. First, you never take custody of the funds: they go directly to a third-party custodian. Second, you do not have any control over the investment of the funds, you cannot direct the funds, and you cannot access the funds. Instead, the funds are invested and directed according to a contractual agreement and are only disbursed to you according to a predefined schedule in the contract.

Legal precedent permits structured fee arrangements. In *Richard A. Childs et al.* v. *Commissioner of the Internal Revenue Service* in 1996, the 11th Circuit Court of Appeals ruled that attorneys can use structured fee arrangements to recognize income in the year(s) that future payments are received from the arrangement rather than in the year the fee is awarded.[1]

The other aspect of IRS law that concerns structured fee arrangements is the doctrine of economic benefit. Under IRS rules, this doctrine holds you liable for tax when you receive an economic benefit. Even if you will not receive property until sometime in the future, you are liable for tax when the right to receive that property is conveyed to you. However, the IRS ruled in Revenue Ruling 79-220 that the right to receive future payments from a structured settlement does not constitute an economic benefit. This same ruling applies to structured fee arrangements.

RULES AND REQUIREMENTS

A structured fee operates in much the same way as does a claimant's structured settlement. Setting up a structured fee arrangement requires cooperation from the defense, and you will want to make sure that you have specific language in your settlement agreement that allows for structuring your fee. A structured fee arrangement needs to be set up carefully to meet IRS guidelines, and a qualified settlement specialist should be utilized.

In terms of mechanics, as soon as the settlement is awarded, your fee is paid to an assignment company. The assignment company then immediately sends the funds to a trust company for custody and management. If you are using an investment advisor to manage the funds, they will then be transferred to the adviser's investment platform to be invested on your behalf. An investment policy statement will guide the investment of the assets; this

---

[1] Childs v. Comm'r of Internal Revenue, 103 T.C. 634, 103 T.C. 36 (U.S.T.C. 1994).

is part of the agreement as well. To avoid constructive receipt, you cannot direct the investment of the funds.

OPTIONS FOR STRUCTURING FEES

Several options are available for what types of vehicles can be used to structure your fee. You can use a fixed or variable annuity offered through an insurance company. Annuities can either provide a fixed rate of return (in a fixed annuity) or be invested in subaccounts that invest in stocks, bonds, and the like (variable annuities).

A more attractive option is a market-based structured fee arrangement. In this arrangement, your fee is invested directly through a brokerage firm like Charles Schwab or E-Trade and managed by an investment advisor. This option is more attractive because it often means lower costs than an annuity, the opportunity to have your money managed by a professional advisor, and potentially higher returns over time.

Structured fee arrangements are an attractive strategy for contingency-fee attorneys looking to minimize taxes. But you can employ yet more strategies than tax deferral. If you are charitably minded, you can use charitable-giving plans to reduce taxes as well. We will explore those strategies next.

CHAPTER 18
Charitable Tax Strategies

One way to reduce your overall tax burden is to take advantage of charitable contributions. Normally, when we think about giving to charity, we think in terms of cash. Taxpayers can deduct charitable cash contributions as itemized deductions up to a percentage (normally 60 percent) of their adjusted gross income (AGI). You can also contribute noncash property such as real estate, automobiles, tangible personal property, appreciated stock, or other items and receive a deduction for those donations. This is a great way to reduce your tax liability without having to write a check.

Giving appreciated stock to charity is one of the most effective ways to give to charity. This is because when you donate stock to charity, you receive a deduction for the current fair market value (which ideally is much higher than your cost basis or original purchase price) and you effectively eliminate the capital gains tax on the gain. If you sold the stock and then gave cash, you would have to pay taxes on the capital gain. Because you are donating the shares directly, you do not have to pay capital gains tax, and if the charity is a tax-exempt nonprofit, they will not be required to pay capital gains tax either when they sell the shares.

TRUST STRATEGIES

Besides direct giving, a trust might allow you to take a more strategic approach to giving, especially when it comes to estate planning. Charitable trusts can be used to reduce income or estate taxes. There are two main types of charitable trust arrangements: charitable remainder trusts and charitable lead trusts.

A charitable remainder trust (CRT) provides you, the donor, with a lifetime income (calculated as some percentage of the trust assets annually), while pledging the remainder of the trust to charity after you are deceased. In a CRT, the asset is divided into two interests: an income interest, which you will retain, and an irrevocable remainder interest, which you will donate to the charity of your choice. The remainder interest is valued based on the annual income payout of the trust and IRS valuation tables.

The CRT has some great benefits. First, you receive an immediate, partial tax deduction when assets or funds are contributed to the trust based on the appraised value of the remainder interest. Even though that interest will not be given to charity until your death, you get the deduction up front. Another benefit is that you can use a CRT to retain the value of appreciated stock. By donating appreciated stock to the CRT, you can avoid paying capital gains tax. When the trust finally receives the remainder interest and sells the property, it is exempt from tax. Finally, the CRT's investment income is tax exempt. Funds within the CRT can be managed by professional investment managers without needing to be concerned with taxes on gains or dividends within the trust.

By contrast, a charitable lead trust (CLT) is a trust through which you donate to charity the income interest for a period of years. After the term of years specified in the trust document ends, the remainder is distributed to you, the donor, or to your beneficiaries, such as a child or grandchild. This system is essentially the opposite of the CRT. These trusts can be funded during your lifetime or upon death through your will. Either you or your estate (depending on when the trust is funded) will receive an immediate income or estate tax deduction for the value of the income interest based on IRS valuation tables. If done correctly, these trusts can be structured to create a charitable deduction equal to 100 percent of the current value of the property.

The CLT is especially advantageous during time periods when interest rates are low. This is because of the different ways in which the IRS values the income interest versus the remainder interest. Lower interest rates produce a lower value for the remainder interest and a higher value for the income interest, which you would donate to charity. In today's low interest rate environment, the CLT may be more advantageous than the CRT.

PRIVATE FOUNDATION

In addition to trusts, private foundations can be a source of charitable deductions. A private foundation is a legal entity set up solely for charitable purposes. In contrast to a public charity which derives its fundraising from the public, private foundations are usually set up and funded by individuals or families for purposes of giving to charities and minimizing taxes.

If the private foundation is set up correctly and obtains tax-exempt status, contributions to the foundation will qualify for a charitable tax deduction when made. Then, you can make grants to charities of your choice through the foundation using foundation funds. Private foundations provide a great deal of flexibility and control. While private foundations must distribute a certain amount of their funds each year, you can be flexible as to how much and when you make distributions. A private foundation can also provide a great framework for educating and involving family members in the charitable mission. Often, private foundation boards are composed of family members and friends.

Private foundations have some disadvantages, however. First, they can be costly to set up and maintain. Start-up costs can easily exceed $10,000 depending on complexity. Second, there are strict IRS rules that private foundations must follow, including annual reporting, and you will want to make sure you follow those rules and regulatory requirements to retain nonprofit status. Third, while private foundations may be granted tax-exempt status, they must pay a 1 to 2 percent excise tax on their net income.

DONOR-ADVISED FUND

A donor-advised fund (DAF) is a great alternative to a private foundation if you want to receive a charitable deduction immediately and give money to charities over time, and you want to avoid the hassle of setting up a private foundation. A DAF is a charitable-giving vehicle set up at a public charity. The charity serves as the custodian of the fund.

Donating to a DAF gives you an immediate tax deduction at the time you contribute funds. However, you do not have to give the funds immediately to any specific charity. Instead, you can recommend grants from your DAF to various charities at your discretion. This allows you to receive an immediate deduction for gifts you would otherwise give over time. Thus, the DAF can be a great tool for contingency-fee attorneys who are charitably minded and are seeking a large charitable deduction in a year in which they receive a large settlement fee. However, because you receive an immediate deduction for your contribution, donations are irrevocable. This means you cannot get them back.

Funds not given away can be invested and will grow over time. The funds held in your DAF can be invested in stocks, bonds, and so on at your discretion, or they can be managed by the public charity itself and grow over time. The public charity will charge an annual fee calculated as a percentage of assets to maintain your fund.

Unlike a private foundation, a DAF involves little time commitment or regulatory red tape and is much easier to set up and maintain. Also, it does not incur an excise tax on investment income. However, in exchange for those benefits, you give up some of the flexibility and control that a private foundation offers. You can only make distributions to IRS qualified charities. Your investment options may be limited, and the public charity that manages your DAF has ultimate legal authority over the use of your funds.

CHARITABLE LIMITED LIABILITY COMPANIES

Another charitable strategy that has become popular in recent years is the limited liability company (LLC). Mark Zuckerberg and his wife Priscilla Chan made this strategy famous. The greatest advantages of the charitable LLC are its privacy and flexibility. Unlike private foundations which must file 990s or 990-PFs and make their information public, charitable LLCs do not have to make any public filings.

A charitable LLC also has much greater flexibility. Private foundations must give or spend at least 5 percent of their funds each year and have strict rules around self-dealing, excess business holdings, jeopardy investments, and taxable expenditures to name a few. Charitable LLCs do not have any of these rules since they are really just LLCs used for charitable purposes. Funds in the LLC can be invested in for-profit opportunities, and ventures do not have to be impact-related or socially responsible.

So, what is the drawback? The LLC is not a tax-exempt entity; rather, it is a pass-through entity like any other LLC. Charitable LLCs are simply LLCs that are used for charitable purposes. Whatever profits or tax deductions the LLC receives flow through to the owners. Unlike a private foundation or DAF, you do not receive a tax deduction for simply putting money in the LLC. However, if you give to charity from the LLC, the tax deduction will flow through to you, the owner, and any other owners.

For the highly compensated and charitably minded attorney, charitable giving strategies can accomplish several purposes: giving you the opportunity to make an impact in the world, boosting your reputation and public goodwill, and reducing your taxes.

We help our clients examine the pros and cons of various strategies and decide which will best accomplish their purposes and complement their overall financial plan. You should also consult your financial advisor and a qualified tax advisor to help you in these decisions.

There is one more vehicle that is often touted for its tax advantages that we have not covered yet: life insurance. We will examine this vehicle next.

CHAPTER 19

Life Insurance Tax Strategies

Throughout this section I have described a variety of vehicles and strategies you can use to reduce your overall tax burden. One additional vehicle worth mentioning is life insurance. Life insurance policies have several tax advantages useful for retirement funding, charitable giving, or education planning.

First, you need to be familiar with the two main types of life insurance: term and cash value. Term life insurance is insurance that only lasts for a specific period of years and then expires. Once it expires, it is worthless. It is meant solely to provide pure insurance protection for a specific, temporary period.

Cash-value life insurance, by contrast, builds cash value over time within the policy. Premiums are higher on cash-value life insurance policies than on term policies. This is because part of the premium will go to pay the cost of pure insurance protection and the rest will remain in the policy to earn interest. Some policies pay a fixed interest rate on the cash value. Others allow you to allocate your cash value to subaccounts that will track different stock market indices such as the S&P 500.

As you get older, the cost of insurance increases because your mortality risk increases. The cash value that builds up within a cash-value life insurance policy will be used to subsidize the rising cost of insurance protection as you get older. This can allow the life insurance policy to last indefinitely. Many policies are guaranteed to last until age 100 or older, making them effectively permanent.

TAX ADVANTAGES OF LIFE INSURANCE

Life insurance has a few tax-advantaged features. First, the death benefit provided by a life insurance policy is income-tax free to beneficiaries. Also, if removed from the estate and placed in someone else's name, the proceeds will not be included in your gross estate—so no estate tax. Second, cash values that accrue in a life insurance policy accumulate on a tax-deferred basis. You do not pay any tax on earnings within the life insurance policy. Third, funds borrowed from the life insurance cash value are not taxable. You can borrow funds from a cash-value life insurance policy through policy loans. Generally, as long as these loans do not exceed the amount of premiums paid, they are not recognized as income by the IRS and therefore are income-tax free.

Because life insurance offers the ability to receive tax-deferred growth and potentially use funds without paying tax on those earnings, life insurance can be an additional vehicle for retirement or education funding. To use a life insurance policy this way, you would contribute funds to the policy over time in excess of your premium (overfunding) and then when you need the funds, you would borrow money through a policy loan. However, you will need to consult a qualified advisor to make sure you do this correctly. If you overfund a life insurance policy too much during the first seven years, it can be classified as a modified endowment contract (or MEC); as a result, any policy loans become taxable, and you lose your tax advantages.

Do you have to pay back policy loans? That is up to you. Borrowing money from your life insurance is like any other kind of loan: you have to pay interest. But this interest is technically being paid to yourself. If you do not pay back the loan, the accrued interest and cost of life insurance could deplete the cash value and cause the policy to lapse—or effectively be canceled. However, if the policy lapses, the loan and interest on the loan will be considered taxable income.

In the case of retirement planning, you probably are not planning to pay back the policy loans. When you die, any unpaid loans will be subtracted from the final death benefit payable to your beneficiaries.

NONQUALIFIED DEFERRED COMPENSATION PLAN

Life insurance is a popular way to fund a nonqualified deferred compensation plan. These plans are retirement plans that companies often offer to their executives or highly compensated employees and can be used by law firms to provide additional benefits to partners or high-paid attorneys at the firm.

Unlike a traditional defined contribution plan such as a 401(k), these plans do not need to be offered to all employees. For this reason they are called nonqualified. A nonqualified deferred compensation plan is essentially a contract whereby an employer agrees to pay the employee their compensation at a later date. This allows the employee to defer taxation on the income.

Companies often fund these arrangements using life insurance. How could a law firm set up a nonqualified deferred compensation plan using life insurance? The firm will sign a contract with the partner to make specified benefit payments upon retirement, death, or disability in exchange for the partner continuing to work at the firm. The firm will then obtain an appropriate amount of life insurance on the employee to cover its expenses should the employee die prematurely, with the firm named as the beneficiary. In order to meet IRS guidelines, the firm must be named as owner and beneficiary, with no interest in the policy given to the partner. The policy must be subject to the firm's general debt obligations, and the firm must pay the premiums.

When the partner retires, the firm makes payments to the partner based on its contractual obligations. The firm can use policy loans to make these payments. The income is reported by the partner when received, and it is deductible to the firm in the year paid. When the partner dies, the firm collects the life insurance proceeds (tax-free) and is reimbursed for part of the cost of the plan.

SPLIT DOLLAR LIFE INSURANCE

A split dollar life insurance plan is a type of nonqualified deferred compensation plan. This type of plan is called split dollar because the firm and the partner will split the costs and benefits of a life insurance policy.

These plans can be designed in several ways, which can be fairly complex. The two basic and popular ways to design these plans are the loan regime and the economic benefit regime. In a loan regime plan, the partner is the owner of the policy, but the firm pays the premiums. These premiums are paid by technically lending the amount of the premium to the partner and then the partner paying the premium. Interest can be charged or not charged on these loans. If not charged, then the loaned amount is taxable as income. When the partner retires, the loan is forgiven and may become taxable to the partner but deductible to the firm. The partner can then use the policy to fund their retirement.

In an economic benefit regime plan, the firm owns the policy and pays the premiums but allows the partner to name the beneficiary of the policy. When the partner retires, the firm transfers ownership of the policy to the partner.

What are the benefits of such a plan? For the partner, there are several benefits: life insurance protection for their beneficiaries, the potential of tax-free income through partial withdrawals or policy loans, and tax-deferred growth of the cash value in the policy. For the firm, plans like this are a form of "golden handcuffs" encouraging the partner to stay with the firm for a period of years. These plans can be designed with vesting requirements, allowing the firm to recoup its investment if the partner quits or leaves prematurely.

DISADVANTAGES OF LIFE INSURANCE

Using life insurance as a tax-deferral vehicle has its downsides as well. First and most obvious are the expenses. In comparison to other types of retirement savings vehicles, life insurance is the most expensive. The cost of insurance to provide the death benefit will increase each year, eating into the cash value of the policy. Most policies also have surrender fees that will apply to any funds withdrawn during the first several years—called a surrender period. These periods can last 10 years or longer. If you withdraw money or surrender the policy during the surrender period, surrender charges will apply.

Another major disadvantage of life insurance policies has to do with growth potential. Life insurance policies do not provide the growth potential that an IRA invested in stocks and bonds can provide. In today's low interest rate environment, cash-value policies that provide a fixed rate of return are simply not competitive. Policies that allow you to "invest" your cash value in subaccounts that track various stock market indices (variable or indexed policies) have some catches as well. While these policies usually will guarantee that you will not lose money if the index loses money, they often apply caps or participation factors that limit the amount of an index's upside potential that you can capture.

CHARITABLE USES OF LIFE INSURANCE

Life insurance can be an effective way to maximize your charitable impact and obtain some tax benefits. You can name a charity as the beneficiary of

Life Insurance Tax Strategies

your life insurance policy. Although this will not give you a tax deduction in the present, it will allow you to retain control of the policy, including taking policy loans. Because the death benefit is going to the charity (although the death benefit will be included in your estate if you own the policy), your estate will receive an estate tax deduction equal to the size of the death benefit, eliminating this problem.

Alternatively, you could gift the policy itself to a charity. This option tends to be a more popular route. While you will give up control of the policy, this will remove the death benefit from your estate, and you can claim a tax deduction for part of the value of the donated policy. If you want to keep paying the premiums to maintain the policy, you can deduct the cost of those premiums going forward. Or the charity can take over the premium payments.

Life insurance can be a valuable alternative vehicle for tax savings due to the tax-advantaged features of life insurance policies: income-tax free death benefits, tax-deferred growth of the cash value inside the policy, and the ability to use policy loans income-tax free. However, life insurance can be a costly way to achieve your financial objectives and may not be an ideal tax-savings vehicle in today's low interest rate environment.

Having covered a variety of tax-deferral and tax-minimization vehicles, we will wrap up this section with a variety of specific, practical ideas for attorneys and law firm owners to minimize taxes in the next chapter.

CHAPTER 20

10 Tax Tips for Attorneys

In addition to some of the more complex strategies we discussed already, there are some small, simple ways to reduce the amount of tax you pay. The tax code is quite complex, but that complexity can work to your advantage if you know how. I am not saying you should shirk your responsibilities as a taxpayer or commit tax evasion. Rather, the complexity of the tax code creates perfectly legal planning opportunities for the financially savvy. To close out the section on tax savings for attorneys, I will show you 10 perfectly legal ideas for tax savings.

PREPAY EXPENSES

One of the simplest ways to reduce your taxes in a particular year is to accelerate your deductions by prepaying expenses early. The local chamber of commerce that I belong to sends out a notice in November each year offering to allow members to pay their dues early. Doing so allows you to deduct your dues for the upcoming year in the current year instead. This strategy is helpful if you have had a particularly high-income year and are looking for extra deductions. What other things could you prepay? Here are some ideas:

- Pay monthly subscriptions a year or two years in advance.
- Make next year's charitable contributions early.
- Purchase an advertising campaign that lasts several years and pay up front.
- Pay estimated fourth-quarter tax payments in December instead of January.

DEFER INCOME

For tax purposes, you could try to defer receipt of income as much as possible until the following year. In this way, you can shift income in the current year to the next year, which might help you reduce the taxes you owe in the current year. Again, this strategy is helpful if you have had more income than you anticipated in the current year and expect less income next year. This will only work, however, if you use a cash accounting method and recognize income when received, as opposed to an accrual accounting method that recognizes income when earned. Here are some ideas:

- Delay collection of accounts receivable until the new year.
- Delay billing of clients until the new year.
- Defer compensation by making additional retirement plan contributions.
- Defer the sale of any property that might result in a capital gain.

HIRE YOUR KIDS

Another simple way to reduce your overall tax rate is to hire your kids. If you are a solo attorney or law firm owner, you may want to consider this strategy. The Tax Cuts and Jobs Act of 2017 made this idea much more attractive because it greatly increased the standard deduction and thereby the amount you can pay your kids without requiring them to pay tax. Any income your child receives up to the standard deduction is not taxable. For 2022, the standard deduction was $12,950 for single taxpayers. And of course, what you pay your kids is deductible to the business.

You of course need to make sure that your kids are actually doing work and are being paid a reasonable wage. If you pay your child nearly $13,000 to fold papers for an hour, the IRS is not going to accept that. Keep a record of the work your child has done and the money you have paid for the work they have done so that you can justify what you have paid if you are audited. Your child could handle administrative tasks, organize paperwork and files, or even manage your social media accounts. Think creatively.

HIRE YOUR SPOUSE

If you are a solo attorney, in addition to hiring your kids, you could hire your spouse as well. Paying your spouse is not quite as lucrative as paying your kids because it will not entitle you to any new deductions. Also, paying your spouse may mean paying more in social security and Medicare taxes, which you may not want to do. However, as I explained before, paying your spouse opens up the door to make 401(k) contributions on their behalf, potentially doubling the amount you can contribute to a solo 401(k).

USE THE AUGUSTA RULE

Often called the Augusta Rule because it originated as a result of lobbying by wealthy homeowners in Augusta, Georgia, who were looking to receive favorable tax treatment for renting their property during the Masters golf tournament, the IRS allows you to rent out residential property for a limited time without paying taxes. Generally, if you rent out residential or vacation property that you also use, you will need to pay taxes on the income you receive. However, the IRS made a special ruling that applies to minimal rental use. If you rent out property that you also use as a residence for a rental period of fewer than 15 days, you will not need to report any income from the rental.[1]

How does this rule help you? You could use your residence or vacation home as a location for a firm meeting or retreat and charge your business for the privilege to do so. The expense is deductible for your business, and the income you receive is not taxable as long as the rental is less than 15 days. This effectively eliminates taxation on that portion of income. To do this, however, you will want to make sure that you are charging your business a reasonable rate for the rental of the space and that there is a business purpose.

DEDUCT YOUR VACATION

Along the same lines, you may be able to deduct some of the expenses related to your family vacation if you are conducting business on your vacation. You may not be a fan of mixing business and pleasure, but this is one way to achieve some extra deductions. To do so, however, a legitimate business purpose must be tied to your vacation. Also, you need to be conducting business for a majority of the time you are there.

---

[1] "Topic no. 415 renting residential and vacation property," IRS, March 5, 2021, https://www.irs.gov/taxtopics/tc415.

For example, let's say you want to attend a three-day conference in Florida. You decide that you will use the opportunity to turn this business trip into a week-long family vacation and save some money on taxes. If your vacation will last seven days, then at least four of those days need to be devoted to business. Travel counts toward your business activity, so you could potentially count two travel days as business days. That would mean you need to spend at least two days at the conference for the trip to qualify as a business trip (while your family relaxes poolside). You can spend the remaining three days with the family at the beach.

What exactly can you deduct? According to IRS topic 511,[2] you can generally deduct some of your travel, lodging, and meal expenses. However, there are some caveats. First, the expenses you deduct need to be necessary and ordinary to your business. You cannot deduct lavish or purely personal expenses. In addition, you can only deduct the portion that applies to you and your business activities. For example, you can deduct your plane ticket, but not the plane tickets for your spouse and children. You can deduct the cost of a single hotel room, but not the entire cost of a five-bedroom beach house. You can deduct your meals while you are engaged in business, but not the family outing to the seafood buffet.

BUY YOUR OFFICE

Instead of leasing your office, you might consider purchasing your office space. While you can deduct the cost of rent used for your office space, purchasing your office may be an even better tax strategy. Additionally, owning your office can be a great way to enhance your long-term wealth accumulation. In today's low interest rate environment, purchasing your office space may make a lot of sense. It provides you with an asset that you can sell later to fund your retirement. However, if your firm grows or your needs change, leasing provides you with more flexibility.

You can deduct the cost of buying business property (not including the cost of the land), but the IRS generally requires you to do so over time through a calculation called depreciation. The simplest method of doing this is called straight line depreciation. In this calculation, you simply spread out the cost of the acquisition over the "useful life" for that type of property according to IRS tables. For example, commercial real estate has a 39-year useful life. So,

---

[2] "Topic no. 511 business travel expenses," IRS, https://www.irs.gov/taxtopics/tc511.

you can deduct 1/39th of the cost of your commercial real estate acquisition over 39 years.

Another type of depreciation, called bonus depreciation, allows you to accelerate the recovery of your costs through tax deduction. Before 2018, bonus depreciation allowed you to deduct up to 50 percent of the cost of property up front and then a smaller amount in years after until it had been fully recovered. However, the Tax Cuts and Jobs Act of 2017 increased this to a 100 percent bonus, allowing you to fully recover the cost in the first year. There is one major catch though: this only applies to property that has a useful life of less than 20 years.

Does this rule out real estate? Not necessarily. Some accounting firms offer what is called a cost segregation study to break down the cost of property into different components that have different useful life periods. This allows you to achieve bonus depreciation on a portion of your property cost.

For example, let's say you purchase an office for $500,000. And let's assume that through cost segregation you were able to break that down to 5-year property worth $100,000, 15-year property worth $100,000, and the rest remaining as a 39-year property or land. This strategy would allow you to enjoy a tax deduction of up to $200,000 in year 1. While these tax advantages are not permanent, this strategy could allow you to greatly increase your deductions in a year when your income is higher than normal, and your taxes would otherwise be much higher. These advantages will not last forever, though. These bonus depreciation rules only apply to property purchased before 2023.[3]

BUY A NEW CAR

Just like buying your office can lower your tax bill, buying a new car through your business can be a great way to lower your tax bill as well. Obviously, buying new cars all the time is probably not a cost-effective way to consistently lower your tax bill. However, if you have a year in which your income is substantially above average, and you might be due for a new car, purchasing a new vehicle could be a great idea.

---

[3] Jason Jobgen, "New depreciation rules create tax planning opportunities," BKD, January 25, 2019, https://www.bkd.com/article/2019/01/new-depreciation-rules-create-tax-planning-opportunities.

Vehicles are generally considered five-year property and are written off over a five-year period. Under straight-line depreciation, you could just write off 1/5th each year. Or under bonus depreciation rules you can accelerate that process and deduct more up front. Because vehicles have a useful life of less than 20 years, they do qualify for the section 179 deduction rules allowing you to deduct up to 100 percent of the cost in year 1 if put in service before 2023. Unfortunately, vehicles are subject to a maximum dollar limit. In 2021, this was $18,200 for passenger vehicles.[4] Still, that would be a nice extra tax deduction.

ESTABLISH A HOME OFFICE

Even if you have an official office that you use solely to conduct business, you probably do some work from home. If that is the case, you may be able to deduct a portion of your home expenses as business expenses. To qualify for this deduction, you will need to set aside a room or part of a room exclusively for work. Many people already have a room in their house that they use as a home office. Then, you will need to calculate what percentage of your home this space represents. Let's say your home office is 10 percent of your overall square footage. In that case, you may be able to deduct 10 percent of various home expenses as business expenses.

The IRS has two basic requirements for the home office deduction. First, your home office area must be used regularly and exclusively for conducting business. Second, your home office area must be a principal place of business. If you have a separate office elsewhere, it is likely you do not qualify but not necessarily. To qualify, you need to show that you use your home substantially and regularly for tasks that are not done anywhere else. For example, you could make your home a secondary location for your business. Many businesses have more than one location.

What expenses can you deduct? You can fully deduct any kind of regular office supplies or other business-related expenses that pertain solely to your home office. You can also deduct a portion of home expenses such as mortgage interest, insurance, utilities, repairs, and depreciation.[5]

---

[4] "Rev. proc. 2021-31," IRS, 2021, https://www.irs.gov/pub/irs-drop/rp-21-31.pdf.

[5] "Publication 587 (2020), business use of your home," IRS, January 15, 2021, https://www.irs.gov/publications/p587.

FILE AS AN S-CORPORATION

Finally, one of the most effective strategies to reduce taxes for highly compensated solo and small-firm attorneys is to file taxes as a subchapter S-corporation. This can allow you to cut back on the amount of money you pay in social security and Medicare taxes.

Many solo attorneys or small firms are set up as sole proprietorships, partnerships, or LLCs. These types of entities are pass-through entities. All income received by the business flows through to the owners and is taxable to the owners. As a result, all the income is potentially subject to self-employment tax or social security and Medicare taxes.

One of the biggest drawbacks to being self-employed is that you pay both the "employer" and "employee" portion of social security and Medicare taxes. Typically, the employer and employee each pay half of the social security and Medicare taxes. The social security tax rate is 12.4 percent and the Medicare tax rate is 2.9 percent, for a grand total of 15.3 percent in self-employment taxes. These taxes apply to income up to $142,800 in 2021.[6] To make matters worse, you can only deduct the employer portion of the self-employment tax from your adjusted gross income in calculating your income tax liability.

The S-corporation filing strategy provides a solution, however. If you file as an S-corporation, you will be able to classify some income as "salary" and some as "distributions." You will pay self-employment tax on the salary portion, but not on the distributions portion. On the distributions portion, you will only pay income tax. This could result in substantial savings on self-employment taxes.

Let's compare the S-corporation to a sole proprietorship. Imagine you are a solo practitioner, you make $120,000, and you have business expenses of $40,000 for a net profit of $80,000. You will pay self-employment tax of 15.3 percent on your net profit less 7.65 percent, which comes to $11,304. Because only the "employer's" portion is deductible, you can only deduct $5,652. The standard deduction in 2021 was $12,550. Therefore, your taxable income is potentially $61,798. At that level, you are in the 22 percent tax bracket for 2021 and you'll pay $13,596 in federal income tax. Your net after-tax profit (I am ignoring state income tax for simplicity) comes to $55,100.

---

[6] "Self-employment tax (Social Security and Medicare taxes)," IRS, June 26, 2021, https://www.irs.gov/businesses/small-businesses-self-employed/self-employment-tax-social-security-and-medicare-taxes.

On the other hand, if you file as an S-corporation, your taxes could be less. As an S-corporation, you will need to pay yourself a reasonable wage, which let's suppose is $50,000. You will pay social security and Medicare tax on that amount, which comes to $7,650. You will pay the rest of your profit to yourself as a distribution—$30,000. This amount will skip social security and Medicare taxation. Your taxable income with the standard deduction and deduction for the employer portion of social security and Medicare tax would be $63,625. At that level, you are still in the 22 percent bracket and pay $13,998 in federal income tax. Your net after-tax profit comes to $58,352. That's a savings of over $3,000.

How is this done? You will need to organize as an LLC and then elect to file as an S-corporation. Then, you will need to run payroll for yourself and pay yourself a reasonable salary. The key here is "reasonable." You cannot make $500,000 and pay yourself only $10,000 in salary. That is a sure way to attract IRS attention. A certified public accountant can help you determine what is reasonable. Setting all this up carries some cost, but usually it is well worth it. Some states, however, impose additional fees and taxes on S-corporations (e.g., California) that reduce the benefit.

In this chapter, I presented you with 10 perfectly legal tips for reducing your overall taxes. Taxes are one of the primary concerns for attorneys that I work with. Solo and small-firm attorneys who are successful pay a lot in taxes and feel the burden of taxes more than some. It makes sense to take advantage of every legal opportunity to reduce them.

PART IV

Protecting Your Wealth

No one expects to die prematurely, become disabled, or to be sued. But these risks are all too real. No discussion on growing your wealth would be complete without a section on protecting it. As you grow your practice, your career, and your wealth, it is important to make sure you have the right protections in place against risks that can derail your financial plan. In this section, we will discuss some of those key risks and how to protect yourself and your future.

CHAPTER 21

Life Insurance Protection

Premature death is one of the biggest risks to your financial plan, especially if you are the major breadwinner in your family or in your law practice. Even if both you and your spouse work, the loss of your income to your family may be a devastating financial blow, leaving inadequate financial resources to meet ongoing obligations and to save for future goals like retirement or college funding. Your surviving spouse will also need funds to service debt, especially mortgage and car payments. Will your spouse be able to continue these payments in your absence?

If you have kids, they will need financial support, especially if college or other postsecondary education is on the horizon. While your spouse may remarry or adjust the family's lifestyle to adapt to a change in resources, your family will still need to replace your income for at least some period of time during any kind of readjustment phase. Additionally, death is not cheap! Your family will need funds to pay for funeral expenses, probate expenses, and perhaps taxes.

Finally, if you are part of a small law firm, your death may impact the survivability of the firm and thereby be a major concern for your partners. If you are a chief rainmaker, this concern will be greatly amplified. Will your firm be able to continue operating if something happens to you? Will your family receive any compensation from the partners taking over your part of the partnership? These are matters that need to be considered and worked out in advance.

THE SOLUTION: LIFE INSURANCE

Premature death creates a large liquidity need for both your family and your firm. The solution to this need is life insurance, which is simply a contractual agreement that provides a cash payout (death benefit) upon your death in exchange for the policy owner's regular payments as agreed upon (premium payments) with the insurance company.

By making a death benefit available if you should die, life insurance creates an estate or inheritance for your dependents or heirs instantaneously, even though your actual assets may be far less substantial. Your premium payment is a function of your risk factors, death benefit, and other considerations. The higher the death benefit you select when you purchase a policy, the higher your premiums will be. And the more at-risk you are in terms of your health and premature death odds, the higher your premiums will be at all levels.

HOW MUCH LIFE INSURANCE DO I NEED?

A few different methods can be used to determine mathematically how much life insurance you should have. At a minimum, you may want to start with an amount that would be able to retire debts such as your mortgage, student loans, vehicle loans, credit card debt, and other debts. This would ease the considerable financial burden placed on your surviving family members. You should also add to that amount any anticipated funeral, medical, and probate expenses. According to the National Funeral Directors Association, the median out-of-pocket cost for a funeral and burial in 2019 was $7,640. According to the National Bureau of Economic Research, the average out-of-pocket medical cost related to end of life was $11,618.[1]

One way to determine how much life insurance you need is the "financial needs" approach. As the name implies, you simply add up all of your family's potential financial needs and subtract current assets to determine your total life insurance requirement. Things to consider include final expenses and debts, mortgage payoff, education costs, emergency expenses, and future income needs.

All of these needs are relatively easy to determine except for the last item—future income. You will need to determine how much income your

---

[1] Gabrielle Olya, "Can you afford to die in your state?" Yahoo! Finance, March 2, 2021, https://finance.yahoo.com/news/afford-die-state-200000934.html.

Life Insurance Protection

family will need going forward. That amount will change over time as your family experiences different phases. During the first few years, total household income should remain the same as it was before; this is often called the "readjustment phase." Next, you will need to consider how much income your spouse will need until the kids are grown, after the kids are grown, and finally in retirement. These needs can sometimes be offset by social security income; children of a deceased parent may be entitled to social security benefits. You will also need to account for inflation. A financial planner can help you make these calculations.

Another method to calculate your life insurance need, the so-called Human Life Value approach, is used to determine the present value of all your future earnings from your career. First, you determine the "family's share" of your earnings. To do this, subtract taxes and personal consumption from your annual earnings. For example, if your annual earnings are $100,000 and you pay 25 percent in taxes, your net after-tax amount would be $75,000. Then, suppose you spend about $20,000 on expenses related only to you (personal consumption). That leaves you with $55,000 as your "family's share." You also need to think about inflation and how your income might rise over time with pay increases.

You would then calculate the present value of this stream of income accounting for inflation, growth rate, and increases in income over time. This is a complicated calculation which may require you to get some outside help. Thankfully, there is an easy way around doing heavy math or using a special calculator. You can simply assume that your income will keep pace with inflation, which will eliminate the need to adjust for inflation and pay raises. This is going to underestimate your insurance requirement, however, because your income will likely outpace inflation over time.

To make up for this underestimation, assume 0 percent growth on your assets (the most conservative assumption). That makes the calculation simpler as you can simply multiply your family's share of income by the number of years it will be needed. For example, if your family's share of income is $55,000 and they will need that income for 20 years, this method would imply that you should have $1.1 million in life insurance.

Other methods may be used to determine how much life insurance you should have; a qualified financial planner can help you do the math and decide how much to purchase. Be sure to consult a fee-only financial planner, not a commission-based life insurance salesperson. A fee-only planner will be able to make an unbiased recommendation.

WHAT TYPE OF LIFE INSURANCE SHOULD I PURCHASE?

Many different kinds of life insurance policies are available, but essentially, they fall into two categories: term policies and cash-value policies. Term life insurance is pure insurance. You pay only the cost of the insurance itself for a predetermined period of time—hence the name. Term policies can be purchased for various periods of time, typically ranging from 10 to 30 years. Usually, the most cost-effective and sensible type of term policy is a level term policy, which is a policy whose premium stays the same (or level) over time. Annual renewable term is a type of term policy that renews each year, which means that the premiums go up each year. Remember: your age is a big determining factor for the cost of your insurance—the older you are, the more expensive it is. I have seen clients hang on to annual renewable term policies until the premiums become unbearable.

Level term life insurance is most often the best insurance option. Life insurance meets a specific need: a liquidity gap due to a lack of funds. This is usually a temporary need. As you age and your portfolio grows, most people eventually reach a point in life where they do not need life insurance at all, for your assets will be plentiful enough to meet the financial needs of your surviving spouse or family. Term life insurance provides protection only during the predetermined term of the policy. Once it expires, you no longer have coverage, but ideally you are in a place where you no longer need life insurance.

The other kind of life insurance is cash-value life insurance, variously also known as whole life insurance, universal life insurance, or permanent life insurance. Essentially, this type of insurance is a term life insurance policy with a savings account attached. Cash-value policies are more expensive because you pay more than the cost of insurance. The additional amount that you pay accumulates in the policy with interest to offset the prohibitive cost of insurance when you are older. For example, a $100,000 whole life insurance policy will start out with a cash value of $0, but the cash value inside the account will grow over time until eventually the policy matures. At maturity, ideally you have accumulated a cash value of $100,000, which is now accessible to you. Usually, these policies are guaranteed for life, or at least until the beneficiary reaches a very old age like 100 years.

Cash-value life insurance policies are often touted for their ability to grow money on a tax-deferred basis and to provide access to those funds through policy loans in a tax-favored way. Through the policy loan feature, you can withdraw funds without needing to pay tax on those funds right away.

On the negative side, these types of policies incur lots of expenses and offer poor investment options that lead to low growth. Premiums are subject to all kinds of costs, including mortality, premium, and administrative charges. If you withdraw money too soon, you may be subject to surrender charges. And in today's low interest rate environment, the cash values do not earn very much interest. Some policies, such as equity indexed or variable policies, seem to offer the ability to invest cash values in the stock market with no downside risk. But do not be fooled: your money is never invested in the stock market. Instead, it is credited with interest using a complicated formula that is tied to stock market performance. This formula often reduces what you can earn through caps or participation rates and other provisions. Moreover, added investment fees reduce what you are able to earn. Even though they may guarantee no downside risk, after factoring in fees you may actually lose money!

In most cases, it is far more advantageous to buy a less expensive term policy and invest the difference in premium in your retirement accounts or a brokerage account. Your expenses over time will be much lower, and your accumulated wealth will likely be much greater. However, in some specialized cases, a cash-value policy may make sense, such as for unique estate planning or tax planning purposes.

POLICY RIDERS

Life insurance policies often offer riders, that is, optional features that can be added for an extra cost. An important one is the waiver of premium rider. If you become disabled, your income may be reduced significantly. Having the waiver of premium rider means you can stop making premium payments without your policy lapsing; it will stay in force.

Another rider worth considering is the accelerated death benefit rider, which allows you to access some or all of your death benefit early. If you are diagnosed with a terminal illness, you may be facing some hefty medical bills and your family may need financial support. By accessing the death benefit early, you can alleviate some of that financial strain.

A third rider, the accidental death benefit rider, will pay out more, sometimes double, if you die from an accident. You may consider this option if you drive a lot. It is usually quite inexpensive because the odds that it will be paid out are very low. However, if your family truly needs more life insurance, you should just buy more insurance. This rider is more akin to gambling than to proper planning.

People often opt for cash-value life insurance instead of term because they are concerned that if they buy a term policy and it expires having never been used, they will have wasted their money. As I explained earlier, the only difference between a term policy and a cash-value policy is that the cash-value policy has a savings account attached to it. Either way, you will be putting money toward the cost of insurance every year. If you are truly concerned about wasting money, you might consider the return of premium rider, which will return your premiums to you at the end of the term policy if the death benefit has not been triggered. However, you do not get these premiums back with interest, and this rider is quite expensive. In my opinion, you would be better off skipping the return of premium rider and investing the difference.

Finally, another rider you can add to a term policy is spouse and child insurance. This rider adds a smaller amount of insurance for the death of a child or spouse. The cost of this rider is usually minimal, and it can help ease the financial burden of potential funeral and burial expenses. This option makes sense if you are young and have young children and limited financial resources.

LIFE INSURANCE FOR THE LAW FIRM

As noted earlier, if you are a partner in a firm or the owner of your own firm, your death may have a significant negative impact on the firm's revenue or ability to operate. In addition, what will become of your ownership share and your clients? Your firm has value, as does your share of the partnership. Your family should receive consideration for that value if you should die. Small law firms should have a buy–sell agreement in place between owners that permits the remaining owners to buy out an owner who passes away.

Having the buy–sell agreement is not enough, however. A funding mechanism is also needed. Otherwise, where will the funds come from for the surviving partners to buy out the deceased partner? In the absence of significant cash reserves, this could be problematic. The best solution, of course, is life insurance. To fund a buy–sell agreement between partners, each partner takes out a life insurance policy on the other. Then, if one partner dies, funds are instantly available to buy out the deceased partner and provide liquidity to the surviving spouse and family.

Premature death risk is just one of the major financial risks you face. Another one that is critical for law firm owners is disability risk, which we will cover next.

CHAPTER 22

Disability Risk

According to a study by the Social Security Administration, the probability of becoming disabled between age 20 and normal retirement age for those born in 2000 is about 25 percent.[1] Disability is defined as being unable to engage in substantial gainful employment for at least 12 months. Your odds of becoming disabled are greater than your odds of death. Disability can be a serious risk to you and your family's financial health. Loss of income due to a disability can be a major detriment to reaching your financial goals and may put your family's financial stability in jeopardy. This risk is especially critical if you are a solo attorney or the primary breadwinner for your family. Additionally, if you are part of a small firm, your disability could put the entire firm in jeopardy, much like premature death risk. You should take steps to make sure you are protected against loss of income due to disability.

DETERMINING YOUR DISABILITY INCOME NEEDS

The first step in assessing your disability risk is to determine your income needs if you should become disabled. Many people estimate their disability income needs at 60 to 80 percent of current income. If you want to be more thorough, start by adding up your monthly nondiscretionary expenses, defined as those expenses necessary to daily living. These include mortgage

---

[1] Johanna Maleh and Tiffany Bosley, "*Disability and Death Probability Tables for Insured Workers Born in 2000,*" Social Security Administration, June 2000, https://www.ssa.gov/oact/NOTES/ran6/an2020-6.pdf.

or rent payments, food, clothing, utilities, medical/dental expenses, personal care expenses, automobile payments and expenses, tuition, and insurance premiums. Some of these expenses may be higher or lower if you become disabled. Then, subtract any income provided by your spouse. Finally, subtract any other sources of income that you may receive or become entitled to such as group disability benefits, mortgage insurance, creditor insurance, disability pension benefits, and investment income. The last-named source is important, for significant investment assets can provide income. But you will want to make sure that using your investments as a source of income rather than allowing them to grow unhindered does not jeopardize your future financial and retirement goals.

You will notice that I have not included social security income in this calculation. This is because while you may be eligible for disability benefits through social security, it is much more difficult to qualify for them. The Social Security Administration has a much more restrictive definition of disability than most disability insurance policies. Thus, you may experience a disability that causes loss of income and still not qualify for disability benefits through social security. Furthermore, social security requires you to wait five months before receiving benefits, to prove that you cannot obtain gainful employment, and to verify that your disability will last 12 months or longer or result in death. If your disability only lasts six months, you may lose a significant amount of income and never receive any benefit from social security.

Disability risk planning integrates closely with retirement planning. A young attorney with few assets may have a much higher need for disability insurance than an older attorney with more significant savings and assets. Ideally, you will reach a point in life where you have accumulated enough assets that you will no longer need disability insurance coverage. Also, your emergency fund may be sufficient to get you through a short-term disability, which is much more common than a long-term disability.

DISABILITY INSURANCE

To meet your disability income need gap, you may consider disability insurance. This type of insurance will replace your income during a period of time if you become disabled. The least expensive type of disability insurance is the insurance you can obtain through your employer if you work at a large firm. If you do not work for a large firm, you may need to purchase an

Disability Risk

individual disability policy. However, employer-sponsored plans terminate if you leave the firm. Therefore, it may be smart to have an individual policy even if employer-sponsored coverage is available.

When obtaining disability insurance coverage, one of the first and most important things to consider is the definition of disability. There are two definitions actually: "any occupation" and "own occupation." Under an any occupation policy, you will qualify for benefits if your disability prevents you from performing the duties of any occupation. Thankfully, the courts have interpreted this to mean any occupation to which you are suited by education, experience, and training. This is a very restrictive definition and makes it much harder to qualify for benefits.

On the other hand, if you have an occupation policy, benefits will kick in if you experience a disability that prevents you from performing the duties of your particular occupation. This policy is much less restrictive and easier to qualify for benefits.

The cost of a disability policy will depend on various factors such as your occupation, health, and other risk factors. Two other factors that have a major impact on price are the elimination period and the benefit period; these are considered the two main features of disability policies. The elimination period is the period of time you must wait between when you become disabled and when benefits begin. Because most disabilities are short term and allow a person to return to work, a longer elimination period will result in a less expensive policy. However, you should make sure you have sufficient emergency reserves to meet your income needs during the elimination period. The benefit period is the length of time that the policy will pay out. Policies can be purchased with benefit periods that last a few years or that last until retirement age. Longer benefit periods will of course be more expensive.

You may also consider some riders, such as waiver of premium and cost-of-living adjustment. Through the waiver of premium, you will not have to pay the premiums on your policy if you should become disabled. This makes a lot of sense, for why would you want to continue making premium payments if you become disabled and are receiving payments from the policy? The cost-of-living adjustment rider will increase benefits over time with inflation. These increases are normally tied to an index like the consumer price index. This is a smart option if you are purchasing long-term disability insurance, as your expenses may increase significantly over time. However, both riders will increase the cost of your policy.

INTEGRATION WITH SOCIAL SECURITY

Even though it is difficult to qualify for social security disability benefits, you may be entitled to apply. If you do indeed qualify, your need for disability insurance income will be significantly reduced. One way to reduce the cost of disability insurance is to purchase a policy that integrates with social security. Such policies will reduce your benefits by the amount you receive from social security. Such a policy is often much less expensive because it dramatically reduces the risk to the insurer.

TAXATION OF BENEFITS

Because individual disability insurance premiums are not tax deductible and are paid with after-tax dollars, benefits received from these policies are not taxable. This is an important consideration when you are determining how much of a benefit you need to apply for in order to have adequate coverage. However, if you purchase disability insurance through your employer, your premiums may be paid on a pretax basis. If this is the case, your benefits, should you qualify, will be fully taxable.

DISABILITY RISK AND YOUR FIRM

In addition to the effect on your family, you need to consider the risk a disability poses to your law firm or practice. If you are part of a small firm, how will the disability of one of your partners affect the firm's ability to generate business or finish the existing caseload? If your disability is long term or permanent, will the partners be able to buy you out? If you are a solo attorney and you experience a long-term or permanent disability, who will buy your practice and where will the funding come from?

Solo attorneys and small-firm partners should consider a few things. First, partners should consider disability income insurance that would permit the firm to receive income and protect the firm's cash flow should one of the partners become disabled. Second, small firms might want to have business or professional overhead expense insurance. This type of insurance can pay the day-to-day costs of running the business if one of the partners or you as the sole owner become disabled. While an individual disability income policy may replace your income, who will pay the business expenses? Things like rent, insurance, and utilities will still need to be paid while you are out of work.

Finally, solo attorneys and small firms should consider a disability buy–sell agreement and disability buy-out insurance to fund the agreement. Like a buy–sell agreement in the case of death as we discussed earlier, a disability buy–sell agreement will allow your other partners or another attorney/law firm to buy out your practice if you should become long-term or permanently disabled. The best practice is to set up one singular buy–sell agreement that covers both premature death and disability. The disability buy-out insurance will provide the liquidity that the other partners or other attorney will need to purchase your practice. You and your family can then use these funds to support your ongoing financial needs.

However, all of these benefits come at a cost. If you insured against every risk under the sun, you might not have any money left to save and invest! Insurance against major risks is prudent, but your decision on whether to insure and how much to insure comes down to a question of personal risk tolerance. How much risk are you willing to accept? If you should be exposed to one of these risks, how much are you willing to adapt and change your lifestyle? You and your family will need to carefully answer these questions together.

To wrap up this section on risk management planning, in the next chapter I will discuss liability risk and how to protect yourself and your firm.

CHAPTER 23
Liability Risk

In addition to premature death or disability, another type of risk that can derail your financial plan is liability risk. As you probably know as an attorney, if you are the cause of injury to another person due to negligence, you can be held monetarily liable and be required to compensate the person for injuries they sustain. In addition, you may in some cases be required to pay punitive damages. If you do not have the funds to pay damages, your assets or future earnings may be seized involuntarily. Obviously, this scenario presents a large risk to your financial future and one that you should be careful to manage appropriately. Liability risk is greatest in three areas: your home, your automobile, and your business or law practice.

PERSONAL PROPERTY AND LIABILITY

Let's imagine that you have some friends over to your house for an outside barbeque. One of your friends trips on the steps that go from your deck to your yard. Your friend falls and breaks her arm and must be rushed to the emergency room. Your friend is a professional gymnast, and now her entire career has been put in jeopardy. It just so happens that this particular step was loose, and you knew that it needed repair. In this simple example, you could be found negligent and held liable. If that happens, you may be required to pay significant damages. And if you do not have the money to pay, you could lose your house.

Your homeowners insurance is the first line of defense against such liability claims. A homeowners policy has six major areas of coverage: the dwelling itself, other structures on your property, personal property in your home, loss of use due to catastrophe, liability, and medical payments to others. The last two would come in handy in our example.

Often people skimp on the liability section because they want to save money. Don't. The liability coverage of your homeowners policy protects you against liability for bodily injury or property damage on or off your premises due to negligence. You read that correctly—on or off. Most policies will cover you for certain negligent acts that may occur off premises. Examples include your dog biting someone at the park or your son hitting a baseball through the neighbor's window.

What does coverage give you? Typically, the insurer will pay all defense and settlement costs associated with a claim. However, you will only be covered for acts of negligence. Intentional acts of harm are not covered, including shooting an intruder. Also, your homeowners policy may deny your claim if it relates to running a business out of your house unless you have coverage specifically for your business.

How much liability coverage should you have? Most policies come with a minimum coverage of $100,000. However, I usually recommend having at least as much liability coverage as the value of your assets—house, car, financial assets, and other assets. Homeowners' policies usually max out liability coverage at $500,000 or in some cases $1,000,000. If you need more, you can purchase an umbrella liability policy.

AUTOMOBILE INSURANCE

The second area where you are most exposed to risk is in the operation of a motor vehicle. There is a reason that the majority of personal injury suits are vehicle related. The primary function of automobile insurance is to protect you against liability when you are at fault and legally responsible. If you cause an accident, you could be held liable for costs related to bodily injury, loss of income, emergency medical aid, and property damage. The insurance company agrees to pay damages you are responsible for up to the policy limits. Additionally, the insurance company will defend you if you are sued and cover defense costs. Usually, these are covered separately and will not reduce your policy limits.

What are policy limits? These are the maximum amounts that the insurance company will pay out—a certain amount per person and per accident for bodily injury and property damage. You should think carefully about how much liability insurance you maintain. Being found at-fault in an automobile accident exposes you to financial risk. The other party can go after your financial assets for compensation. Let's say you have minimum coverage, and your liability limits are only 25/50–$25,000 per person and $50,000 per accident. If you cause an accident and the other party has medical bills of $100,000, your insurance policy will only pay out $50,000. The other party could potentially come after your personal assets for the remaining $50,000. The more money you have, the more risk you are exposed to in an accident.

UMBRELLA INSURANCE

Your liability coverage should match your total assets in most cases, unless you have a high risk tolerance and are comfortable with some of your assets being at risk. However, if you have a lot of assets, you may not be able to obtain enough liability insurance through your homeowners or automobile policy.

This is where an umbrella liability policy is helpful. An umbrella policy provides additional liability coverage above and beyond what your homeowners and automobile policies cover. For those with significant assets, an umbrella policy is a prudent idea. Obtaining additional liability through an umbrella policy can be more cost effective than maxing out the liability coverage available through your homeowners or automobile policies. However, most umbrella policies will require you to maintain a certain level of coverage on your underlying homeowners or automobile policies.

BUSINESS LIABILITY RISK

Now that we have covered the personal side of risk, if you own a law firm, you may also be exposed to business liability risk. First, in the general operation of your day-to-day business, there is the potential for liability. For example, if a client slips and falls on ice walking into your office, you could potentially be liable if found negligent.

Several types of business liability insurance are available that can protect you from liability in operating your business. A business owners policy is designed for small to midsized businesses and would fit the needs of small law firms well. This type of policy usually covers buildings, property, and liability from bodily injury or property damage. There are business auto policies that will cover the use of vehicles by the business. If you use your personal vehicle in the operation of your business, you need to make sure that your personal auto insurance covers you while performing business duties. Otherwise, if you are in an accident, your claim could be denied.

Additionally, there are business umbrella policies which, like personal umbrella policies, will cover additional liability above and beyond the coverage of your firms' basic liability policy.

PROFESSIONAL LIABILITY

In addition to the general operation of your business, you can be exposed to liability in your professional duties. If a client is unhappy with your work and can prove negligence on your part, they can come after you for damages. There have been some high-profile attorney malpractice cases over the years. In 2017, for example, celebrated civil rights attorney Gloria Allred was sued for $1 million by a former client claiming she had negotiated a secret TV deal with the company that he was suing while she was representing him. This case is still being litigated as of the time of this writing.

Professional liability insurance is not required in most states. Many attorneys do not carry insurance, but you should strongly consider obtaining liability insurance. All it takes is one disgruntled client to make your professional life exceedingly difficult and cost you a lot of money.

Certain areas of law, such as securities, personal injury, intellectual property, and trusts and estates, are more exposed to malpractice liability than others. The amount of malpractice insurance you should carry will vary depending on your area of practice and the volume of your practice. Most attorneys at larger firms are covered by their firm's own liability insurance. However, if you are a solo attorney or part of a small group, you may need to purchase your own policy.

When purchasing a policy, be sure to read the details very carefully. Be aware of all the provisions and requirements of your policy, including notice provisions that explain when and how you must inform the insurance company of a potential claim. "Claims made" policies only cover incidents that occur and are reported while the policy is in force. By contrast, "occurrence" policies provide lifetime coverage for incidents that occur during a policy regardless of when the incident is reported.

The American Bar Association is a great resource for additional information on professional liability. You can visit their website at: https://www.americanbar.org/groups/lawyers_professional_liability.

Liability for damages you cause to others in your personal life or business can be very costly and put your financial plan at risk. Liability insurance should be used to protect yourself, your family, your business, and your future.

PART V

Running Your Own Practice

Starting and running your own law practice is a true act of courage. But the reward can be great. Although the practice of law has changed as firms have gotten larger, more corporate, and more international, most attorneys still practice either as solo practitioners or as partners in small law firms. Running your own practice has the appeal of greater flexibility, more control, and the chance to build more wealth. In today's entrepreneur-driven economy, that appeal may be greater than ever. In the subsequent chapters, we will explore different ways to structure your business, steps to improve your bottom line, planning for business continuity, and steps to ensure your firm can survive difficult times.

CHAPTER 24

Choosing a Business Structure

When starting your business, you may be wondering, should I form an LLC or a corporation or should I just operate as a sole proprietor? You can choose from several different legal entities, and the requirements for law firms will vary from state to state. What entity you decide to organize as will depend on a number of factors, such as the size of your practice, the type of practice you have, and taxes, to name a few.

SOLE PROPRIETORSHIP

A sole proprietorship is the simplest form of business structure. This is a business that is owned and controlled by one person who alone is responsible for all debts and claims against the business. I started my business as a sole proprietorship because it was the simplest thing to do, and I was not terribly concerned about taxes at the time. I expected losses in the first few years. The IRS does not treat sole proprietorships as separate entities. Thus, you (the owner) report all income and losses on schedule C of your 1040. Although it is a smart idea to maintain separate books for business and personal items, the business does not file a separate tax return.

The greatest advantage of the sole proprietorship is its simplicity and flexibility. If you want to discontinue your business, you can simply shut it down. You have ultimate control. However, it has a few major disadvantages. First, you have unlimited personal liability for any debts or claims against the business. Second, you may end up paying more in taxes than other forms of business. This is because of the self-employment tax, which is just a fancy name for the Medicare and social security taxes paid by self-employed people.

Typically, if you work for a company, the company pays half and you pay the other half of your social security and Medicare taxes. But as a self-employed person, you pay both halves. See the section on tax minimization for more information on this topic.

PARTNERSHIP

A partnership is like a sole proprietorship with more than one owner. It is an association of two or more individuals who operate as co-owners. Typically, partners will draft a partnership agreement that outlines the partners' ownership, roles, and responsibilities. There are two types of partnerships: general partnerships and limited partnerships. General partnerships have only general partners: each partner is a full owner of the business and can act on behalf of the business.

Limited partnerships have at least one general partner and one limited partner. The limited partner, unlike a general partner, does not participate in the management of the partnership and enjoys limited liability. They are only liable for the business's debts to the extent of the capital they have contributed. General partners have unlimited liability and can be personally liable for the debts or acts of the business and obligations made by the other general partners.

For taxes, like sole proprietorships, partnerships are flowthrough entities. The net income or losses from the business flow through to the partners' personal tax returns. Each partner receives a K-1 describing their share of income or losses. Income received by general partners is considered self-employment income and is subject to self-employment taxes. However, limited partners' income is considered passive income and is not subject to the self-employment tax.

LIMITED LIABILITY PARTNERSHIP

One of the biggest disadvantages of sole proprietorships and partnerships is the fact that owners are exposed to unlimited liability for debts and claims against the business. Other forms of business provide some protection against owner liability. A limited liability partnership is similar to a general partnership, but it provides liability protection to the partners. This business form is designed for professional service businesses and can only be used by certain professionals such as attorneys or accountants. The limited liability partnership (LLP) is a popular business structure for law firms and protects attorneys in a firm from being held liable for the acts of other partners in the firm. Partners are personally liable for the own acts, but personal assets outside the partnership entity are protected from claims arising from the acts of other partners.

Management of an LLP is similar to a general partnership, and LLPs are treated similarly for tax purposes. The LLP is a conduit or flowthrough entity where the net income or losses from the business flow through to the partners' personal tax returns. Each partner receives a K-1 to report their share of the income or loss for the year.

C-CORPORATION

Whereas the business structures we looked at earlier are flowthrough entities, a corporation is a separate entity. There are two types of corporations. The first one, which most people are familiar with, is the C-corporation. These corporations are formed under state law and are treated separately from the owners (often called shareholders). Because the corporation is a separate entity, it offers limited liability to owners (shareholders). Shareholders can only lose the amount of money they have invested and do not put their personal assets at risk. Also, as a separate entity, the corporation is taxed separately and pays corporate income taxes.

Shareholders can receive distributions from the corporation in the form of dividends. Dividends are then taxable to the shareholder. The major disadvantage of the C-corporation is that dividends face double taxation. The net income of the corporation is subject to corporate income taxes, and dividends paid to shareholders are not tax deductible to the corporation but are taxable to the shareholder. However, dividends usually receive favorable tax treatment under long-term capital gains tax rates and are not subject to social security or Medicare taxes.

For a law firm forming as a C-corporation, the law firm partners would be the shareholders. Each partner would receive a salary, which would be subject to social security and Medicare taxes shared by the company and the employee. These salaries would reduce the corporate income tax to the business because wages are deductible. Then, additional profits could be distributed as dividends and taxed at potentially more favorable rates. Corporations that operate exclusively in the field of law and where stock is almost exclusively owned by employees are classified as "personal service corporations."

Under pre-2017 tax law, the corporate income tax applied to personal service corporations was a flat 35 percent. All other corporations paid the tax based on graduated rates, with lower rates imposed on those in lower income brackets. This law was originally designed to encourage owners of personal service corporations to take more salary rather than rely on dividends by reducing some of the potential tax benefits of the C-corporation form. The Tax Cuts and Jobs Act of 2017 established a flat rate of 21 percent for all corporations, potentially making this form of business more attractive.

S-CORPORATION

The other type of corporation is the S-corporation, which is a special kind of corporation formed like a regular corporation under state law as a separate entity but treated like a partnership for tax purposes. Like a C-corporation, the S-corporation offers limited liability to shareholders (owners) who only risk the amount of capital they have invested in the corporation. Unlike a C-corporation, all corporation income and losses pass through to the owners and are reported on their personal tax returns. The S-corporation will file a separate tax return for informational purposes only. Owners receive a K-1, just like a partnership does. However, the K-1 income is not subject to self-employment income.

This is a big advantage because it offers you the ability to reduce the amount you pay on self-employment tax by paying yourself through distributions (not subject to self-employment tax) instead of regular wages (subject to self-employment tax). See chapter 23 for more details.

LIMITED LIABILITY COMPANY

That brings us finally to the LLC, or limited liability company. The LLC is a relatively new form of business that is created under state law by filing articles of organization with the secretary of state. Owners are called members. As the name implies, the LLC offers limited personal liability to members like a corporation.

Unlike a corporation, though, an LLC is treated as a flowthrough entity like a partnership or an S-corporation. Sole-member LLCs are taxed as sole proprietorships, and multiple-member LLCs are generally taxed as partnerships. However, an LLC can elect to be taxed as an S-corporation. This is a popular strategy for solo attorneys setting up a business because they benefit from the simplicity of the LLC and the potential tax savings of the S-corporation.

You can structure your business in a variety of ways, each of which has implications requiring careful consideration. One of the main reasons why attorneys start their own firms is to maximize profitability. In the next chapter, I will discuss ways that solo attorneys and small firms can monitor and improve profitability.

CHAPTER 25

Improving Your Bottom Line

Let's face it. If you have launched your own practice or are considering launching your own practice, one of the biggest motivating factors is the opportunity to earn more money. Working for yourself, you can control your overhead and keep more of the fees you bill for your services. While the first few years could be quite lean, going solo can certainly be lucrative. According to the Martindale Avvo's 2020 Attorney Compensation Report, the average solo or small-firm attorney earned an annual full-time compensation of $192,000 in 2019.

RUN IT LIKE A BUSINESS

Launching and running your practice is a business venture. While some attorneys may be naturally gifted in business operations, for others running a business requires a completely different skillset. Some attorneys, for the sake of professionalism, may protest the idea of running a practice like a business. After all, lawyers are supposed to be professionals, not business moguls, right? I would argue that lawyers can do both. In fact, plenty of other professions behave professionally, while running their businesses to maximize profitability.

As a business, you need to pay close attention to your numbers and plan strategically for the growth and development of your firm. I would recommend using budgeting or business accounting software to monitor your financials. Lots of free programs are available, such as waveapps.com, or there are others you can pay for like QuickBooks.

You should create a business plan that outlines your goals for the upcoming quarter, the current year, and the next five years. My business plan is a one-page paper with several columns. The quarterly column shows my projections and goals for the current quarter in terms of revenue, expenses, and net profit, along with the specific actions and marketing activities I need to engage in this quarter. There are similar columns for the current year, the next 3 to 5 years, and the next 5 to 10 years or more. I review and update my business plan on a quarterly basis.

MARKETING

One of the biggest keys to success is marketing. You cannot post your website, sit back, and expect the phone to ring. You have to get your message out there. Whether you do that through networking in the local community, billboards, or seminars, the key to successful marketing is activity and consistency. As my dad always says, "Activity, activity, activity!" Develop a marketing strategy that centers around reaching your target client and execute that strategy with diligence and consistency. You will not see results right away. Remember that marketing is like farming: you plant seeds, they grow, and down the road you collect the harvest.

The goal of your marketing is simple: get prospective clients to meet with you or your staff. You should set a goal for the number of new consultations you want to have per week or per month and monitor how you are doing. Meeting with new prospective clients is the first step to signing a new client. If you are not having new consultations with prospective clients, you are not going to have new clients. It is that simple.

As your case load ebbs and flows, you may be tempted to pull back on your marketing activities when business is going well. You must avoid this pitfall. This will inevitably result in a constant boom-and-bust cycle for your business. If you neglect marketing for new clients when your case load is high, you will eventually find yourself in a position where business is slow and you are scrambling to find new clients. Consistency is key. You may want to outsource some of your marketing activities to a marketing consultant or agency that specializes in working with attorneys or your particular niche. This will help with consistency. For example, I outsourced the publication of my monthly blog and social media management so that I could focus on meeting with new prospective clients and serving existing clients and so that my marketing efforts would not fall by the wayside.

As your business grows, you will likely obtain more and more clients through word-of-mouth referrals. The best source of new business is your existing client base. Make sure you are being proactive about asking clients for referrals. Let them know that you are accepting new clients. And make sure you are staying top of mind with current and former clients through a regular, educational email campaign.

IMPROVING PROFITABILITY THROUGH EFFICIENCY

As a business owner, your goal is to maximize profitability. To do so, you need to be constantly evaluating your business and looking for ways to improve profitability. One of the best ways to improve profitability is to improve your efficiency. What tasks can you make more efficient and less time consuming?

Start with your own efficiency. Your time is extremely valuable and perhaps your most valuable asset in your law firm. You need to find ways you can maximize the value of your time. What is your time worth? What is your billable rate for your time? If your hourly rate is $250 an hour, why would you spend time working on $15 an hour work? You need to make the most valuable and most profitable activities of your practice your focus. Delegate the less valuable tasks to office staff or assistants. Outsource low-value work to consultants or virtual assistants who can free up your time.

Another way to improve efficiency is to make sure you have written processes, procedures, and templates for handling cases or work items. You should not reinvent the wheel each time you deal with a similar issue. Having checklists for tasks or clients will enable you and your office to execute your workflow quickly, avoid wasting time, and make sure nothing falls between the cracks. You should consider software that can help you manage clients, cases, and billing. Software can help you automate workflows, delegate tasks, and make sure things get done in a timely fashion. I remember when I finally gave up my excel spreadsheets for a client relationship management software. I improved my efficiency exponentially. Now, I do not know what I would do without it!

KEY PERFORMANCE INDICATORS

Key Performance Indicators (KPIs) are metrics used in different industries to monitor and improve efficiency. KPIs are very popular in manufacturing, for instance, to measure the efficiency of a process and minimize cost. These metrics can also be used to identify weak points or to diagnose problems. The idea is simple and can apply to all types of business, including law firms. Here are some sample KPIs that you may want to use for your law firm:

- **Income and Expenses per Month** – Financial KPIs tell you how you are doing financially. One of the most basic KPIs for law firms is to simply keep track of income and expenses each month and make sure they are hitting your targets. If you want to hit your profit goals for the year, you need to constantly be aware of your income and expenses throughout the year. It is easy as a business owner to spend too much on your business. We justify this to ourselves as "investment" in the business. I am guilty of this very rationalization! But you do not want to be wasteful with your spending. Periodically, you should look for ways you can cut costs. Are you paying for products and services that you are no longer using? Do other vendors offer better rates? Can you pay up front and save money?
- **Effective Billing Rate** – This is another financial KPI that you can use to measure profitability. To determine your effective billing rate, keep track of all the time spent on a client or case, including flat fee or contingency cases. Then, divide the actual bill by the number of hours to determine your effective billing rate in dollars per hour. You can use this KPI to determine if you are spending too much time on a particular item and ensure that you are staying profitable. Your effective billing rate should ideally rise over time. Periodically, you may want to evaluate your fee structure and increase your rates. After all, as time passes, you gain valuable experience, your time becomes worth more, and thanks to inflation the dollar becomes worth less.
- **Average Billing per Client or Case** – In addition to keeping track of your effective billing rate, you should note the average bill per case. To improve profitability, you need this number to increase. As your reputation and practice grow, your average billing should grow as well.
- **Accounts Receivable and Age of Accounts Receivable** – One more financial KPI is to keep track of outstanding bills that are owed to you and the age of those bills. One of the most basic ways to improve your

profitability is to collect on outstanding bills. As accounts receivable age, they become less and less likely to be collected. You should strive to keep the age of your accounts receivable as young as possible. To increase the likelihood of getting paid, make it easy for clients to pay you by accepting many forms of payment and bill them right away. Do not delay: the longer you wait, the more difficult it becomes to collect. Finally, consider hiring a collections agency to go after those old accounts receivable. It may not seem like the "nice" thing to do, but you are running a business and you need to get paid for your work.

Number of New Consultations per Month – Now come the marketing KPIs. Because new consultations lead to new clients and new clients lead to revenue, you should keep track of the number of new consultations you are having per month. If this number is slipping, you know that your revenue may dip as well, and you might want to ramp up some marketing efforts. This is a leading indicator that will tell you early if you are on track to meeting your goals.

Conversion Rate – How many of those new consultations turn into new cases or clients? This is called your conversion rate: number of new cases divided by number of new consults. In addition to tracking new consultations, you need to also track the number of new clients or cases. If none of your consultations result in new cases or clients, you are in trouble! Monitor your conversion rate and make it your goal to improve this conversion rate over time. That will improve your profitability.

Marketing Budget per New Client – To evaluate the effectiveness of your marketing budget, you should track the ratio of marketing dollars to new clients. Take your total marketing budget and divide it by the number of new clients you obtained during a given period. You can improve your profitability by improving the effectiveness of your marketing budget. If this ratio goes up, you are spending too much on marketing and something is not working. If this ratio goes down, you will know that whatever changes you have made are working and are effective.

Client Satisfaction – One final KPI that is less numeric and more subjective is client satisfaction. You should be aware of how satisfied your clients are and how likely they are to recommend you to others. Develop a client survey that you can send out at some point during or after the client engagement to measure their satisfaction and find ways you can improve your service.

This is not a book on marketing or on running a law practice, but these ideas will get you started on the pathway to improving your profitability. It will let you maximize your earnings as well as the potential future value of your practice, which may be a key factor in your retirement plan.

But even the best business plan is subject to the ups and downs of the economy and other risk factors. In the next chapter, I will discuss how you can ensure the survival of your business through proper business continuity planning.

CHAPTER 26

Business Continuity Planning

If you were hit by the proverbial bus, who would keep your business running? Or if you suddenly lost one of your firm's partners, what would happen? A business continuity plan ensures that the operation of your business will continue despite interruptions caused by death, disability, or disaster. Business continuity planning is an important part of running any business. Unfortunately, many law firm owners neglect this important aspect of business planning.

WHY YOU NEED A CONTINUITY PLAN

There are several reasons why you should have a business continuity plan. Most obviously, a business continuity plan is important to your family's financial well-being, and it is an integral part of a complete financial plan. If your income suddenly stops because you die or become disabled, how will your spouse or children continue paying the bills? A business continuity plan can ensure that your family continues to receive income to meet financial obligations and provide liquidity to your estate if needed.

Second, if you have employees or partners in your firm, a business continuity plan ensures that the firm will continue to operate. If you care about the people you work with, you should have a continuity plan. Furthermore, a continuity plan protects you if one of your partners dies or becomes disabled. It can also help you avoid nasty disputes, or worse, the dissolution of your firm.

Finally, having a continuity plan is important for your clients. If you are an estate planning attorney, you may have a vault of wills and estate documents that you have prepared for clients. What will become of those documents if you die unexpectedly? You need to have a plan in place. In this way, you will serve as a true fiduciary to your clients—putting their best interests first.

THE BUY–SELL AGREEMENT

A buy–sell agreement is a key piece of the business continuity plan. It is a binding agreement between co-owners who agree to buy each other's ownership stake in the event the other owner dies or becomes permanently disabled. In the case of solo attorneys, you could set up a buy–sell agreement with a colleague who has a similar practice in your area.

In the case of firms with more than two partners, a special type of buy–sell agreement called a "cross-purchase" agreement is appropriate. This is an agreement for the remaining partners to buy out a partner who has died or who has become permanently disabled. Each partner is responsible for funding a portion of the buy-out proportionate with their equity stake. If you have three partners each of whom has equal ownership and one passes away, the remaining two partners will each buy half of the deceased partner's ownership stake.

The more partners your firm has, the more complex and difficult a cross-purchase agreement becomes. Also, if there is a wide range in the ages of the firm's partners and you fund the agreement using life insurance, the younger partners will end up paying more.

One solution to the complexities of a larger firm is an entity purchase agreement. Under this type of agreement, the law firm itself will buy out the deceased or disabled partners' stake, thereby avoiding some of the complexities of the cross-purchase agreement. However, you may lose some tax advantages. Because the partner is an owner of the entity that is buying out their stake, there is no step-up in the cost basis and the purchase price can be included in the deceased partner's estate. It is important to consult a qualified CPA.

KEY CONSIDERATIONS

When setting up your buy–sell agreement, you need to consider several important aspects. One key consideration is the method for valuing the firm. The firm's value will change over time. The purchase price to be paid to buy

Business Continuity Planning

out one of the partners will also change over time, but hopefully in a positive direction. The most accurate method for valuing your firm is to hire a qualified valuation expert to determine your firm's actual value. However, this is expensive and must be done on a regular, recurring basis to keep track of the firm's value over time. An easier method is to simply base the value on the annual gross earnings or the average of gross earnings over the last two or three years.

Another key consideration is the payment structure. Is payment for the buy-out to occur as one single lump sum or as a series of payments over a period of years? A lump-sum payment provides greater liquidity and may be desirable to the seller. However, an installment payment provides an incentive to partners to make sure that the buy–sell agreement is effective and that business operations and client relationships will continue in their absence.

Lastly, you need to decide on and clearly define the events that will trigger the buy–sell agreement to go into motion. Death is an obvious trigger and is easy to define. However, disability is a bit fuzzier. Your agreement should clearly spell out what a disability is and what types of disability will trigger the agreement. Other types of triggering events could be divorce or retirement.

FUNDING THE BUY-OUT

Funding the buy-out is one of the biggest considerations and merits some special attention. Having a buy–sell agreement or cross-purchase agreement in place is not enough. You need to have a mechanism for funding the buy-out. If triggered, a buy–sell agreement may require a considerable sum of money. What if one of the partners does not have the funds sufficient to complete the buy-out? The obvious choice would be to borrow funds to complete the buy-out. However, this solution may not be as easy as it sounds. Obtaining a loan for a business where one of the partners is now absent may prove difficult. Banks and other lending institutions may be skeptical of the firm's ability to generate sufficient cash flow. Borrowing is usually not the best option.

If you set up a buy–sell agreement, you need to institute a plan to fund the transaction ahead of time. You may think that this plan can be put in place by simply setting aside funds over time. This approach may work if the triggering event (death or disability) happens in the far future. But what if it happens tomorrow? It may take a long time to accrue enough money to fund a buy-out by simply setting aside money. Also, this funding can be a big drain on resources.

Another option is to structure the payout as an installment rather than as a single lump sum, as we mentioned earlier. This method is preferable to the buyers and may permit the transaction to be paid for out of current cash flow. However, even this type of arrangement can put a lot of squeeze on cash flow, especially if profits are down. Further, depending on your valuation method, inhibited cash flow could alter the value of the business.

As we mentioned before, life insurance is the generally preferred method for funding buy–sell agreements, including cross-purchase agreements and entity purchase agreements. Life insurance guarantees that sufficient money will be available to fund the buy–sell agreement whenever it happens, especially if the agreement is triggered much earlier than expected. This is the biggest advantage of using life insurance. Also, life insurance proceeds are generally not subject to income tax.

Using life insurance to fund these agreements has some downsides. First, life insurance premiums are paid with after-tax dollars and are generally not a tax-deductible expense. These premiums represent an ongoing, added expense to the law firm partners. If there are large age discrepancies between owners, the cost to each partner may vary. And as we mentioned before, in cross-purchase agreements, having each partner purchase a policy on each of the other partners can be burdensome and expensive.

The entity purchase agreement is one solution. Another option is sometimes called a "trusteed cross purchase." In this type of arrangement, each partner transfers their stake in the business to a separate trust. The trust then purchases a single life insurance policy on each partner. The trust is the owner and beneficiary of the policies. If one of the partners passes away, the trust collects the proceeds, pays the deceased partner's estate or family in exchange for the partner's ownership interest, and then allocates that ownership interest to the remaining partners. This approach eliminates the need for each partner to purchase a life insurance policy on each of the other partners.

If you do use life insurance to fund your buy–sell agreement, what type of life insurance should be purchased? Term insurance, as we have discussed, is usually the most cost-effective way to provide life insurance coverage. However, this type of insurance does expire after a certain number of years and may need to be replaced. At that point, it may become cost prohibitive.

Another solution would be to buy convertible term life insurance. This type of insurance can be converted to a cash-value policy at maturity without requiring a new application process and medical exam. Cash-value insurance may be preferable because it can remain in force indefinitely. Also, the cash values that build inside the policy can eventually be used to buy out the partner when the partner retires or decides to withdraw from the partnership.

To fund the disability provision of a buy-sell agreement, insurance companies can provide specific disability buy-sell policies. These policies will provide a lump sum of cash in the case of an owner experiencing a permanent disability, so the other party (or parties) of the buy-sell agreement can buy out the disabled owner.

A buy-sell agreement is an important component of your business continuity plan and will ensure the continued operation of your business if you or one of the other owners dies or becomes permanently disabled.

Another event that can cause significant business disruption is the economic cycle. Our economy naturally goes through ups and downs. In the next chapter, we will discuss ways you can recession-proof your business.

CHAPTER 27

Surviving a Recession

Ups and downs, expansions and recessions, bull markets and bear markets are part of the natural business cycle. Throughout your career, you will undoubtedly experience your share of economic booms and busts. Perhaps you have already lived through some of the most recent ones, including the pandemic of 2020 and the Great Financial Crisis of 2008.

Some areas of law practice are more affected than others by the economic tides. Law firms that are heavily involved in business transactions and corporate law will perhaps be the most affected, while law firms that focus on things like credit repair and bankruptcy may actually do better during recessions. In any case, you will face periods of prosperity and periods of scarcity. In this chapter, I will show you how to insulate yourself from these ups and downs.

WHAT IS A RECESSION?

A recession is part of the normal and natural business cycle, and as defined by economists, it is two consecutive quarters of negative GDP growth. Despite the technical definition, there can be shorter time periods of slow or negative economic growth that may affect your firm. Most recessions do tend to be short-lived. The average economic expansion lasts 38.7 months (or just over three years), while the average recession lasts 17.5 months (or about a year and a half).[1]

---

[1] "What's an average-length boom and bust cycle?" Investopedia, November 19, 2018, https://www.investopedia.com/ask/answers/071315/what-average-length-boom-and-bust-cycle-us-economy.asp.

CAN YOU PREDICT A RECESSION?

Recessions are notoriously hard to predict, and most experts get it wrong when they try to predict when the next recession will occur. However, there are a few clues that can indicate a recession may be on the way. First, recessions are typically preceded by and coincide with declines in the stock market. In the 11 recessions that took place between 1945 and 2012, nine of them were preceded by stock market declines. The average recession was preceded by a stock market decline of −7.90 percent. The average lead time between the peak of the stock market and the peak of the business cycle was 5.4 months. However, this statistic can be misleading because many other stock market declines have not been followed by recession.[2]

Second, recessions are typically preceded by an uptick in unemployment. This is difficult to quantify, but as you can see in Figure 27.1, recessions usually occur following a flattening and sharp rise in the unemployment rate. However, this can also be deceiving because there have been periods of time where the unemployment rate curve has flattened or ticked up without an ensuing recession.

A third indicator often used to signify a recession, the yield curve, is the result of graphing the difference between short- and long-term treasury yields. Typically, long-term yields are higher than short-term yields. However, on rare occasions, this order flips, and long-term yields decline below short-term yields. This is known as an "inversion." Figure 27.2 shows the difference between 10-year and 2-year yields over time. Whenever the line is below 0, 10-year yields are lower than 2-year yields—the curve is inverted. As you can see, every recession since 1976 has been preceded by an inversion in the yield curve.

However, this too can be deceiving because it is hard to predict the length of time between yield curve inversion and the start of a recession. The lead time can be years or months. Although certain clues do precede recessions, recessions are notoriously hard to predict.

HOW RECESSIONS AFFECT LAW FIRMS

The Great Recession of 2008 coincided with a decline in the stock market of over 50 percent and lasted 18 months. During this time, many companies,

---

[2] Jeremy Siegel, *Stocks for the long run: The definitive guide to financial markets and long-term investment strategies* (New York: McGraw-Hill, 2014).

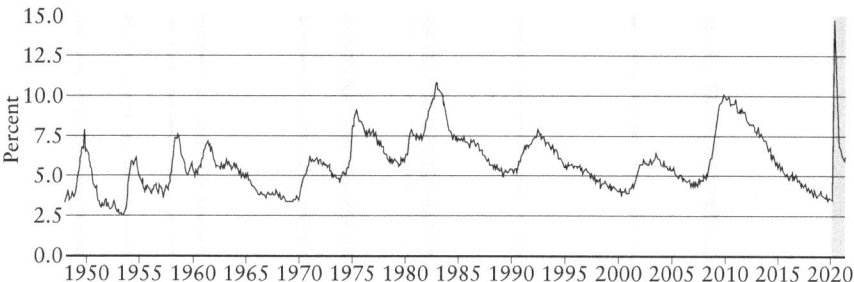

U.S. recessions are shaded; the most recent end date is undecided.

Figure 27.1 Unemployment Rate.

Source: US Bureau of Labor Statistics

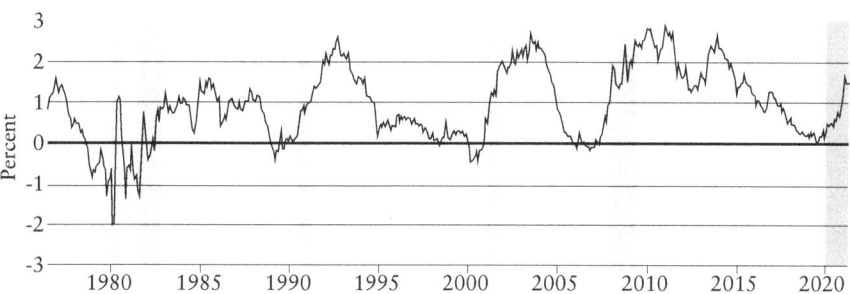

U.S. recessions are shaded; the most recent end date is undecided.

Figure 27.2 10-Year Treasury Constant Maturity Minus 2-Year Treasury Constant Maturity.

Source: Federal Reserve Bank of St. Louis

forced to cut costs, started looking for alternative legal service providers and so they reduced their legal budgets. Corporate law firms felt the squeeze, facing competition from in-house legal counsel, pressure on fees, and an erosion of client loyalty. Although the economy recovered, demand for legal services did not expand as quickly as the broad economy. A 2018 Georgetown Law Report found that lawyers were billing an average of 156 fewer hours than prerecession levels even 11 years after the Great Financial Crisis of 2008.[3]

---

[3] Elizabeth Olson, "Lawyers bill fewer hours than a decade ago: Report," Bloomberg Law, January 22, 2018, https://news.bloomberglaw.com/daily-labor-report/lawyers-bill-fewer-hours-than-a-decade-ago-report.

In 2020, the world was hit with the COVID-19 pandemic and the ensuing global recession due to economic shutdowns around the world. This recession affected an even broader swath of the legal industry as courtrooms across the country were closed and companies hit the pause button on many legal proceedings. Personal injury firms and other firms that are typically more recession-resistant were caught off-guard as jury trials were paused indefinitely. Despite the government's relief efforts to keep businesses afloat, many law firms were forced to close their doors for good because they simply did not have the resources to wait for the economy and courtrooms to reopen.

Recessions affect law firms of all kinds in all areas of law. What we learned from the pandemic of 2020 is that no law firm is truly "recession-proof." Still, there are some things you can do to boost your odds of survival during the next recession or lull in your firm's activity.

RECESSION-PROOFING YOUR LAW FIRM

One of the most important ways to insulate your firm from the effects of a recession is to strengthen your cash flow beforehand. Make sure you are using software to track your income and expenses and always forecast your cash flow over the next several months. Be sure that you have a sufficient liquidity cushion should there be an interruption to business. Establish an emergency line of credit well in advance that you can use in an absolute emergency. A line of credit will be much harder for you to qualify, for if there is a downturn in the economy, banks become reluctant to lend. Finally, make sure you are charging what you are worth and are collecting on your accounts receivable. It will be much harder to collect from clients if a recession should develop. Firms with strong cash flow and cash reserves are more likely to survive a recession.

Another way you can prepare and improve cash flow is to become more efficient. When times are good, invest in technology that can make you more productive and reduce waste. Perhaps consider cutting unprofitable services and clients and focus on the core of your business that is most profitable. Also, look for ways you can improve your practice structure. Make sure that high-paid attorneys, especially you, are not spending time on low-value tasks.

Also consider things you can do to improve the perceived value of your brand and the value you are delivering to clients. It may sound counterintuitive, but firms that deliver greater value are more likely to survive recessions.

Greater value increases client loyalty and allows you to charge more for your services. A strong well-differentiated brand will be more likely to survive a downturn. And beef up those client relationships, looking for ways you can develop a stronger tie between your clients and your firm, such as engaging them with additional services. As I am sure you know, it costs a lot more to gain a new client than it does to keep an existing one.

Additionally, you may want to consider diversifying your practice. Through diversification you can manage risk in both your investments and your practice. If you are focused solely on one practice area, your firm will face all the risk associated with that one practice area. Adding a different practice area that may thrive during times when your main practice area is suffering may give you a better chance of surviving the ups and downs in the economy. However, whatever practice area you add needs to be profitable, and you want to be careful not to dilute the branding of your firm.

If a recession occurs, modify your cash flow to improve your ability to stay afloat. Plan ahead. Stretch out payments as far as possible. Revert to monthly pay plans rather than pay-ahead plans. Deepen your client relationships and make the most of your current clients. Work to attract the competition's clients. Firms that market aggressively even during downturns and work to win over clients from competing firms are more likely to survive a recession. And, of course, be willing to adapt.

RECESSION-PROOFING YOURSELF

In addition to recession-proofing your law firm, you can take certain steps to ensure your own survival during a slow business period. We have already discussed strategies to manage irregular income, including creating a cash flow account, having sufficient emergency savings, and looking for ways to maximize your interest on those emergency savings. Setting aside a sufficient emergency fund is one of the best ways to make sure you are prepared for a slow period.

You may also explore additional sources of income to diversify your revenue stream. Other sources of income can help when your business goes through a rough patch. One way to do this is through traditional investments such as dividend-paying stocks, bonds, real estate investment trusts (REITs), master limited partnerships, or other asset classes in a taxable account. If you build up a portfolio of $100,000 in high-yield bonds paying 12 percent interest, you will have set up an additional income stream of $1,000 a month.

You can reinvest those dividends until you need them to keep your income stream growing.

Another option is real estate. Many attorneys that I know are involved in real estate through either flipping or rentals. Rentals can be a nice alternative source of consistent revenue. You can stash away the income until you need it. However, real estate does involve additional work and can incur expenses that may take away from your net income.

Or how about a side hustle? Do you have a hobby that you really enjoy? You may be able to turn an enjoyable hobby into a side hustle that generates revenue. Perhaps you have a wood-working hobby or you are a flea market flipper. You could sell items that you create or refurbish for additional cash. However, this is probably a last resort for most attorneys.

All law firms are subject to ups and downs in business, even practice areas that are "recession-proof." Recessions are notoriously difficult to predict. However, with some careful planning, you can improve both your firm's probability of survival and your own.

PART VI

Planning for Retirement

What is your idea of retirement? Do you picture white sandy beaches and streets lined with palm trees? Or do you envision working until you finally expire at your desk, writing your last court brief? Some have a concrete picture of retirement and perhaps a specific retirement date or age in mind. For others, retirement is more nebulous. They know they will probably retire someday, but they have no definite plans to do so. You may fit into one of these camps. If the latter applies to you, perhaps instead of planning for retirement, you are aiming for a "work-optional" lifestyle or financial independence. That is, you want to reach a stage where you could retire if you want to, even if you decide to continue working. Whether your goal is true retirement or a work-optional lifestyle, ultimately you need to build a large enough nest egg. This section will show you how to get there.

CHAPTER 28

How Much Do I Need to Retire?

All retirement planning really boils down to this one simple question: how much money do you need to be able to stop working and not run out of money? For most people who are contemplating retirement, their biggest fear is running out of money. The best way to protect yourself against this risk is to make sure you retire with a sufficient nest egg. In this chapter, I will demonstrate how to calculate how much you need for retirement.

RETIREMENT CHALLENGES FACING ATTORNEYS TODAY

Retirement for attorneys has become more challenging in recent years. This is due in part to broad changes in our society such as longer lifespans and the disappearance of pension programs. Undeniably, people are living longer today. According to the Centers for Disease Control and Prevention, the average life expectancy at birth in the United States was 78.8 years in 2019, with males having a slightly lower life expectancy and females slightly higher.[1] However, this figure is for newborns and so does not provide the entire picture. According to the Social Security Administration's actuarial tables,

---

[1] Elizabeth Arias, Betzaida Tejada-Vera, and Farida Ahmad, "Provisional life expectancy estimates for January through June, 2020," U.S. Department of Health and Human Services, Centers for Disease Control and Prevention, February 2021, https://www.cdc.gov/nchs/data/vsrr/VSRR10-508.pdf.

as of 2019, the life expectancy was about 83 years for 65-year-old males and about 85 years for 65-year-old females.

But these are averages. Consider instead the number of people living to extreme old age these days. The number of centenarians is growing and is expected to grow exponentially in the coming years. If you retire at 65, it is very reasonable to expect that you could spend 30+ years in retirement. With pensions programs now largely a thing of the past, the responsibility for planning and preparing for a potentially long retirement rests on your shoulders—with some modest help from social security.

Another issue facing attorneys and retirees at large is a lower expected future return on stocks and investments. With global economies and governments extremely leveraged and debt-laden, there is growing concern that growth may be limited in future years. As of the writing of this book, stocks are overvalued when compared with the long-term historical averages of many valuation metrics. This could mean limited upside going forward.

Attorneys face their own unique challenges as well. Larger firms are pushing attorneys to retire earlier to get high-paid attorneys off their payroll and make room for younger talent. Solo and small-firm attorneys have difficulty walking away from their practices and may be so heavily invested in their businesses that they have neglected to invest in their retirement accounts. Finally, as busy professionals who often are business owners as well, you may simply not have had the time to think about and plan for life after the law.

YOU ARE UNIQUE

So how much exactly does it take to retire? Occasionally, you may see an article in the news or online with a prominent financial guru pronouncing how much people need to accumulate to retire comfortably. News flash: they are all wrong. Everyone is different, and your retirement needs are unique to your own individual financial circumstances. Your retirement needs will depend on several different factors including when you want to retire, your life expectancy, other sources of income, and your lifestyle. I often joke that I could have retired at the age of 25 if I only expected to spend about $100 a year for the rest of my life. So specifically, how much do you need to be able to retire? Here are the steps you can follow to find out.

Step 1: Determine Your Future Expenses

First, you need to determine your retirement budget. To get started, you need to think critically about what your life in retirement will look like.

How Much Do I Need to Retire?

What are your goals for retirement? Where will you be living? What sort of activities will you be engaged in? Will you be downsizing, upsizing, or purchasing an additional residence? These determinations are critical because they will tell you what your spending in retirement will look like. If you plan to sell your home and downsize, your spending will be much less than if you plan to purchase a vacation home and spend your retirement as a snowbird.

After you have done some dreaming, it is time to crunch the numbers and calculate your anticipated retirement spending. Start off by examining your current spending. If you keep a budget or track your expenses, you can begin with this information. If not, you should go through an entire year and categorize your spending. Once you have a good idea of your annual spending, adjust your categories based on how you expect life to be different in retirement. Some expenses such as health care costs, hobbies, and travel may increase. To get a better understanding of future health care costs, visit www.medicare.gov. Other expenses, such as work-related expenses, may decrease. I spend a lot of time on this step with clients because it is so important to get it right.

Step 2: Subtract Future Income Streams

Now that you have a good understanding of your future spending, you need to subtract any future income streams from this number to determine your future retirement income gap. These include social security benefits, pension payments, rental income, and any other income sources that you expect to continue throughout your retirement. The number left over represents the income you will need to generate from your investment portfolio. For example, if your retirement budget is $100,000 and you expect to receive $30,000 from social security, your future retirement income gap is $70,000.

A word of caution, however: this is a simplistic approach that does not consider the timing of different elements. This approach assumes everything starts at once—retirement, social security, and so on. Things may occur at different times. You may retire a few years before you begin social security. To understand the nuances of timing, you may need the help of a professional financial planner.

Step 3: Adjust for Inflation

Your retirement income gap needs to be adjusted for inflation. As you probably well know, the prices of goods and services generally increase over time.

This phenomenon is called inflation, and it is caused by the devaluation of our currency over time. The rate of inflation has varied throughout history, but the long-term historical average rate of inflation is around 3 percent. Thanks to inflation, your retirement budget will need to be higher when you actually get to retirement, and it will need to increase over time. The longer the time between now and when you actually retire, the bigger the adjustment. For example, if you calculated a retirement income gap of $70,000 in step 2, but you do not plan to retire for another 10 years, you will actually need more than $70,000 in 10 years.

To make the inflation adjustment, you will use something called a compound interest calculator. An internet search for "compound interest calculator" will likely yield one quickly. You can find a compound interest calculator at www.moneychimp.com/calculator/compound_interest_calculator.htm.

In the box labeled "current principal," you will put your future retirement income gap. I am using $70,000 from our example above. In the box labeled "years to grow," you will put the number of years from now until when you plan to retire. And in the box labeled "interest rate," you will put your assumed inflation rate. See Table 28.2 for the example inputs.

Click the button that says "calculate" and voila: if my retirement income gap is $70,000, in 10 years I will actually need about $94,000, assuming a 3 percent inflation rate.

Table 28.1

Inputs	
Current principal:	$70,000
Annual addition:	$0
Years to grow:	10
Interest rate:	3%
Compound interest:	1 time annually
Results	
Future value:	$94,074.15

Step 4: Calculate Capital Needs

Now that you have determined your inflation-adjusted retirement income gap, you can use that figure to determine how much money you will need at retirement. We are going to determine the sum of money that would be needed to generate that income, with adjustments for inflation, for the duration of your lifetime.

To make this calculation, you are going to use a different calculator called a "present value annuity" calculator. Again, an internet search for this term will likely yield one that you can use. You can find one on www.moneychimp.com/calculator/present_value_annuity_calculator.htm.

In the box labeled "annual payout," I have put my inflation-adjusted retirement income gap, $94,074.15. In the box labeled "growth rate," I have put my inflation-adjusted growth rate. This is how you will account for inflation—by adjusting your growth rate. If my assumed average return on my investments in retirement is 6 percent and my assumed inflation rate is 3 percent, I can use 3 percent (or six minus three) as my inflation-adjusted growth rate. It is very important that you adjust for inflation because you could be retired for a long time and prices may increase dramatically over the duration of your retirement. This is a simplified calculation, but it will work for your purposes. You may think 6 percent is too low a growth rate, but we want to err on the side of caution here and assume less than we think we might actually achieve. Finally, in the box labeled "years to pay out," I have put the estimated number of years I expect to spend in retirement. If I retire at 65 and my life expectancy is 95, that would be 30 years. See Table 28.2 for the example inputs.

Table 28.2

Inputs	
Annual payout:	$94,074.15
Growth rate:	3%
Years to pay out:	30
Results	
Present value:	$1,899,211.71

Once again, click the button that says "calculate" and the calculator will spit out the answer. Based on the inputs I entered, I will need approximately $1.9 million at retirement.

Step 5: Determine If You Are on Track

Finally, you are ready to determine if you are on track to retire. Before doing that, however, there is one adjustment you need to make. If you expect to receive any lump-sum cash payments at retirement, you should subtract these from the amount you arrived at in step 4. Examples include the sale of assets such as real estate or your law practice.

Let's suppose I expect that I will be able to sell my law practice for $500,000. Then I would subtract this amount from the $1.9 million I calculated in the step above to arrive at $1.4 million. This is the amount that my investment portfolio needs to reach before I can sell my practice and retire. Determining whether your practice will be marketable and estimating a reasonable future sale price will be tricky. We will cover these matters in more detail later. You may even wish to leave them out of your calculation if you want to err on the side of caution.

To see if you are on track for retirement, you are going to revisit the compound interest calculator we used before. This time, simply enter your current portfolio value in the "current principal" box, total annual contributions to your investment accounts in the "annual addition" box, and the number of years you have from now until retirement in the "years to grow" box.

Instead of adjusting for inflation, this time you are going to use your nominal assumed growth rate and enter that in the "interest rate" box. I have used 7 percent for illustrative purposes. Then, click the calculate button and the calculator will tell you the eventual value of your portfolio based on the assumptions you have entered. If you are on track, it should be equal to or greater than the number you got in step 4. You can go back and adjust your inputs in order to achieve the number you need, such as increasing the number of years until retirement (delaying retirement) or increasing the annual additions (saving more). I would caution you against assuming that you can earn more on your investments as you have little control over this input. See Table 28.3 for the example inputs.

You, of course, have to consider many nuances that make retirement planning much more complex than what we have outlined here. Things will change over time. Your annual additions will go up naturally as your

Table 28.3

Inputs	
Current principal:	$500,000
Annual addition:	$20,000
Years to grow:	10
Interest rate:	7%
Compound interest:	1 time annually
Results	
Future value:	$1,279,247.67

income increases. Investment returns and inflation will likely deviate from your assumptions. And events may not occur simultaneously as this method assumes. You may retire several years before starting social security or taking a pension. You may sell assets such as real estate later in retirement. You may downsize. Or you may even upsize. The key is to monitor your progress over time by revisiting this calculation regularly—perhaps annually. For help with the finer details of retirement planning, you should consult a qualified financial planner. However, this chapter should give you a good start.

CHAPTER **29**

Retirement Income Planning

Determining how much you need to retire and making sure you are on track to reach that goal are not all that goes into retirement planning. The other critical piece is careful planning of your cash flow in a way that will maximize your income over your lifetime and minimize taxes. Decisions you make regarding your pension distributions, social security benefits, and withdrawals from your investment accounts will have a major impact on the success of your retirement plan.

PENSION DISTRIBUTIONS

Although less common, generally, and even less common in the legal field, some companies still offer pension plans to their employees. However, if you are entitled to pension benefits, you will have to make some key decisions about when and how you take benefits. Most pensions will offer either a lump-sum distribution which will give you all your money at once, or a variety of annuity options that will guarantee income for you over a certain period or for life.

A life annuity option will guarantee benefits for as long as you live, but benefits will cease when you die. Companies may offer a single life annuity that is based solely on your life or a joint life annuity that will continue to pay benefits as long as either you or your spouse is living.

A period certain annuity option will provide income guaranteed for you for a specified period of years. For example, a 10-year certain option will guarantee income to you and your beneficiaries for 10 years. If something happens to you before the 10 years have passed, the income will continue to be paid to your beneficiaries until 10 years have been completed. Some 10-year certain options will stop paying benefits altogether at the 10-year mark. Others are continuous, meaning they will continue paying benefits as long as you are still alive.

Most pensions also offer a lump-sum distribution, which gives you the option to take all your benefits immediately in one lump sum. Why would you do this? You might consider this option if you believe that you could invest the full amount and achieve a higher income or net wealth over time than any of the pension annuity options will provide. Some pensions do not offer very attractive annuity options, especially in today's low interest rate environment. If you do not need the income and simply want to invest the funds, this would be an attractive option as well. Obviously, the downside is that you assume all the investment risk yourself, whereas with an annuity option, the pension company assumes the investment risk.

SOCIAL SECURITY INCOME

Another source of retirement income is social security, which is available to most people in the United States. You can claim your benefits as early as 62 years of age or as late as 70 years of age. When you claim your benefits determines the amount of your benefit. Thus, if you claim early, your benefit will be reduced, whereas delaying benefits will result in a permanently increased benefit. Choosing the date for benefits to begin is a critical decision that you will face. (Social security is covered in depth in the next chapter.)

PLANNING DISTRIBUTIONS FOR TAX EFFICIENCY

The other obvious key source of income is your investment accounts. Distributions from these accounts will make up the difference between social security and other income and your spending needs. You may choose from a variety of accounts, including IRAs, Roth IRAs, after-tax brokerage accounts, and annuities. Distributions from each of these types of accounts are treated differently for tax purposes.

Distributions from IRAs are generally treated as pretax dollars, so anything you withdraw from an IRA will be counted as income, reported on your annual tax filing, and taxed at your ordinary income tax rates. This is why retirees often move to states like Florida that do not have state income taxes. There is one exception: after-tax IRA contributions. These contributions are treated as after-tax dollars and so are not subject to income tax. If after-tax dollars are part of your IRA balance, your distribution will be treated on a pro-rata basis. For example, if your IRA comprises 10 percent after-tax contributions and 90 percent pretax contributions or earnings, anytime you take a distribution, 90 percent of it will be taxed and 10 percent will be counted as after-tax dollars until the after-tax portion is completely withdrawn.

On the other hand, distributions from Roth IRAs after 59½ years of age are tax-free. Contributions you have made were made from after-tax dollars and earnings are not taxed. This is the big advantage of the Roth IRA.

If you have an after-tax brokerage account, distributions will also not be taxed simply because you took a distribution. However, if you have to sell assets to take that distribution, those sales will be subject to capital gains taxes. After-tax brokerage accounts are not tax deferred. That is, sales or dividend payments are taxed annually at your dividend and capital gains tax rates.

Annuities have their own unique tax treatment. Contributions to an annuity are not tax-deductible and are therefore made with after-tax dollars. However, annuities are tax-deferred. You do not pay taxes on gains or dividends as long as the money stays in the annuity. So, all your contributions are not taxable, but all your earnings are taxable. If you simply take a withdrawal from an annuity, this is treated on a last in, first out basis for tax purposes (LIFO). That is, withdrawals will come from earnings first and be fully taxable at your ordinary income rates. Once all your earnings are spent, your contributions will come out tax free. If, however, you annuitize your annuity—or select a guaranteed annuity option much like a pension plan—distributions will be treated on a pro-rata basis. Each distribution will be a proportional amount of tax-free basis and taxable earnings.

Which account should you draw from first? In general, it is best to spend pretax dollars first and let tax-free dollars grow. If you spend your tax-free dollars first, you'll be allowing your pretax dollars as well as your tax liability to grow. By spending the pretax dollars first, you will permit the growth of more money that will become tax-free income in the future, and you will also minimize taxes over your lifetime.

RETIRING BEFORE 59½

Those relatively few people who wish to retire early and need access to their retirement accounts before the 59½ mark can do so in a couple of ways. First, any contributions to Roth IRAs are accessible at any time for any reason. When you make a withdrawal from a Roth IRA, it is treated as contributions first. However, you will want to keep a careful record of your contribution amounts as the IRS will not do this for you.

Second, through Roth conversions you can turn traditional IRA money into tax-free money that can be accessed at a later date. The trick here though is to do so at least five years before you retire. There is a five-year waiting requirement on conversions before they can be accessed tax free.

Finally, there is the relatively unknown 72(t) rule. According to this rule, you may start taking distributions from your IRA before age 59½ without penalty (although still subject to income tax), but there are some restrictions. The most important requirement is that you need to take approximately the same amount for at least five years. The IRS describes this as "substantially equal periodic payments." There are various ways to calculate these payments to qualify for the rule. If you are considering this option, you should consult a qualified CPA.

REQUIRED MINIMUM DISTRIBUTIONS

One unique aspect of IRAs and other pretax retirement accounts is that at a certain age, you must start taking required minimum distributions. Required minimum distributions (RMDs) were invented to provide a way for the government to start taxing the vast wealth that people in our country have built up in these accounts. RMDs apply to IRAs, 401(k)s, and 403(b)s, each of which is treated a little bit differently.

RMDs now begin at age 72 instead of age 70, as formerly mandated. At this age you must start taking distributions from pretax accounts based on your age and life expectancy. The IRS has created an RMD table to tell you what percentage you must withdraw. That percentage increases each year as you get older. There is one big exception, however. RMDs do not need to be taken from an employer plan (401(k) or 403(b)) if you are still working for that employer. If you leave that employer or if you have an employer plan but no longer work there, you will need to begin RMDs. Be sure to get your RMDs correct. The IRS penalty is steep—50 percent of the RMD you were supposed to take if you forget.

Another key consideration is that Roth or after-tax dollars in an employer plan will count toward your RMD calculation. If you want to minimize the amount you must withdraw, you will want to remove these portions from your plan. Some plans will allow you to withdraw just these amounts or roll them over to a Roth IRA. Roth IRAs are not subject to RMDs.

MANAGING CASH FLOW

You need to carefully monitor and manage your cash flow to make sure you are not overspending and that you are sticking to your plan. The best approach is to set up your distributions on autopilot. Have an automatic monthly or biweekly distribution set up from your investment accounts to simulate having a paycheck. This will help you stick to your budget and keep you from overspending. On an annual basis, you should revisit your automatic distribution setup, crunch the numbers again, and see if any changes need to be made.

When setting up your income plan, determine first the accounts you will be drawing from, then your after-tax amount, the tax, and the gross distribution. Your selection of what account you will draw from has a big impact. If you are drawing from your Roth IRA, your gross distribution can match your spending need. However, if you are drawing from a traditional IRA, your gross distribution will need to be larger to account for the taxes to be paid. Your account custodian can withhold these taxes for you.

CASH RESERVES

Whereas financial planners generally recommend three to six months in liquid cash for clients, perhaps more if your business is volatile, retirees should generally keep at least 12 months in liquid cash. Some planners recommend more. Some planners recommend keeping five years of spending in cash. However, with interest rates on deposit accounts virtually zero today, this can expose you to a high degree of inflation risk. Also, removing five years' worth of funds from stocks or bonds to put in cash can have a significantly detrimental impact on your portfolio growth. Remember that growth is just as important in retirement as at any other time.

If your investment strategy is set up appropriately for your age and risk tolerance, I do not believe you need to have such high amounts in cash. If you are so concerned about risk that you need to have five years of savings in cash, your investment strategy is too risky. However, it is prudent to put some of your portfolio into cash deposits. I would suggest no more than 2 to 5 percent. Your annual withdrawals should not exceed 4 percent or so. This would keep plenty of cash on hand as part of your portfolio.

One alternative to bank deposits is a separate investment account. While investing does entail risk, this account should allow you to invest in a very conservative strategy designed to minimize drawdown risk. This strategy may not earn as much as your retirement accounts, but it might at least earn more than a low-interest rate bank account.

CHAPTER 30

Getting the Most Out of Social Security

One of the most important aspects of retirement planning, as suggested earlier, is deciding when to take your social security benefits. Social security benefits are a critical component of the retirement income planning of most people. In fact, for some, these benefits make up the bulk of their retirement income. How are your benefits calculated?

ELIGIBILITY AND BENEFIT CALCULATION

To be eligible for social security benefits, you must have 40 quarters of wages that were subject to social security payroll taxes. This equates to 10 years of consistent employment, and the quarters need not be consecutive. Your benefits are based on the average of your 35 highest years of income. If you do not have 35 years of earnings, years of zero earnings will be counted toward your average. For example, if you have only 30 years of earnings, you will have 5 years of zero earnings that count toward your average earnings. To maximize your social security benefits, you need to have at least 35 years of earnings.

In determining your actual benefits, the Social Security Administration adjusts your earnings record for inflation and averages together your 35 highest years. Then, that average is divided by 12 to determine your average indexed monthly earnings or AIME. Your AIME is then plugged into a formula designed to replace a higher proportion of income for low-income earners. The formula replaces 90 percent of the first $996 of earnings, 32 percent of earnings up to $6,002, and 15 percent of anything over that, up to a limit (these numbers are as of 2021). This formula determines your primary insurance amount (PIA), the monthly benefit that is available to you at full retirement age.

Your full retirement age is based on when you were born. For anyone born in 1960 or later, your full retirement age is 67. If you were born before 1960, your full retirement age may be somewhere between 65 and 67.

MAXIMIZING YOUR BENEFITS RULE #1: PATIENCE PAYS

The first rule of social security benefits is that it pays to be patient. Even though your full retirement age may be 66 or 67, you can file for benefits as early as age 62 or as late as 70. What's the difference? As noted earlier, filing earlier or later can increase or decrease your benefit. For each year that you file earlier than your full retirement age, your benefit is reduced by about 8 percent. If your full retirement age is 66 and you file at 62, your benefit will be reduced by 25 percent. On the other hand, if you delay filing for your benefits, your benefit will be increased by about 8 percent for each year you delay. So, if you file for benefits at 70 and your full retirement age is 66, your benefit will be about 32 percent higher. This could make a huge difference in your retirement plan.

Unfortunately, most people claim their benefit as early as possible. According to a study by the Center for Retirement Research at Boston College in 2015, 42 percent of men and 48 percent of women file at 62. Only 2 percent of men and 4 percent of women wait until 70.[1] Why is this? It could be that people are taking this benefit early because they need it at the time. Or perhaps they are simply taking it because it is available to them. However, in my conversations with clients, I have heard a lot of people discuss taking benefits early simply because they are concerned about "missing out" on their benefits if they die too early.

Do they have a point? If you delay social security until 70, might you miss out on benefits if you die too early? It is possible. One way to answer these questions is to calculate your "break-even age." This is the age to which you

---

[1] Alicia Munnell and Anqi Chen, "Trends in social security claiming," Center for Retirement Research at Boston College, May 2015, https://crr.bc.edu/briefs/trends-in-social-security-claiming.

Getting the Most Out of Social Security

must live in order for delaying your filing to be the more profitable option. For example, if your full retirement age is 66 and your monthly benefit at that time will be $2,000 a month, you could file as early as 62 for a reduced benefit of $1,500. If you file early, you will get $1,500 a month for four years—money you would miss out on if you waited until full retirement age.

However, if you forgo those four years of benefits and take your benefit at 66, your benefit will be a permanently higher $2,000 a month. How long does it take for that higher benefit to accumulate to a higher amount than if you took benefits at 62? The answer is about 12 years. In this example, your break-even age would be 78. Filing for benefits at 66 instead of 62 results in a higher cumulative benefit if you live to at least age 78. What about age 70? In that case, you will forgo benefits for a longer period, but your benefit once you start receiving it will be permanently higher at about $2,640 a month. In this case, your breakeven age is 82.

I caution clients to ignore break-even ages and instead think about social security as insurance against living too long. The truth is that people are living much longer today than when social security was first created. You may easily live into your 90s or 100s and could spend 30 years or more in retirement. Living longer than you anticipate puts more stress on your investment portfolio and raises the risk of depleting your assets because you will have to contend with inflation over a long period of time. If you live into your 90s or beyond, delaying social security benefits until 70 could mean hundreds of thousands of dollars more in cumulative benefits over your lifetime than if you claim early. In the example above, if that individual lives to 100, filing at 70 would result in $266,760 more in benefits over time than filing at 62.

But here's the real kicker: when you file affects not just your benefit, but also your spouse's benefits and other potential benefits. Filing early reduces your benefit, but it also permanently reduces the spousal benefit to which your spouse may be entitled. Spousal benefits are 50 percent of your benefits. Your spouse can receive the higher of their full benefit or a spousal benefit that is equal to 50 percent of yours. If your spouse's own benefit is greater than 50 percent of yours will ever be, this may not be something you need to consider. However, filing early will also permanently reduce any survivor benefit to which your spouse may be entitled. When you pass away, your spouse can begin receiving a survivor benefit equal to your benefit if it is higher than theirs. Delaying social security benefits past full retirement age will increase the survivor benefit that your spouse can potentially receive.

MAXIMIZING YOUR BENEFITS RULE #2: GET ALL THAT'S YOURS

When you claim social security, you may be entitled to various types of benefits. The general rule, however, is that you only get one benefit: whichever benefit is higher. You also need to be aware that when you file you cannot pick and choose the benefit you want to receive (except for widow and widower benefits). When you file, you will be "deemed" to be filing for all benefits to which you are entitled, and social security will give you the highest one to which you are eligible.

Above we introduced spousal and survivor (or widow) benefits. Generally, spousal benefits are 50 percent of the other partner's benefit. To be eligible for these benefits, you must be at least age 62 and your spouse must have already filed for and begun receiving their own benefits. You can receive whichever is highest: 100 percent of your benefit or 50 percent of your spouse's benefit.

Survivor benefits (sometimes also called widow or widower benefits) are 100 percent of your deceased spouse's benefit. You can receive survivor benefits as early as age 60 instead of 62, though for a reduced amount. If you are already receiving spousal benefits, your benefit will be automatically switched over to the survivor benefit amount. But these benefits have a unique feature. If you are eligible for either your own or your deceased spouse's benefit, you can claim one early while delaying the other and allowing the other to accrue delayed filing credits. For example, you might claim your own benefit at 62 and delay your survivor benefit until full retirement age. Doing so would allow you to collect your own benefit for a few years (albeit a reduced benefit because you are taking it early) and then switch over to your deceased spouse's full benefit at full retirement age.

You also need to be aware of divorced benefits. These benefits apply to those who were married for at least 10 years, who have been divorced for at least two years, and who are currently unmarried. These benefits are equal to 50 percent of your ex-spouse's benefit. Please note that these benefits do not in any way affect your ex-spouse or their ability to receive benefits! Clients often ask me if they are taking money away from their ex by claiming divorced benefits; they are not. Additionally, divorced survivor benefits can kick in if your ex-spouse dies. These benefits apply if the marriage lasted at least 10 years and you did not remarry prior to age 60. For survivor and divorced survivor benefits, remarrying after age 60 does not affect your eligibility to receive survivor benefits.

Finally, you should be aware of other auxiliary benefits. Most of these benefits apply to situations involving children. These include spousal benefits if you have a child of a retired worker in your care, mother/father benefits if you have a child of your deceased spouse or ex-spouse in your care, divorced spousal benefits if you have a child of a retired social security-entitled spouse in your care, and child benefits for children of disabled, retired, or deceased workers.

MAXIMIZING YOUR BENEFITS RULE #3: TIMING IS EVERYTHING

Timing is everything, especially as it relates to couples. Spouses need to evaluate their options together to decide when to file for benefits to maximize their collective benefits. As I mentioned earlier, when each spouse files can have a major impact on the other's benefits. Below are some scenarios that may apply to you.

First, if your full retirement benefit is larger than half your spouse's full retirement benefit, generally it makes sense to wait until age 70. This is because you will not ever be entitled to a spousal benefit, since yours is higher than 50 percent of your spouse's. The Social Security Administration will force you to take your own benefit whenever you file since it is larger.

But what if your own benefit is less than half of your spouse's benefit? In these situations, it may make sense to take your spousal benefit at full retirement age. Spousal benefits do not increase past full retirement age, so delaying a spousal benefit beyond full retirement age will provide no additional benefit. The test to determine if this is the right approach is to compare your spousal benefit at full retirement age to your own benefit at age 70. If the spousal benefit is greater, then it's usually best to take your spousal benefit at full retirement age. Social Security will automatically give you this benefit because it is higher, provided your spouse has filed for their benefit.

Remember, though, in order to be eligible for a spousal benefit, your spouse must be currently receiving benefits. Therefore, you could file for your benefit early before your spouse files for their benefit. Then, when your spouse files for their benefit, you can begin receiving your spousal benefit. But this may not be the best approach because your spousal benefit may be permanently reduced as a result of having filed early.

Finally, let's suppose your age 70 benefit is more than your spousal benefit, but your full retirement age benefit is less than your spousal benefit.

This situation requires more in-depth analysis. It may be best to file for your spousal benefit at full retirement age. You will never be able to collect your higher age 70 benefit, but you will pick up three to four years of spousal benefits that you would otherwise lose. However, this will not be the case if your age-70 benefit is significantly greater.

Of course, these decisions need to be made within the context of your overall retirement plan and when you plan to retire. Does delaying to age 70 make sense based on when you plan on retiring and your investment portfolio? If you are not planning to retire until 70, this may be fine. But if you plan an earlier retirement, you will need to compensate for the lack of social security income by withdrawing more from your portfolio while you wait for your benefits. Will this alternative put too much strain on your portfolio and endanger your retirement plan? Sometimes it can make sense for one spouse to file for benefits at full retirement age and the other to wait until 70. This provides some of the benefits of waiting while reducing the strain on the portfolio during the waiting years.

Social security is just one part of the retirement puzzle. It is important to understand how social security, your investment portfolio, pensions, and other assets will work together in your retirement plan. We help our clients create a cohesive plan that ties all these elements together to achieve the most optimal outcome.

PART VII

Law Firm Succession

How will you bow out from the practice of law? Will you leave a legacy that can continue in your absence? Will you reap the rewards of all these years of labor? In exploring the topic of retirement planning, I mentioned factoring in the future sale of your law firm into your calculations. If you are a solo practitioner or an owner of a small firm, you may be able to sell your firm or your stake in the firm to fund part of your retirement. Unfortunately, however, most do not take advantage of this opportunity because, admittedly, selling a law firm and planning for law firm succession is difficult and tricky. In this section, I will show you how it can be done.

CHAPTER 31

What's a Law Firm Worth?

Can you sell a law firm? In short, the answer is yes! And selling your firm is something you should seriously consider as part of your retirement plan. If you are a law firm owner, your firm or ownership stake has value, and that value could be a key component of your overall retirement plan. Think about it: you have invested tons of capital and energy over the years in building up your business. If you can obtain compensation for all that work, why not? Law firms are more difficult to sell than other types of business but not impossible. While law firms may not sell for as much as other types of businesses generating similar revenues, getting something is better than nothing.

WHAT MAKES SELLING A FIRM DIFFICULT?

Selling a law firm is more challenging than selling other types of businesses. The first challenge is marketability. In most, if not all, states, law firms can only be owned by attorneys (although some states like Arizona are now opening up to nonlawyer ownership of law firms). Already your potential customer base is drastically reduced. Not just anyone can buy your business; it must be a lawyer. That presents another problem. Most attorneys who might have the resources to purchase a law firm are more focused on their own approaching retirement and uninterested in purchasing someone else's firm. The attorneys who generally are interested in purchasing a practice are younger and may have less capital available. Furthermore, because the marketability of a law firm is limited, this makes a law firm much less liquid than other types of businesses. Someone purchasing your firm is in it for the long haul. They cannot just turn around and sell the firm to someone else. Also, ethical rules generally require that law firms be sold in their entirety and they cannot be bought simply to be resold. This lack of marketability and liquidity makes law firms less valuable to buyers.

The second big challenge is that most small and solo law firms are personality driven. The identity of the firm is tied to the identity of one or more attorneys. Most law firms are named after their founders after all, and the business of law is often very personal. Your clients work with you because they want you specifically to be their attorney. They are tied to the attorney personally, and not necessarily to the firm itself. That creates a big problem. If all of your clients are working with your firm because they like working with you and you retire, what happens to all the clients? Will they want to stay on and work with a new attorney? Someone purchasing your firm needs to retain those client relationships. If they cannot retain the clients, there is little to no value in purchasing the firm.

Because law firms are generally small, closely held businesses that depend on client relationships, they tend to be high-risk businesses for buyers to purchase. In addition, most firms have greater income volatility than other types of businesses, especially personal injury firms. Income unreliability is a major risk factor. Finally, most law firms operate with a backlog of unbilled work of about eight to nine months. All of these various risk factors reduce the potential valuation of a law firm to a potential buyer. However, do not despair. Despite a potential lower valuation than other types of businesses, law firms still have value and can be sold.

WHAT HAS VALUE?

Your law firm does indeed have value. First, there are the physical assets: your office or building if you own it, leases, equipment, desks, furniture, and so on. The sale of your building could be the largest contributor to your valuation. Or you could sell the firm and retain the building and lease the building back to the new owner. This would provide you with a stream of income in retirement.

Second, all of your digital assets, such as your website, online presence, and social media accounts, have value. If your website consistently gets a lot of traffic or ranks high in Google's search results and you consistently get clients through your online presence, this is a major asset carrying a lot of value. People spend a great deal of money to improve their Google ranking.

What's a Law Firm Worth?

According to an article in *Forbes*, websites by themselves can be worth 24 to 36 times your firm's monthly earnings![1] Your digital assets do indeed have immense value.

Other valuable nontangible assets include your reputation, brand awareness, and goodwill. Does your firm have a good reputation in the community? How is your brand awareness? Do people in your area immediately recognize your "jingle" or your firm's name? These assets can have great value. Reputations are difficult to build and can only be built slowly over time. You have invested many years and lots of dollars into building your reputation and goodwill in the community. There is much value in attaining a good reputation or quick brand awareness. If you are one of the most well-recognized firms in your area, your firm already has significant value to a potential buyer.

Next, there are your information assets, which include your processes and procedures, proprietary information and systems, workflows, intellectual property, and databases. Proprietary systems for accomplishing certain tasks have value. Databases of current and past clients, referral partners, vendors, and key outside partners also have value. To maximize your firm's value for potential sale, you should make sure all of your databases are well maintained and that all your processes and procedures are carefully documented and organized.

The biggest chunk of value, of course, lies in your relationships, not only client relationships, but also relationships with past clients, referral partners, and colleagues. These are the most difficult assets to "sell" because they cannot truly be sold. Rather, they have to be carefully and deliberately transitioned to the new buyer over time. The new firm owner or attorney should be slowly introduced to existing clients and referral partners and brought into the relationship. Herein lies the big secret of selling law firms: selling a law firm is a slow transition not a quick transaction.

Finally, there are accounting assets such as cash, cash-like items, costs advanced to clients, work in progress, and accounts receivable. Cases that you are currently working on have potential value. Personal injury cases can be valued based on an analysis of the risk and potential outcome. In fact, if you are a personal injury attorney, you may be aware that you can sell these types of cases to settlement companies for immediate cash payment to offset

---

[1] Haris Bacic, "How much is my website worth and how do I sell it?" *Forbes*, September 20, 2017, https://www.forbes.com/sites/allbusiness/2017/09/20/how-much-is-my-website-worth-and-how-do-i-sell-it/?sh=22fb0df625ec.

costs. Your accounts receivable have value as well, depending on the collectability and age of the account.

VALUING A LAW FIRM

So, what is a law firm worth? As I have mentioned, valuing a law firm can be tricky. All of the assets I have mentioned have value and should be considered in determining your firm's overall value and potential sale price. You can hire a valuation expert to perform a formal appraisal of your business. This person will examine the assets of your business and determine their value based on various factors, including risk and liquidity. For example, office furniture has value, but it will be priced based on its age and replacement value and not on the amount you paid for it. Your accounts receivable will be valued based on quality and age. Older accounts receivable are less likely to be collected and therefore are worth less.

One of the biggest factors in valuating a law firm is what is often called "going concern." This term refers to how much cash the firm can be expected to generate for the new owner, assuming the former owner is no longer part of the firm. Going concern is really a function of client loyalty. Are clients loyal to the lawyer or to the firm? If client relationships are strongly bonded to the individual lawyer and not the firm, they are less likely to stick around during a transition.

The problem with hiring a valuation expert to do a formal appraisal of your firm is that your firm's value will change over time, and so the appraisal will have to be done more than once. An alternative to this process is to simply use an earnings multiplier. In the stock market, the value of a company can be measured in terms of its price-to-earnings ratio, which is simply the current stock price divided by earnings per share. These ratios vary over time but have generally ranged between 10 and 25 throughout much of history. If a company's price-to-earnings ratio is 25, that means the value of its stock is 25 times annual earnings.

Unfortunately, law firms are riskier, smaller, and a lot less liquid than publicly traded companies on the New York Stock Exchange. These factors reduce the potential earnings multiple of a law firm. In general, most law firms sell for somewhere between one and two times gross annual earnings. That is a far cry from 25 times earnings, but it is more than nothing! Your firm's multiple will depend on various factors such as location, current market environment, and firm-specific characteristics such as going concern.

Your succession plan is a key part of your retirement plan and can enable you to fund part of your retirement through the sale of your firm. However, as I mentioned before, selling a law firm is more of a slow transition than a quick transaction. In the next chapter, we will discuss the mechanics of how to sell a law firm.

CHAPTER 32

How Do You Sell a Law Practice?

As baby boomers age and enter retirement, an unprecedented number of attorneys are approaching retirement in our country. Failing to plan for succession has important consequences for both the firm and the individual attorney. Firms face the loss of senior talent and leadership as attorneys retire. Without a clear succession plan in place, they also face the potential loss of key clients. The result can be a major disruption to the firm's cash flow, putting partners, employees, and clients at risk. Failure to plan for succession can also create division within the firm and lead to defections and firm breakups.

A succession plan ensures that leadership and management are in place to allow the firm to continue for the next generation. It will also help the firm to retain existing client and referral relationships so that the firm can maintain profitability. And of course, a succession plan provides the ability to finance the buy-out of retiring partners.

For the individual attorney, failing to plan for succession means an inability to capitalize on goodwill and sweat equity—all that hard work you have put in to building up your practice and clientele. A properly executed succession plan can help you fund your retirement and protect your family's wealth by providing additional funds for you and your family.

Every attorney needs a succession plan that deals with both short-term risks and long-term goals. Your succession plan should describe in detail everything that happens with your business and clients, and who fills your shoes if something unexpected happens to you such as premature death or disability. Your succession plan should also outline your exit strategy for retirement. This part of your succession plan will describe who will take over the business for you, terms of payment, and clear steps for the succession process.

BASIC SUCCESSION STRATEGIES

You can design your succession plan in a variety of ways. The most basic approach to succession is an outright sale of the practice to a third party. This fast and immediate transaction provides maximum liquidity, but for most businesses, let alone law firms, it is difficult to achieve. Law firms, as I have discussed, are often tied to the identity of the practicing attorney and have little annual repeat business. Also, locating a desirable candidate to fill your shoes can take some time. In addition, your state's rules of professional conduct may limit your ability to do this. An outright sale works well for businesses in which the owner has little involvement in the day-to-day activities and whose owners are ready to quit immediately. Law firms do not usually fit this description.

A more applicable succession strategy for law firms is an internal transition, that is, one in which the firm is handed over to an existing member of the firm—perhaps a younger partner or junior associate within the firm. This type of transition will likely be much smoother than selling to an outside party. The identity of the firm remains intact and consistent, and client service is less likely to be interrupted. However, because this transition would be slower, it will take time (perhaps several years) and will not provide as much liquidity.

Similarly, you could pursue an apprenticeship transition. If there is no qualified candidate already part of your firm who is willing and able to assume control, you could bring on a junior associate for that specific purpose. This associate would spend a year or longer becoming part of the firm, learning all your processes and procedures, and solidifying client relationships. Then, the associate would gradually assume control.

Another approach to succession is practice continuation with another firm—or essentially a merger. This would involve merging your firm with another firm—perhaps a larger firm or a younger attorney's existing firm—and forming an "of counsel" relationship with that firm. You would continue working with your existing clients while attempting to transition your existing relationships to the new firm and other attorneys at the new firm. This is a great option for solo attorneys who want to gradually phase down but want to continue working. It also provides a great deal of flexibility for that phase-down period. Since you will still be available to work with your clients, the odds of retaining your clientele are greatly improved, thereby increasing the firm's value to the buyer. And the merged firm is a committed buyer. Finally, this type of transition, which depends on the arrangement with the new firm, can provide immediate liquidity for retirement, while still giving you the ability to continue working and earning.

Larger firms should consider creating an orderly succession plan that all partners will participate in when they reach a certain age. A firm-wide succession plan could require partners to resign equity status at a certain age but allow them to continue practicing law on a reduced schedule. Retiring partners could be paid a salary plus a bonus or be paid based on a formula using collections and fees. But whatever plan is adopted, the partners need to formally agree to it ahead of time, and it must be carefully crafted to avoid claims of age discrimination.

FUNDING THE BUY-OUT

A critical component of the succession plan is funding for the buy-out, or how the buyer is going to pay the seller. Ideally, the buyer should be able to self-fund the buy-out with their own existing assets. This approach may work if you merge your firm with an existing firm, but a junior associate will probably not have the liquidity to manage a self-funded buy-out.

A loan is the next most obvious alternative. However, obtaining financing from a bank to purchase a law firm may be a tall order. As I have mentioned, buying a law firm is a riskier proposition than purchasing other types of businesses for a variety of reasons. Because law firms often have highly variable revenue and are dependent on the identity or identities of individual attorneys, banks may not be willing to provide funding.

Instead, the buyer and seller could arrange a loan between themselves. Essentially, the seller will act as the lender to the buying partner. The buyer and seller will structure an agreement detailing the principal amount, interest rate, term, and amortization schedule. The seller sells the firm in exchange for this agreement, and the buyer makes payments as described by the agreement. However, the one glaring problem with this strategy is that it provides little incentive for the seller to stay involved. If the seller now has an agreement providing a guaranteed stream of revenue for the sale of the firm, what is the incentive to ensure the success of the new attorney? Having the retiring attorney involved in the firm for a period of time after the sale is critical to the success of the transition. If the transition is not successful, the firm could lose revenue and the buyer may default on the loan.

A more attractive approach is an "earn-out." In this type of arrangement, the purchase price of the business is determined in terms of a percentage of revenues over a period of time. The buyer will make payments to pay off the "loan" based on the future revenue of the firm. For example, if the value of the firm is two times gross annual revenue, the buyer could agree to pay the seller 50 percent of revenue for four years. At the end of the term, the agreement will be complete and the payment satisfied regardless of whether or not the sum of the payments equates to the original value. The actual amount paid may be more or less than original value depending on the success of the firm. If the firm is not successful, the selling attorney will receive less than anticipated. On the other hand, if the firm is successful, the selling attorney could receive more than the agreed-to original purchase price. This provides a strong incentive for the retiring attorney to stay involved and ensure the buyer's success. This is a much more attractive proposal to a buyer.

ANNUITIES

Firms with multiple partners might pursue other structures to buy out partners when they retire. Buying out a retiring partner could require a significant amount of cash which the firm may not have on hand. To avoid this difficult circumstance, firms should plan ahead to fund the buy-out of a retiring partner.

One easy method of doing this is through insurance annuities. The firm can purchase annuity contracts over time to fund the retiring partners' eventual retirement. At retirement, the retiring partner would sell their ownership interest in exchange for an annuity or series of annuities and begin receiving the annuity payout. Before then, the annuities remain an asset of the firm, and if the partner leaves prematurely, the annuities can be surrendered for cash value, which the firm would retain.

NONQUALIFIED DEFERRED COMPENSATION PLANS

Firms with multiple partners might also use a nondeferred compensation plan to buy out a retiring partner. These types of plans are often referred to as "golden handcuffs" because they are designed to retain key employees in other types of businesses. A nonqualified deferred compensation plan is essentially an informal retirement arrangement. In order to be legal, these plans have to be "informal," which means they technically cannot be formally funded. However, there are ways to fund these plans that satisfy this requirement.

One method of funding such an arrangement is through a "rabbi trust"—an irrevocable trust set up to fund nonqualified deferred compensation plans. The firm contributes a certain amount of money each year to the trust on behalf of the partner covered by the plan. The trust structure protects the assets from being used by the firm during periods of financial hardship. However, it does not necessarily protect against creditor's claims in the event of insolvency or bankruptcy. At a certain date, the trust is used to fund a stream of income to the retiring partner. If the partner leaves the firm prematurely, the funds can revert back to the firm. However, these types of arrangements are complex and should be handled with the help of a qualified tax attorney.

A second method of funding a nonqualified deferred compensation plan is through a stock transfer, which needs to be planned well in advance. When the firm is established, the partners establish a fixed number of ownership shares. Each founder contributes a fixed amount of cash to finance the startup in exchange for a certain number of shares. New partners who are admitted later must contribute cash upon admittance as partners in exchange for shares that are deducted from the other owners. When a partner retires, the firm pays them an amount equal to the current cash value of their ownership shares. This approach carries a great tax advantage since much of the later buy-out may be classified as a tax-free return of capital.

Alternatively, deferred compensation plans can be funded through a cash-value life insurance policy. In this more common, simpler approach, the firm purchases life insurance on the partner. When the partner retires, they can sell their equity stake back to the firm in exchange for all or part of the life insurance policy. When the partner retires, they can withdraw the cash value to fund their retirement needs. If the partner dies prematurely, the firm can collect the death benefit to fund a buy–sell agreement if one has been set up and provide liquidity to the deceased partner's estate. (See chapter 22 for more details.)

QUALIFIED RETIREMENT PLANS

Finally, qualified retirement plans may also be used as a source of financing if the other partners have built up significant balances and if the plan permits borrowing. A qualified retirement plan is a plan that applies firm-wide, such as a 401(k) or profit-sharing plan. When one partner retires, other partners can borrow from their retirement plan to fund the buy-out of the retiring partner. Most 401(k)s will allow you to borrow at the prime interest rate or better, which makes this an attractive financing option. And, instead of paying back a bank, you are technically paying yourself back over time.

Law firm owners should create a plan for both the succession strategy and funding of the buy-out. These plans should be established well in advance. But it is not enough to have a plan. Some important steps need to be taken to ensure the success of the transition. We will cover those next.

CHAPTER 33

Making the Sale Successful

Pulling off a successful sale of your law firm and transition into retirement is no small task. As we have noted, selling a law firm is difficult. Not only do you need to have a well-thought and carefully crafted plan, but you also need to prepare your firm for sale in order to make the transition as successful as possible.

PREPARATION FOR SALE

Selling a law firm is more of a transition than a transaction, and transitions take time. Because of the difficulties inherent in selling a law firm, you need to start your planning well in advance. You should ideally start the planning process at least five to eight years before the transition begins. If you are bringing on a new attorney to take the reins, they will need time to learn the ropes and develop relationships with your new clients before they can start assuming control. If you are merging with another firm, you and the other firm will need time to get to know each other and evaluate whether you are good fit for each other.

In the time leading up to the transition, there are steps you ought to take to make your firm more viable for sale. First and foremost, you need to clarify your ownership details. Make sure your operating agreement is current. If you do not already have an operating agreement with your other partners, if you have partners, you need to put one down on paper. The operating agreement should detail who the owners are, and how ownership is structured, new partners are admitted, and their equity stake is determined.

Next, take steps to maximize the long-term sustainable value of your firm. You may want to go through some rebranding to breathe some new life into your brand, or to better position your brand so that someone new can take over. If your firm is named after you, you may want to change the name of your firm to ensure better continuity of the firm when the new owner takes over. This is an important consideration. If the name of your firm is Jane Smith, Attorney at Law, you might have some difficulty finding a buyer. You should try to make the name less specific. You may consider adding your practice area and the term *associates* or *group*. You could try something like Smith Injury Law Group or Smith & Associates Injury Attorneys. If your jurisdiction allows brand names, this might be the best option. A brand name is one that does not include personal names, such as Main Street Injury Lawyers. However, some jurisdictions require you to include your personal name. If that is the case, many jurisdictions will allow the name of a retired partner to remain part of the firm's name for a period of time and as long as certain requirements are met.

Ultimately, your most valuable asset is your relationships with clients and referral sources. Take time to cultivate these relationships. Are there clients and referral partners whom you have not spoken with in a long time? Set up a lunch meeting to keep these relationships fresh. You may even consider joining new networks and getting back out into the networking scene. Any new connections you can cultivate may have value to the new buyer. And as the more seasoned attorney, it will be much easier for you to cultivate these connections.

Invest in new technologies that can improve work-flow efficiency. You may have a great system that works for you, but will it work for the new buyer? If you are running your business from a legal pad, sticky notes, and an Excel spreadsheet, how easy will it be for a new owner to take over? Not very. Make sure you are up to date on all the latest software and technology to streamline your operations and make it easy for a new owner to fill your shoes.

Along the same lines, take steps to clean up databases and document everything. Your client and contact databases are going to be valuable assets in the transition; spend time making sure these are in order and complete. If you are still using a physical filing cabinet, you may want to take this opportunity to transition to the cloud. Be sure to carefully document all your processes and procedures for administrative and law-related tasks. And document the day-to-day functions of your firm. Who is responsible for handling specific tasks? You may want to update (or create) your organizational chart and set of job descriptions. Also, be sure to clean up your financial records, including your balance sheet, profit and loss statements, and accounts receivable. If you have not done so, you may want to invest in software that can keep these up to date for you.

Make sure you have a clearly written business plan. Many attorneys and law firm owners neglect putting together a business plan, but it will be a key piece of your transition. A business plan is a roadmap for your firm's future. It should have clearly defined goals for revenue and growth and specific marketing efforts and other actions that you will undertake to reach those goals. A big part of your business plan is a clearly defined brand: your practice areas, your niche, your brand promise, your brand aesthetic, your values, and your story. Get very specific about what niche and practice areas you serve best and make that front and center. It pays to specialize. In today's world, clients are not looking for general practice lawyers; they are looking for specialists who understand their unique circumstances. This will also make you a more appealing acquisition by a potential buyer.

Truthfully, your marketing plan is your business. A potential buyer is buying your business for two possible reasons (and perhaps both): (1) loyal clients who will continue to generate repeat business or (2) a great marketing plan that continues to bring in new business. Many law firms do not generate repeat business and rely on a steady stream of new clients. Those clients come to you because of your marketing efforts. A buyer needs to know how to continue to work that marketing plan and be assured that your marketing plan will continue to generate results.

Finally, identify your key employees and communicate with them early about any of your transition plans. Ideally, you will be able to retain them through the transition as they may be a key part in assuring a smooth transition and retaining clients.

RETAINING CLIENTS

Retaining clients is one of the paramount goals of your succession plan, whether that is ongoing work or long-time clients who bring repeat business. You also need to retain other important relationships such as referral partners, vendors, experts, and colleagues whom you rely on. Start by making sure your client database is complete, detailed, and up to date. Create a specific plan for when and how you will communicate the transition to your clients and introduce clients and other relationships to the buyer.

For your biggest and most valuable relationships, you might consider creating an individualized plan for each individual client and how you will attempt to transition that relationship to the buyer. Be sure to communicate with the client that your succession plan will be a lengthy transition process and that you will continue to work with the clients and be available to answer any questions. A relay race is a great analogy. In a relay race, each runner completes one leg of the race and then hands off the baton to the next runner. But it is not an instantaneous switch. Rather, as the first runner approaches, the second runner takes off. The two runners run until they are close together and at the same speed. Then, as they are running together, side by side, the first runner hands the baton to the second runner. This is what you are doing: you and the buyer will work together for a time during the transition with the existing clients to ensure a smooth hand-off.

FINAL TIPS

Once you have identified a possible successor or merger candidate, you and the candidate will need to decide on a sale price for the buy-out and a strategy for funding (whether that is an earn-out or other strategy), and a specific timeline. In this process, be sure to retain competent counsel in transaction and tax law who can assist you. Do not represent yourself. Make sure to put everything in writing, even (and especially) if you are working with family members. When drafting the buy–sell agreement, you would be wise to retain the ability to regain control of the firm if the buyer should default, commit malpractice, die, or if for any other reason things go awry. Your plan should allow you to gradually cede control over time. Four to five years is a good time frame. Finally, make sure you do your due diligence and properly vet and get to know your buyer well before you commit yourself to the any agreement.

Selling a law firm is difficult, but if you start planning well in advance, the sale of your law firm could be a significant part of your retirement plan and your pathway to financial independence and a confident future.

Conclusion

With the information in this book as your starting point, you're now ready to begin your journey to financial independence and a confident retirement! No matter where you are in your journey, now is the time to start putting your financial house in order to maximize your wealth over time. It's never too late to begin building your wealth. But remember: your most valuable asset is time itself. So don't delay!

I counsel my young attorney clients to start by simply opening an after-tax brokerage account and stashing away as much money as they can. This gives you ultimate flexibility. Let the student loans and mortgage debt take care of themselves over time by sticking to the payment plan and being strategic with high-interest rate debts. You can worry about retirement accounts and tax maneuvers later. The important thing is to start investing now while you are young. Be aggressive with your investments. Time is on your side if you are young, and you can afford the risk.

Start with the end in mind. Write down a financial plan for yourself. Avoid costly financial products like annuities and insurance products that masquerade as investments. Calculate how much you'll need to retire and make sure you are setting enough aside to reach that goal. Make that your priority. You can pay your debts over time as your income grows. But you will never be able to make up for lost time in the market. Keep increasing the amount you are saving as your income grows as well. And, of course, make sure you put the right protections in place, such as life insurance, disability insurance, and proper liability insurance, to prevent disaster.

Start thinking early about your eventual succession strategy and how you plan to bow out. As you earn more money over time, proper tax planning will become increasingly more important as well. Don't let the fast pace of your schedule allow you to neglect your financial planning. Improving your tax efficiency can make a dramatic difference in your net worth over time and your eventual ability to achieve financial independence and a confident and happy retirement.

I wish you the best in your journey. Please feel free to reach out to me with questions you may have. The practice of law is a noble profession. It's also a business. And there's no reason you should be ashamed of running it like a business to maximize profit and wealth, and to achieve your lifelong dreams. Here's to you, and your success!

About the Author

Darren Wurz, MSFP, CFP® is a financial planner, investment advisor, and co-owner of Wurz Financial Services, specializing in working with attorneys and law firm owners. He is also the podcast host of The Lawyer Millionaire Podcast, available on all podcast platforms. Wurz Financial Services (www.wurzfinancialservices.com) is a family business that has spanned three generations and includes his dad, Richard, and his brother, Travis. Darren grew up in the financial services industry working with his dad. He is a graduate of Golden Gate University with a master of science in financial planning. He is a Certified Financial Planner™ (CFP®) Professional. He has a series 65 investment license and is an investment adviser representative with Schmerge Executive Planning Services, Inc., a registered investment adviser. Darren lives and works in the Cincinnati, Ohio, region, but he has worked with attorneys and law firm owners across the country. He is a member of the American Bar Association and is active in his local bar association, the Northern Kentucky Bar Association. Darren can be reached at (859) 291-9879 or by email at dpw@wurzfinancialservices.com. He is also on social media, including LinkedIn (www.linkedin.com/in/darren-p-wurz), Twitter (@wurzfinancial), and Facebook (www.facebook.com/wurzfinancial service).

Index

Note: *f* indicates figure; n indicates note; and *t* indicates table.

4 percent rule, how to calculate retirement savings with, 8
12b-1 fees, mutual funds and definition of, 55
72(t) rule, when to start taking distributions from your IRA, 204
401(k)
   advantage for small law firm or solo attorney, 108–109, 108n3
   customized options for, 108–109
   Roth option for employee contributions, 98
   "safe harbor plan" for, 109
   type of tax-deferred account, 97–98
401(k) account, make backdoor contribution to Roth account with, 104–105, 105n1
401(k) loan, convert student loan to, 22
403(b)
   Roth option for employee contributions, 98
   type of tax-deferred account, 97–98
501(c)(3) organization, forgiveness of student loan debt if employed by, 21–22
529 account, college savings plan, 11
1031 like-kind exchanges, defer taxes on sale by buying new property, 84
1099 form, to report capital gains from retirement account, 97

A

Accelerated death benefit rider, life insurance definition of, 149
Accidental death benefit rider, life insurance definition of, 149–150
Accounting assets, examples of law firm's, 217–218
Accounts receivable, profitability and age of, 176–177
Adjusted gross income (AGI), 123
Advantages
   of 15-year versus 30-year mortgage loan, 32–33, 33*t*
   of 401(k) for small law firm or solo attorney, 108–109
   of auto pay, 17
   of cash balance pension plan, 109–110
   of cash-value life insurance, 148, 182–183
   of C-corporation business structure to shareholders, 169
   of charitable limited liability companies (LLC), 126–127
   of charitable remainder trust (CRT), 123–124
   of consolidation of student loan debt, 21
   of convertible term life insurance, 182
   of direct real estate investment, 83–84
   of diversification, 58–59
   of donation of shares of stock to charity, 123
   of donor-advised fund (DAF), 125–126
   of early filing for social security benefits, 208
   of employer-based disability insurance, 154–155
   of estate planning with Roth account, 101
   of fee-only planner versus commission-based life insurance salesperson, 147
   of fixed rate versus variable rate mortgage, 33
   of Health Savings Account (HSA), 114
   of home flipping, 83, 83n1

Advantages *(continued)*
　of investing in bonds over equities and stocks, 48
　of investing in stock and bonds, 39
　of investing in stocks, 86
　of level term life insurance, 148
　of life insurance for tax purposes, 130
　of limited liability partnership, 168–169
　of making larger mortgage down payment, 34, 34*t*
　of nonqualified deferred compensation plan, 130–131
　of private foundations, 124
　of private mortgage insurance (PMI), 33–34
　of purchasing exchange-traded funds (ETFs), 86
　of purchasing rather than renting your office space, 138–139
　of purchasing real estate investment trust (REIT), 85–86
　of purchasing real estate mutual funds, 86
　of real estate over equities and fixed income, 53
　of renting a house, 30
　of Roth account, 98–99, 101
　of S-corporation versus sole proprietorship, 141–142
　of SEP IRA for small law firm or solo attorney, 107
　of SIMPLE IRA for small law firm or solo attorney, 107
　of sole proprietorship business structure, 167–168
　of "solo" 401(k), 108–109
　of split dollar life insurance to partner/firm, 132
　of structured fee arrangement, 118–119, 119*t*
　of tangible asset (real estate) versus intangible (stock), 84
　of target-date funds, 80–81
　of tax-deferred retirement accounts with tax, 97–98
　of traditional IRA and income limitations, 103
　of using Certified Financial Planner (CFP®) from independent firm, 13–14
　of using debt to create leverage, 16
　of using financial leverage to gain financial, 16
　of using life insurance to fund buy-out agreements, 182
　of using trusteed cross purchase to buy life insurance, 182
Age. *See* Young attorney; Midcareer Attorney; Preretirement; Postretirement
AGI. *See* Adjusted gross income (AGI)
AIME. *See* Average indexed monthly earnings (AIME)
Allred, Gloria, 162
Amazon stock, outsized gains for early investors in, 57
American Bar Association, professional liability information on website of, 163
Annual renewable term life insurance policy, definition of, 148
Annuity, structured fee arrangement uses fixed or variable, 121
"Any occupation," court's interpretation of, 155
Apprenticeship transition, definition of and strategy for succession plan, 222
Asset allocation
　by age, 71–81
　portfolio should include REITs and ETFs, 86
Asset class, drawdown risk present for every, 66
Asset classes
　tactical asset allocation to change weight of different, 62
　types of investable, 47
Assignment company, role in settlement fee, 120
ATTOM Data Solutions, average gross profit from flipping a home, 83, 83n1
Attorney
　run law practice as a business, 173
　tax tips and savings for, 135–142
　See also Lawyer
Attorney Compensation Report of 2020, author Martin Avvo, 173
Attorney Student Loan Repayment Program, from Department of Justice, 22
Augusta rule, report no income from brief rental of your residence, 137, 137n1
Automobile liability insurance, why needed, 160

Index 237

Auto pay, advantages of, 17
Average billing per client or case, profitability and, 176
Average indexed monthly earnings (AIME), 207–208
Avvo, Martindale (*2020 Attorney Compensation Report*), 173

B

Back-end loads, mutual fund commissions of, 55
Back-testing, also known as data-snooping or overfitting, 80
Bankruptcy
  even "blue chip" companies can declare, 58
  individual company stock worthless in, 66
  retirement funds of IRAs and 401(k)s protected from creditors during, 17
Banks, above-average interest rates offered by some, 25
"Bear market," stock market drawdown of 20 percent of more, 67
Behavioral finance theory, tactical asset allocation and definition of, 62
Benefit period, definition of disability insurance, 155
Benefits, life insurance with income-tax free death, 133
Bill, treat savings as non-negotiable autopayment of a, 12
Billing rate, financial KPI to tract monthly effective, 176
Bloomberg International Treasury Bond ETF (BWX), 73
"Blue chip" companies, bankruptcy can occur even with, 58
Bogle, John (*Common Sense on Mutual Funds*), 59–61
Bonds
  advantages over equities and stocks, 48
  classified as short, intermediate, or long term, 48
  definition of, 47
  rate of yield reflects risk of, 48
  recession raises value and interest rates on, 49
  use as diversifier and risk hedge in portfolio, 49

Bonus depreciation, does not apply to property purchased before 2023, 139, 139n3
Boom and bust cycle, 185n1
Bottom line, ways to improve your, 173–178
Brand awareness, recognizing "jingle" associated with your law firm, 217
"Break-even age," retirement and definition of, 208–209
Brokerage account, 97
Budget, debt payments must be part of nondiscretionary, 17
Budgeting, being purposeful with your money, 11
Buffett, Warren, 60
Business continuity planning, 179–183
Business cycle, recession as part of normal, 185
Business liability insurance for law firm, types of, 161–162
Business meeting, tax advantage of using your residence for, 137
Business plan, how to create a, 174
Business structure, types of and choosing a, 167–171
"Buy and hold," another name for strategic asset allocation, 61
"Buy and sell recommendations," stock experts seldom recommend to sell, 92
Buy-out
  methods for funding a, 181–182
  option for funding of law firm, 223–224
Buy-sell agreement
  component of business continuity plan, 180, 183
  considerations in setting up, 180–181
  what triggers a, 181
Buying a house, additional costs involved in, 30
BWX. *See* Bloomberg International Treasury Bond ETF (BWX)

C

California, additional taxes on S-corporation in, 142
Capital appreciation, company's profits as value of shares increase, 49–50
Capital gains, concerns over taxes on, 93
Capitalizing, definition of, 19

Car
  in year of high income lower tax bill by purchasing a new, 139–140
  maximum dollars allowed by IRS for purchase of new, 140, 140n4
Career, lawyers later than others in starting, 3–4
Cash balance pension plan, description, cost, and contributions, 109–111, 110n4
Cash flow
  list annual discretionary versus nondiscretionary expenses for irregular, 23–24
  minimize effects of recession by strengthening, 188
  mistake saving only what is left over with unpredictable, 12
  rental property vacancies and problems with, 85
  See also Irregular income; Unpredictable income
Cash flow account
  help even out irregular income with, 24
  law firm partners/owners use of, 26
  to recession-proof yourself, 189
Cash reserves, in retirement keep three to six months in liquid cash, 205–206
Cash-value life insurance
  advantages of, 182–183
  also known as universal life insurance or permanent life insurance, 148
  definition of, 129
Cash-value life insurance policy, term life insurance policy versus, 148
C-corporation, definition, business structure, and advantages/disadvantages of, 169–170
Cent-billionaire, definition of, 7
Center for Retirement Research, age when men/women file for social security, 208, 208n1
Centers for Disease Control and Prevention, average life expectancy in US, 193
Certificate of deposit (CD), do not put emergency funds into, 25
Certified Financial Planner (CFP®)
  advantage of independent firm as, 13–14
  experience and credentials of, 13
  website where to find, 13
  See also Financial advisor; Financial planner

Certified Financial Planner™, commission-based sales representative versus, 40
Chamber of commerce, pay your dues early to, 135
Chan, Priscilla, 126
Charitable lead trust (CLT), 123–124
Charitable remainder trust (CRT), advantages of, 123–124
Charitable tax strategies, 123–127
Charitable trust, can reduce income tax or estate tax, 123
Charitable trust agreements, types of, 123–124
Charity, 132–133
Charles Schwab (low-cost, online brokerage firm)
  for investments, 94
  for market-based structured fee arrangement, 121
  zero commissions for ETFs, 56
Children in your care, auxiliary social security benefits for, 211
"Claims made," professional liability type of policy, 162
Client base, word-of-mouth referrals best source of new business from, 175
Client loyalty, minimize effects of recession with new services to strengthen, 189
Client relationship management software, definition and use of, 175
Client satisfaction, profitability and, 177
Clients, succession plan and how to retain, 229–230
Close, Glenn, 3
Closing costs, 35
CLT. *See* Charitable lead trust (CLT)
CNBC
  annual rate of increase of median home value according to, 86–87, 87n3
  do not listen to experts or market commentary on television, 92
College savings plan, 529 account for, 11
Commission-based life insurance salesperson, fee-only financial planner versus, 147
Commission-free ETF trading, online trading platforms and, 55
Commodities
  annual gross return (1970–2017; 2009–2017), 52, 52n3
  definition, value, and examples of, 51

Index

perform well during economic stagnation, 52
traded using futures contracts, 52
ways to purchase, 52
Common Sense on Mutual Funds (Bogle), 59
Company-specific risk, stock risk from company's business activities/finances, 50–51
Compound interest, importance of building wealth with, 3–4
Compound interest calculator, how to use and website for, 196, 196f
Compounding interest, 44, 44t
Concentration, definition of investor, 57
Consolidation, advantages and disadvantages of student loan, 21
Constructive receipt
  description of IRS doctrine of, 119–120
  you cannot direct the investment of funds for structured fee arrangement, 120–121
Consultations
  profitability and number of new monthly, 177
  set business goal for number of new customers and, 174
Contingency basis, attorney should structure legal fees when working on, 117–118
Contingency fee, reasons to defer, 119
Contingency-fee attorney
  donor-advised fund advantages for, 125
  high taxes from large settlement fee, 4–5
  how to manage irregular income, 23–27
  salary for, 4
  unpredictable income of, 5
Contingency-fee tax deferral, 117–121
Continuity plan, reasons and need for business, 179–180
Conversion rate, profitability and definition of, 177
Convertible bonds, definition of, 47
Convertible term life insurance, advantages of, 182
Corporate America, materialism and greed encouraged by, 10
Corporate bonds, issued by companies, 47
Corporations, types of, 169
Corrections, stock market drawdowns of 10 percent or more, 67

Correlation, comparison of two different asset classes, 51
Cost-of-living adjustment rider, disability insurance definition of, 155
Cost segregation study, definition of and accounting firms can do, 139
COVID-19 pandemic (2020), percent fall of S&P 500 during, 66
Crash of 1919, percent fall of S&P 500 during, 66
Credit cards, pay off balance monthly before interest charged on, 25
Credit history, loan for house based on borrower's, 31
Credit score, before buying home reasons to improve your, 35
Cross-purchase agreement, definition of, 181
CRT. *See* Charitable remainder trust (CRT)
Currency, devaluation of our, 7

D

DAF. *See* Donor-advised fund (DAF)
Damages (television program), 3
Data-snooping, 80
Death
  charitable remainder trust (CRT), to charity after your, 124
  creates liquidity need for your family/your firm, 146
  funeral and probate expenses from, 145
Death benefit
  in life insurance policy, 146
  provisions of life insurance, 130
Death of spouse or child rider, life insurance definition of, 150
Debt
  advantages of using, to create leverage, 16
  how the wealthy think about and use, 16
  when to pay off, early based on interest rate, 18
  See also Student loan debt
Debt-to-income ratio
  before buying home lower your, 35
  loan for house based on borrower's, 31
Default risk, bonds and definition of, 48
Defer receipt of income, how to reduce current taxes by, 136
Department of Justice, Attorney Student Loan Repayment Program, 22

Depreciation
  calculation of "useful life" of property for IRS is straight-line, 138
  definition of bonus, 139
  of a new car using straight-line or bonus, 140
Developed countries, examples of, 51
Digital assets, examples of law firm's, 216–217
Direct real estate investment, 84–85
Disability
  definition of, 153
  definition of "any occupation" and "own occupation" for, 155
  estimating income needs after, 153–154
  impact on family and law firm, 153
  risk of developing a, 153–157
Disability insurance
  advantages/disadvantages of employer-based, 154–155
  benefits are not taxable for individual, 156
  for each partner in law firm, 156
  integrated with social security disability benefits, 156
Disability insurance policy, 155
Disability risk planning, integrated with retirement planning, 154
Disadvantages
  of 15-year versus 30-year mortgage loan, 32–33, 33t
  of cash-value life insurance, 148–149
  of C-corporation business structure, 169
  of charitable limited liability companies (LLC), 126–127
  of consolidation of student loan debt, 21
  of direct real estate investment, 84–85
  of donor-advised fund (DAF), 125–126
  of employer-based disability insurance, 154–155
  to employer of cash balance pension plan, 109–111
  of fixed rate versus variable rate mortgage, 33
  of Health Savings Account (HSA), 114–115
  of home flipping, 85
  of illiquid commercial real estate, 39
  of investing in real estate, 53
  of life insurance as investment product, 94
  of life insurance as tax-saving vehicle if interest rate is low, 133
  of life insurance as expensive retirement savings and poor growth potential, 132
  of momentum-based investment strategy, 63
  of paying off debts with retirement savings, 16–17
  of paying off smallest loan balance first, 19–20, 19t
  of private foundations, 125
  of private mortgage insurance (PMI), 33–34
  of purchasing real estate investment trust (REIT), 86
  of Roth account, 98, 101, 101n2
  of SIMPLE IRA and "employer" only contributions, 107–108
  of sole proprietorship business structure, 167
  of sole proprietorships and partnerships, 168
  of split dollar life insurance, 132
  of stock picking, 91–92
  of structured fee arrangement, 120–121
  of target-date funds, 80–81
  of term life insurance, 148
  of using life insurance to fund buy-out agreements, 182
  of withdrawing money during down stock market, 68
Distributions
  IRA and age of mandatory minimum, 204
  manage cash flow in retirement with investment accounts' automatic, 205
  planning for tax efficiency in, 202–203
Diversification, advantages of, 58–59
Dividends, 49–50
Divorce, effect on social security benefits of, 210
Donor-advised fund (DAF), definition and advantages/disadvantages of, 125–126
Double taxation, of dividends to C-corporation shareholders, 169
Down payment
  advantage of making larger mortgage, 34, 34t
  mortgage lenders want 20 percent, 33
Drawdown, definition and amount of risk for, 66

Index

E

E-Trade, brokerage firm for market-based structured fee agreement, 121
"Earn-out," option for funding of law firm, 224
Economic benefit, description of IRS doctrine of, 120
Economic benefit regime plan, 132
Economic cycle, periods of positive or negative economic growth, 50
EEM. *See* iShares Emerging Markets ETF (EEM)
Effective billing rate, how to determine, 176
Efficiency
  distribution and planning of tax, 202–203
  maximize profitability by, 175
  of written policies and procedures, 175
Efficient market hypothesis, strategic asset allocation and definition of, 61–62
Elimination period, definition of disability insurance, 155
Emergency fund
  before buying a house increase, 35
  considerations when investing, 25–26
  irregular cash flow requires six months of nondiscretionary expenses in, 24
  short-term disability and use of, 154
Emerging markets, examples of countries, 51
Employer 401(k) match, contribution to retirement savings by, 9
Entity purchase agreement, definition of, 182
Equities
  do well during economic growth, 51
  preferred term for *stocks*, 49
Equity indexed life insurance, 149
Estate tax, charitable trust can reduce, 123
Exchange-traded funds (ETFs)
  advantages of purchasing, 86
  Charles Schwab zero commissions on, 56
  definition of, 54
  use in portfolio of, 72, 72t, 73t
  way to purchase commodities, 52
Expansion, length of average economic, 185
Expense ratio, 54–55
Expenses
  deductions from salary/mortgage and leftover for other, 31
  financial KPI to tract monthly, 176
  for retirement determine your goals and future, 194–195
Exponential growth, money and linear growth over time versus, 45, 45t

F

Federal Reserve
  increases interest rates to combat inflation, 52
  recession and market interest rates lowered by, 49
Fee deferral, legal basis for, 119–120
Fee-only financial planner, commission-based life insurance salesperson versus, 147
Fidelity, low-cost brokerage firm for investments, 94
Fidelity Emerging Markets (FEMKX), 72
Fiduciary, definition of, 13
Financial advisor, 12–13. *See also* Certified Financial Planner (CFP®)
Financial challenges
  of legal profession, 3–6
  unpredictable income, 5
Financial crisis of 2008–2009, home values fell during, 29
Financial goal, disability as detriment to reaching, 153
Financial independence
  definition of, 8
  goal of most lawyers, 7–8
  some risk needed for good returns and, 68
Financial lesson, reasons to spend less than you make, 9–10
Financial leverage, way to gain financial advantage, 16
"Financial needs" approach, how much life insurance is needed using, 146
Financial plan
  mistake of not having a, 39–40
  most common mistake of a hodgepodge or no, 89
  setting goals as first step of, 7
  what to include in, 39
Financial planner, 40. *See also* Certified Financial Planner (CFP®)
Financial planning, contingency-fee tax deferral as aid to, 118

Financial risk, expenses of being found at-fault in auto accident, 161
Fixed income, from bonds, 47
Fixed income securities, definition of asset class of, 48
Flexible Spending Accounts, forerunner of Health Savings Account, 114
Flipping, advantages/disadvantages of home, 83, 83n1, 85
Flowthrough entity, types of, 168, 169, 171
Forbes
   REITs outperform direct investment according to, 86, 86n2
   websites may be worth many times firm's monthly earnings, 217, 217n1
Foreign bonds, issued by foreign governments or companies, 47
Foreign stocks, developed countries versus emerging markets for, 51
Forgiveness, types of student loan debt, 21–22
Front-end loads, mutual fund commissions of, 55
Full retirement age, based on birth year, 208
Furniture, new home and cost of buying, 35, 35n1
Futures contracts, definition and commodities traded using, 52

G

GDP. *See* Gross domestic product (GDP)
General partners, income received subject to self-employment taxes, 168
General partnership, definition and type of business structure of, 168
Georgetown Law Report (2018), billable hours fewer during recession, 187, 187n3
"Going concern," definition of and valuing law firm based on, 218
"Go to cash," take all money out of investments to, 91
"Golden handcuffs," examples of use by law firm of, 132, 224–225
Gold Trust (GLD), 73
Google stock, outsized gains for early investors in, 57
Government, forgiveness of student loan debt if employed by, 21–22
Government bonds
   issued by federal government, 47, 49
   low rate of return of, 49
Great Financial Crisis (2008)
   mortgage-backed bonds and, 47
   percent fall of S&P 500 during, 66, 67*f*, 67n1
   recession and, 185, 186
   S&P 500 percent decline during, 50
   variable-rate mortgages and, 33
   yield of State Street's SPDR® S&P 500 ETF (SPY) during, 74
Gross domestic product (GDP), recession and relation to, 185
Growth stock
   definition and example of, 51
   valued for potential company expansion, 60

H

HDHP (high-deductible health insurance plan), 113
Health insurance, HSA and high-deductible, 113–114, 114n1
Health Savings Account (HSA)
   advantages and disadvantages of, 114–115
   description, cost, and contributions, 113
   legislation (2003) and purpose of, 113, 114
   must be enrolled in HDHP to qualify for, 113–114
   using it as an IRA, 114
Herbert S. Garten Loan Repayment Assistance Program, 22
Herd behavior, behavioral finance theory and, 62
Hewes, Patty, 3
HGTV, real estate investing as seen on, 83
Hollywood, portrayal of legal profession by, 3
Home buyer, financial assistance from state for expenses by first-time, 36
Home equity loan, convert student loan debt to, 22
Home flipping, 83. *See also* Flipping
Home office, IRS rules for deducting percentage of home as business expense, 140, 140n5
Homeowner Association (HOA) fees, 31
Homeowners insurance, major areas of liability coverage for, 159–160

Index

House
    cost of buying versus renting, 29–30
    guidelines on how much to pay for a, 31, 31*t*
    how to prepare finances before purchasing, 35
HSA. *See* Health Savings Account
Human Life Value approach, calculates life insurance for absent future earnings, 147

I

Income
    financial KPI to track monthly, 176
    lawyers with unpredictable, 5
    spending should be less than, 9–10
Income needs, after disability estimating, 153
Income streams, for retirement subtract future, 195
Income tax, charitable trust can reduce, 123
Individual retirement account (IRA)
    funding purchase of house with, 36, 36n2
    type of tax-deferred account, 97–98
Inflation
    abnormally high in 1970s, 52
    adjust your income gap for, 195–196
    definition and cause of, 52, 196
    law school tuition higher than general rate of, 15
    retirement savings and effect of, 9
Inflation hedge, real estate and commodities as, 53
Information assets, examples of law firm's, 217
Initial public offering (IPO), 49, 57
Injury, monetary liability of compensation to person plus punitive damages for, 159
Insufficient income, use stock, REITs, real estate, etc., during recession to raise, 189–190
Insurance annuity, funding law firm sale with, 224
Intentional acts of harm, not covered by liability insurance, 160
Interest, capitalized, 18
Interest rate
    convert student loan to home equity loan to decrease, 22
    do not pay down all debts if low, 16
    first pay off loan with highest, 19
    pay off debt early based on, 18
Interest rate risk, of a bond, 48
Internal Revenue Service (IRS), doctrines of constructive receipt and economic benefit, 120
Internal transition, definition of and strategy for succession plan, 222
Intuit's Mint.com, organizes credit card transactions, 11
"Inversion," long-term yields decline below short-term yields, 186, 187*f*
Investing
    emergency funds and advice on, 25–26
    mistake of paying off debt instead of saving and, 38
    reasons people do not start early, 90
    See also Investment
Investment
    advantages of direct real estate, 83–84
    in commodities, 51–52
    difference between gambling and, 65
    disadvantages of direct real estate, 84–85
    in equities, 49–51
    in fixed income assets, 47–49
    introduction to types of, 47–56
    maximize tax deferrals through tax-advantaged, 39
    in mutual funds, 54–56
    poor decisions made on emotion, 91
    in real estate, 52–53
    See also Investing
Investment account, regular schedule to move money automatically to, 12
"Investment grade," bonds, 48
Investment mistakes, commodity of time robbed by making, 89
Investment portfolio, do not chose strategy based on avoiding expenses, 93
Investment portfolio loan, convert student loan to, 22
Investment strategies, 57–63
Investment strategy
    disadvantages of a momentum-based, 63
    lack of patience so constant change of, 91
    meeting your risk level and financial goals, 57
Investor psychology, 62
IPO. *See* Initial public offering (IPO)

IRA. *See* Individual retirement account (IRA)
Irregular income
   analyze annual not monthly income, 23–24
   create a cash flow account for, 24
   managing, 23–27
   See also Unpredictable income
IRS rule
   deducting percentage of home office as business expense, 140, 140n5
   private foundations and, 125
IRS Topic 511, deductions for dual vacation/business expenses, 138, 138n2
iShares 20 Plus Year Treasury Bond ETF (TLT), 72
iShares Emerging Markets ETF (EEM), 72
iShares Investment Grade Corporate Bond EFT (LQD), 73

J
John R. Justice Student Loan Repayment program, 22
Junk bonds, high yield but high risk, 48

K
Key performance indicators (KPIs), types of, 176–177
Kids, reduce taxes by hiring your, 136
Kochis, Tim (*Managing Concentrated Stock Wealth*), 58, 58n1

L
Land values, Department of Agriculture 2019 summary of, 43n1
Large-cap stocks, total market capitalization of, 59
Last in, first out (LIFO), withdrawal from an annuity based on, 203
Late start, for lawyer in career and savings, 3–4
Law firm
   buy-sell agreement if one owner dies, 150–151
   challenges in selling a, 215–216
   coverage and need of business liability insurance for, 161–162
   determining the value of your, 181
   disability insurance on each partner in, 156
   financial impact of your death on partners in, 145
   life insurance on each partner in, 150–151
   missed saving and investing by starting own, 4
   need business strategy for growth and development of, 173
   negative effects of recession on, 186–187
   pushes high-paid attorneys to retire, 194
   recession-proofing your, 188–189
   salary for partners and owner of, 4
   time needed to prepare for successful sale of, 227
   valuing a, 218–219
   See also Law practice
Law firm owners, how to manage irregular income, 23–27
Law firm partners, responsible for own estimated quarterly taxes, 5
Law firm partners/owners, required to pay own quarterly estimated taxes, 26
Law practice
   benefits of running your own, 165
   how to sell a, 221–226
   See also Law firm
Law school, average annual tuition and fees at private versus in-state public, 15
Lawyer, 4, 4n2. *See also* Attorney
Legal Aid, Herbert S. Garten Loan Repayment Assistance Program from, 22
Legal fees, large settlement increases tax bracket, 117
Legal profession, financial challenges of, 3–6
Legal Services Corporation, student loan forgiveness through, 22
Lender, capitalizing of student loan debt by, 19
Level term life insurance policy, definition of, 148
Leverage, definition of and using debt to create, 16
Liability insurance, have coverage that equals the value of assets, 160
Liability risk, home, automobile, your business/law practice areas of greatest, 159
Life annuity option, pension plan retirement with, 201
Life expectancy, males versus females, 193–194, 193n1

Index 245

Life insurance
  advantages of cash-value, 182–183
  advantages of convertible term, 182
  charitable uses of, 132–133
  how much do you need, 146
  include income amount your family needs in future, 146–147
  insurance product not an investment vehicle, 93
  lack of growth potential with, 132
  most expensive retirement savings vehicle, 132
  not tax-saving vehicle if interest rate is low, 133
  preferred method for funding buy-out, 182
  premature death and protecting your wealth with, 145–151
  premium payment as function of your risk factors, 146
  purpose of, 93
  tax advantages for retirement funding, charitable giving, or education planning, 129–130
  types of, 129, 131
  using a "trusteed cross purchase" to buy, 182
  why cost increases as you age, 129
  See also Life insurance policy
Life insurance policy
  types of, 148–149
  types of riders for, 149–150
  way to fund nonqualified deferred compensation plan, 225
  See also Life insurance
Life insurance tax strategies, 129–133
Lifestyle, reasons for living too large a, 38
Life-time income, charitable remainder trust (CRT) provides, 124
LIFO. *See* Last in, first out
Limited liability company (LLC)
  advantages/disadvantages of charitable, 126–127
  can elect to be taxed as S-corporation, 171
  how to create a, 170
Limited liability partnership (LLP), 168–169
Limited partners, income received not subject to self-employment taxes, 168
Limited partnership, definition and type of business structure of, 168
Line of credit, minimize effects of recession with emergency, 188
Liquidity
  definition of, 55
  maintaining some level in portfolio, 92–93
  Roth IRA early distribution penalty not applied to direct contributions so potential, 99
Liquidity cushion, minimize effects of recession with, 188
Loan
  advantages/disadvantages of 15-year versus 30-year mortgage, 32–33, 33*t*
  borrowing funds from cash-value life insurance policy by, 130
  first pay off highest interest rate, 19
Loan balance, disadvantage of first paying off smallest, 19–20, 19*t*
Loan regime plan, 131–132
Location, unsystematic risk of real estate investment in, 85
LQD. *See* iShares Investment Grade Corporate Bond EFT (LQD)
Lump-sum payment, pension plan retirement with, 201–202

M

Malpractice, professional liability insurance to protect against claims of, 162
Malpractice liability, areas of law practice more exposed to, 162
Managing Concentrated Stock Wealth (Kochis), 58, 58n1
Manhattan Island
  purchased by Dutch from Native Americans (1626), 43
  real estate worth today of, 43, 43n2
Margin calls, 22
Marketing, types of and developing strategy for, 174
Marketing budget per new client, profitability and, 177
Market risk, stock risk associated with economic cycle, 50
Mason, Perry (television program), 3
Maturity, definition of bond, 48
MEC. *See* Modified endowment contract (MEC)
Mega-backdoor Roth account, 104–105

Members, limited liability of LLC and owners as, 170
Merger, succession plan for law firms doing, 222–223
Mid-cap stocks, 59
Midcareer attorney, moderate risk basic and full portfolios for, 74–76, 75t
Minimum hold times, ETFs versus mutual funds for, 55
Minuit, Peter, 43
Mistakes
  annuities used as an investment, 93–94
  avoid biggest investing, 89–94
  do not listen to "buy and sell" individual stock recommendations, 92
  having no investment plan, 89
  having too much money in real estate, 39
  inaction and too much planning, 40
  insufficient liquidity for an emergency, 92–93
  lack of patience with investment strategy, 90–91
  listening to television or website stock experts, 92
  making emotional investment decisions, 91
  money and attorneys' biggest financial, 37–40
  not having a financial plan, 39–40
  not investing early enough, 90
  not maximizing tax advantages, 38–39
  not saving enough money for retirement, 37
  obsessing over taxes or expenses, 93
  paying off debt instead of saving and investing, 38
  picking individual stocks for investments, 91–92
  portfolio with too much or too little risk, 90
  saving only what is left over with unpredictable cash flow, 12
  using life insurance as an investment, 93–94
Modern portfolio theory, strategic asset allocation and definition of, 61
Modified endowment contract (MEC), when overfunding life insurance changes it to, 130
Momentum, concept and definition of, 63

Money
  biggest financial mistakes attorneys make with, 37–40
  time value of, 43–47
Morningstar, mutual fund five-star rating by, 91, 91n1
Morningstar.com, third-party research site for stocks and funds, 56
Mortgage
  advantages/disadvantages of fixed rate versus variable rate, 33
  select lowest possible monthly payment for, 32
Mortgage-backed bond, 47
Mortgage payment, factors that affect amount of monthly, 31, 31t
Municipal bonds, issued by states, 47
Mutual funds
  definition of, 54
  difference between ETFs and, 54
  short-term reserves in conservative asset allocation, 26
  way to purchase commodities, 52

N

National Association of Homebuilders, average cost of new home furniture, 35, 35n1
National Bureaus of Economic Research, average medical expenses at end of life, 146, 146n1
National Center for Education Statistics, average debt of law school graduate, 4, 4n1, 15
National Funeral Directors Association, median cost for funeral (2019), 146
Negligence, definition of, 159
New York Stock Exchange, law firms riskier that publicly traded companies on, 218
Nonqualified deferred compensation plan
  buy out retiring law firm partner with, 224-225
  can be funded by life insurance, 130–131
  definition as type of retirement plan, 130
  does not have to be offered to all employees, 131
  ways to fund, 224–225
Notice provisions, professional liability insurance and required, 162

Index

O

Occupation disability insurance, definition of, 155
"Occurrence," professional liability type of policy, 162
Office, purchase instead of leasing your, 138–139
Off premises, most liability policies cover bodily injury or property damage, 160
One-participant 401(k), 108n3
Options trading, risk of, 90
Outsourcing, of law firm marketing activities, 174–175
Overfitting, 80
Overfunding, contributing to life insurance policy in excess of the premium, 130
Owners-only 401(k), features of, 108
Owning a house, monthly and deductible expenses for, 30

P

Pandemic, 2020 recession due to, 185, 188
Partnership, types of, 168
"Passive investing," another name for strategic asset allocation, 61
Pass-through entities, sole proprietorships, partnerships, and LLCs as, 141
Patience, tolerate market ebb and flow with, 90–91
Payment, when to make more than minimum debt, 18
PCRIX. *See* PIMCO Commodity Real Return Strategy (PCRIX)
Pension benefits, 4 percent rule supplemented by, 8
Pension plans, lump-sum distribution of payment versus life annuity options, 201–202
Pension Real Estate Association, correlation of stocks and bonds to real estate, 53, 53n4
Period certain annuity option, retirement and definition of, 201–202
Permanent life insurance. *See* Cash-value life insurance
Personal finance, spending less than income is foundation of, 10
Personal injury attorney, high taxes from large settlement fee, 4–5
Personal property, liability and, 159–160
"Personal service corporation," definition of and corporate income tax for, 170
Physical assets, examples of law firm's, 216
PIMCO Commodity Real Return Strategy (PCRIX), 73
Plan, 179–183. *See also* Financial plan
Planning
  consequences of lack of time for, 5
  mistake of inaction and too much, 40
PMI. *See* Private mortgage insurance (PMI)
Policies, maximize efficiency with written procedures and, 175
Policy limits, liability insurance and definition of, 160–161
Portfolio
  "buy and hold" simpler than momentum-based, 63
  having too much or too little risk in, 90
  See also Modern portfolio theory
PortfolioVisualizer.com, free online tool, 72
Postretirement attorney, moderate risk basic and full portfolios for, 78–80, 78t, 79t
Preapproval letter, before looking for house get lender's, 35
Prepaying expenses, examples of how to reduce taxes by, 135
Preretirement attorney, moderate risk basic and full portfolios for, 76–77, 76t, 77t
Present value annuity calculator, how to use and website for, 197–198, 197f
Pretax dollars, in retirement first spend your, 203
Pretax income, bank lends up to monthly payment of 28 percent of, 31
Principal, reason early payment of debt should go toward, 18
Private foundation, 124–125
Private mortgage insurance (PMI), reason for and advantages/disadvantages of, 33–34
Professional liability insurance, when client proves negligence of your professional duties, 162
Profitability, factors that affect, 176–177
Profit sharing, contribution to retirement savings by, 9

Property insurance, on owned properties, 84
Public charity, difference between private foundation and, 125

Q

Qualified dividends, REIT dividends are not, 86
Qualified retirement plan, way to fund nonqualified deferred compensation plan, 225–226
QuickBooks, accounting software for law firm business, 174

R

"Rabbi trust," definition of and use of, 225
Rate of yield, reflects the risk of the bond, 48
"Readjustment phase," family income needed after your death, 147
Real estate,
  advantage of tangible asset versus intangible (stocks), 84
  advantage over equities and fixed income, 53
  disadvantage of illiquid commercial, 39
  high returns comparable to stock market (1984–2018), 53, 53n3
  illiquid investment versus liquid investment of stocks, 85
  mistake of having too much money in, 39
  risks and disadvantages of investing in, 53
Real estate agent, closing costs include commission of, 35
Real estate investing, 83–87
Real estate investment, advantages of direct, 83–84
Real estate investment trusts (REITs)
  advantages of purchasing, 85–86
  disadvantages of purchasing, 86
  may outperform direct investment, 86
  how to invest in, 53
Real estate mutual funds, advantages of purchasing, 86
Recession
  cut unprofitable services and clients during, 188
  diversify profitable areas of law practice during, 189
  economists' definition of, 185
  length of average economic, 185, 185n1
  predicting a, 186
  stock market decline sometimes precedes, 186, 186n2
  surviving a, 185–190
  yield curve inversion as predictor of, 186
Recession-proofing, your law firm and yourself, 189
Refinance, 21
Relationships, client/colleagues, as asset of law firm, 217
Rental property
  investing for long-term capital appreciation, 83–84
  rental income not subject to payroll taxes, 84
  vacancies and cash flow problem with, 85
Renting a house, 30
Required minimum distributions (RMDs), 204
Retire, how much do you need to, 193–199
Retirement
  4 percent rule to calculate money needed for, 8
  before age 59½, 203–204
  challenges facing attorneys before, 193
  determining if you are financially on track for, 198–199
  late start for lawyers in saving for, 3
  longer life expectancy increases number of years in, 194
  mistake of not saving enough money for, 37
  mistake of paying off debt instead of saving for, 38
  planning for, 191
  portfolio should have less risk nearing, 90
  start planning at least five years before, 5–6
  See also Retirement planning; Retirement savings
Retirement account
  chief way to reduce taxes, 97
  payments to student loan debt instead of to, 4
  unpredictable income effect on, 5
  withdrawals reduce compounding effect in, 46

Index

Retirement income
  inflation-adjusted, 197
  pension plans for, 201–202
  social security for, 202
Retirement income gap, determine your future, 195
Retirement income planning, 201–206
Retirement planning
  based on age when career began, 9
  decisions needed for, 5
  legal profession and challenges of, 3–6
Retirement savings
  disadvantages of paying off debts with, 16–17
  employer 401(k) matches and/or bonuses, profit sharing in, 9
  key is starting early, 9
  supplemented by Social Security and pension benefits, 8
Return of premium rider, life insurance definition of, 150
Revenue Ruling 79-220, IRS ruling about structured fee arrangement, 120
Revenue stream, during recession and irregular income, diversify your, 189
"Reversion to the mean," definition of, 60, 60n2
Richard A. Childs et al v. *Commissioner of the Internal Revenue Service*, 120, 120n1
Rider
  accelerated death benefit, 149
  accidental death benefit, 149–150
  cost-of-living adjustment, 155
  death of spouse or child, 150
  disability insurance policy, 155
  life insurance policy, 149–150
  return of premium, 150
  types of disability insurance policy, 155
  types of life insurance, 149–150
  waiver of premium, 149, 155
Risk, definition and types of, 65–66
"Risk attitude," definition and psychology of, 68–69
"Risk capacity," function of age and income, 68
Risk management, based on personal risk capacity and risk attitude, 69–70

Risk tolerance
  assessing your level of, 65–70
  components of, 68
  determining your, 68–69
RMDs. *See* Required minimum distributions (RMDs)
Roth account
  advantage of estate planning with, 101
  conversion of traditional IRA funds to, 103–104
  differences between traditional retirement account and, 98
  income limits for eligibility to make contributions to, 101, 101n2, 103
  provides "tax insurance" against future higher taxes, 101
  at retirement can take money out tax-free, 98–99, 101
  subject to some income limitations, 98, 98n1
  tax advantages of traditional 401(k) retirement account versus, 99–100, 100*t*
  tax-deferred but early withdrawal penalty, 98
  type of tax-deferred account, 98–99
  See also Roth IRA
Roth account backdoor, 103–104
Roth IRA
  contributions to, accessible at any time for any reason, 204
  funding purchase of house with, 36, 36n2
  turn traditional IRA into tax-free money with conversion to, 204
  type of tax-deferred account, 97–98
  See also Roth account
Roth, Senator William, 98
RPIBX. *See* T. Rowe Price International Bond (RPIBX)
Rule of 72, how quickly investment doubles depends on growth rate, 45
Russell 2000, small-cap index, 59

S

S&P 500, 2008–2009 financial crisis and percent decline of, 26
S&P Goldman Sachs Commodity Index, 52
Salary, lawyer median, 4, 4n2
Sale, 227–229

Sale price, deciding on timeline and law firm's, 230
Saving, buying house should not prevent, 31
Savings, 9t. *See also* Retirement savings
Schedule K-1 form, partners' share of income or losses reported on, 168, 169, 170
S-corporation
  definition and advantages of, 170
  offers limited liability to shareholders, 170
  reduces self-employment tax by paying through distributions, 170
  reduces taxes by filing as, 141
Sears, bankruptcy of retail company (2018), 58
Section 179, deduction rules for new car, 140
SECURE Act (2019), did away with old stretch IRA rules, 101
Self-employed, 141, 141n6
Self-employment tax (Social Security and Medicare taxes), 141n6
SEP (simplified employee pension plan), 108n2
SEP IRA, 107–108, 108n2
Settlement fees, contribution to retirement savings by, 9
Settlement specialist, to set up structured fee arrangement use a, 120
Shareholders
  C-corporation pays dividends to, 169
  C-corporation and S-corporation offer limited liability to shareholders, 170
  rights of a stock owners as, 49
Short-term treasuries, bulk of emergency fund in, 26
Siegel, Jeremy (*Stocks for the Long Run*), 49n1, 67–68, 67n2
SIMPLE IRA, 107, 107n1
"Small-cap premium," small-cap outperform large-cap stocks over time, 59–60
Small-cap stocks, total market capitalization of, 59
Small law firm, should have disability buy-sell agreement and disability buy-out insurance, 157

Social security
  determining eligibility for, 207
  eligibility and difficulty obtaining, 154
  filing early reduces spousal and your personal benefits, 209
  getting the most out of, 207–212
  how to get all that's yours in benefits, 210–211
Social Security Administration
  actual benefits calculated by, 207
  average life expectance from actuarial tables, 193–194
  probability of being disabled between age 20 and retirement, 153, 153n1
  restrictive definition of disability, 154
Social security benefits
  4 percent rule supplemented by, 8
  advantage of early filing for, 208–209
  can file as early as age 62, 208
  deciding when to file for self/spouse collective, 211–212
Social security disability benefits, integrated with disability insurance, 156
Sole proprietorship
  advantages/disadvantages of, 167–168
  how to report income and losses on schedule C of 1040 for, 167
"Solo" 401(k)
  features of, 108
  no IRS testing requirements for, 109
Solo attorney, should have disability buy-sell agreement and disability buy-out insurance, 157
Solo practitioner, unpredictable income of, 5
Speculation, risk with individual stock, 90
Spending, tools to track income and, 10–11
Split dollar life insurance, definition and types of, 131–132
Spousal benefit, equals 50 percent of your social security benefit, 209, 210
Spouse
  financial impact of your death on spouse, 145
  reduce taxes by hiring your, 136–137
Stagnation, characterized by weak economic growth, rising interest rates, high inflation, 52

Index

Standard & Poor 500 (S&P)
  companies average dividend (1871-1960; 2009-2019), 50, 50n2
  comprised mostly of tech companies, 50
  less risk investing in diversified, 65
  large-cap index, 59
State Street's SPDR® S&P 500 ETF (SPY), gross expense ratio of, 55, 55n6, 73-74
Stealth IRA, HSA plus way to save for retirement, 113-115
Stock, advantages of charitable donation of shares of, 123
Stock market
  disadvantage of withdrawing money during down, 68
  frequency of drawdowns, 67
  historical average rate of return from, 18
  impending recession with decline of, 186
  maximum monthly drawdowns of, 67f, 67n1
  most growth over time from capital appreciation, 50
Stock-picking
  definition and disadvantages of, 91-92
  diversification has lower risk than, 65
Stocks
  better long-term investment than real estate, 86-87
  categorized by growth or value, 51
  definition of, 47
  examples categorized by sectors with different growth opportunities and risks, 51
  ownership securities as shareholder in a company, 49
  portfolio to have no more than 5 percent in individual, 58
  preferred asset class for long-term growth and wealth creation, 49, 49n1
  reason why companies issue, 49
  risker investment than bonds and subject to investor whims, 50
  small, mid, and large categories of, 51
  ways to make money owning, 49
Stocks and bonds, advantages of investing in, 39
Stocks for the Long Run (Siegel), 49n1, 67-68, 67n2
Stock transfer, way to fund nonqualified deferred compensation plan, 225

Strategic asset allocation, 61-62
Structured fee arrangement
  constructive receipt avoided by, 120
  cooperation from defense needed to set up, 120
  description and advantages of, 118-119, 119t
  legal precedent (1996) permits, 120, 120n1
  vehicles to help structure, 121
Student loan debt
  advantages and disadvantages of consolidation of, 21
  converted to home equity loan, 22
  guidelines for paying down, 17
  law school graduate and average, 4, 4n1, 15
  paying off, 15-22
  ways to obtain forgiveness of, 21-22
  when to refinance, 20-21
  years of loan, loan balance, and amount of monthly payment of, 19t
Subsection-S-corporation, reduce taxes by filing as, 141
Succession plan
  for large law firm, 223
  purpose of and details to include in, 221-222
  retaining clients as important goal of, 229-230
  strategies for design of, 222
Surrender period, life insurance definition of, 132
Survivor (or widow/widower) benefits, social security and, 210
Systematic risks, based on the stock market, economy, and inflation, 65

T

T. Rowe Price International Bond (RPIBX), 73
Tactical asset allocation, 62-63
Target-date funds, 80-81
Tax advantages
  mistake of not maximizing, 38-39
  of S-corporation versus sole proprietorship, 141-142
Tax benefits, of flipping a home or purchasing a rental property, 84
Tax bracket, large settlement fee and higher, 5
Tax brokerage accounts, concern over taxes, 93

Tax Cuts and Jobs Act (2017)
  bonus depreciation rate of, 139
  C-corporation and personal service corporation tax rate changed by, 170
  reduce overall tax rate by hiring your kids, 136
Tax deduction, contribution of cash and noncash property to charity for, 123
Tax deferral, turbocharged, 107–111
Tax drag, capital gains/dividend, 100, 100*t*, 118
Tax law (2017), cap lowered on deducting mortgage interest and property tax, 30
Tax planning, lack of time and missed opportunities for, 5
Tax Relief Act (1997), 98
Tax strategies, life insurance, 129–133
Tax tips, savings for attorneys and, 135–142
Tax-deferred, definition of gain or dividends, 98
Tax-deferred accounts, concept and types of traditional, 97–98
Taxable account, also known as *brokerage account* or *standard account*, 97
Taxes
  contingency-fee and personal injury attorney income and high, 4–5
  examples of deferring income to following year to reduce, 136
  foremost concern of lawyers to reduce high, 5
  law firm partners responsible for own estimated quarterly, 5
  mortgage interest and property taxes as deductible expenses for, 30
Tech bubble, percent fall of S&P 500 in aftermath (2000) of, 66, 67*f*, 67n1
Tech companies, invest in innovation instead of paying dividends to investors, 50
Tech start-up companies, time needed to go public and percentage of, 58
Term life insurance
  cash-value life insurance versus cost of, 11
  definition of, 129
Term life insurance policy, cash-value life insurance policy versus, 148
Time
  billable hours versus taking, to plan and save, 5
  bonds have lower rate of return than stocks over, 49
  most valuable asset for saving and investing, 3
  secret to riches by maximizing money's investment over, 46
Time horizon, definition of, 68
Time value of money, concept of, 44
TLT. *See* iShares 20 Plus Year Treasury Bond (TLT)
Tracking spending, stay current with, 11–12
Traditional IRA, eligibility not subject to income limitations, 103
Trust company, role in settlement fee, 120
"Trusteed cross purchase," life insurance and, 182
Tuition, private versus in-state public law school average annual, 15

U

Umbrella liability insurance policy, when to purchase, 160–161
Underwriting standards, of lender bank, 31
Unemployment, impending recession with rise in, 186, 187*f*
"Unicorn status," percentage of tech start-ups that reach, 58
Universal life insurance. *See* Cash-value life insurance
Unpredictable cash flow, 12. *See also* Unpredictable income
Unpredictable income
  finances and retirement account affected by, 5
  See also Unpredictable cash flow; Irregular income
Unsystematic risk
  location of real estate as, 85
  based on business operations of individual companies, 65
Urban area, tax abatements for revitalization of, 84
U.S. News & World Report, average annual tuition and fees at private law school, 15, 15n1
US Global Investors Gold and Precious Metals (USERX), 73
US stock market, 8, 8n1. *See also* Stock market
"Useful life of property," IRS tables for calculation of, 138–139, 138n2

Index

V

Vacation, how to deduct expenses if conduct business along with, 137–138, 138n2

Value, determining law firm assets and their, 216–217

"Value premium," value stocks that did well in 1980s and 1990s, 60

Value stocks
definition and example of, 51
undervalued by the market, 60

Vanguard Growth Index Fund Admiral Shares (VIGAX), percent return of, 61, 61n3

Vanguard Intermediate-Term Investment Grade Corporate Bond (VFICX), 72–73

Vanguard Intermediate-Term Treasury (VFITX), 73

Vanguard Long-Term Treasury (VUSTX), 72, 80, 80n1

Vanguard Real Estate Index (VGSIX), 73

Vanguard Real Estate Index Fund ETF (VNQ), 73

Vanguard Value Index Fund Admiral Shares (VVIAX), percent return of, 61

Vesting, 401(k) and, 108

VFINX, 80, 80n1

Volatility
diversification decreases risk and, 59
risk defined as, 66

W

Waiver of premium rider
disability insurance definition of, 155
life insurance definition of, 149

Wall Street, IPOs offered in the past by brokers on, 57

Wealth
being serious about savings is building, 12
compounding interest powerful in creation of, 44
equation of savings multiplied by time for building, 16
live below your means to build, 38

Withdrawal, penalty for IRA or 401(k) premature, 98

Work-optional lifestyle, definition of, 8

Y

Yield curve, definition of, 186

Yield curve inversion, as predictor of recession, 186

Young attorney, moderate risk portfolio for, 72–73, 72*t*, 73*t*

Z

Zuckerberg, Mark, 126